THE PRINCIPLES OF

ARCHITECTURAL DRAFTING

THE PRINCIPLES OF
ARCHITECTURAL DRAFTING
A SOURCEBOOK OF TECHNIQUES AND GRAPHIC STANDARDS

HUGH C. BROWNING

WHITNEY LIBRARY OF DESIGN
AN IMPRINT OF WATSON-GUPTILL PUBLICATIONS/NEW YORK

For my son who died too young.

ACKNOWLEDGMENTS
Special thanks to Lynn Bahrami for her tenacious editorial help at critical points and to Paul Laurence for his patient word processing.

Senior Editor: Roberto de Alba
Editor: Micaela Porta
Designer: Abigail Sturges
Production Manager: Ellen Greene
Layout conceived by Hugh C. Browning

First published in 1996 by Whitney Library of Design, an imprint of Watson-Guptill Publications, New York, NY 10036.

Cataloging-in-Publication Data is on file with the Library of Congress

Distributed in the United Kingdom, Eastern Europe, Russia, and the Middle East by Windsor Books International, The Boundary, Wheatley Road, Garsington, Oxford OX44 9EJ, England.

Distributed in Western Europe (except the United Kingdom), South and Central America, the Caribbean, the Southeast, and Asia (except P.R. of China) by Rotovision S.A., Route Suisse 9, CH-1295 Mies, Switzerland.

Manufactured in the United States

First printing, 1996

1 2 3 4 5 6 7 8 9 /02 01 00 99 98 97 96

CONTENTS

INTRODUCTION

Architectural drafting is a form of communication. Just as in any other language, simple and complex ideas are conveyed in a standard, structured, and recognizable manner. How well you draw depends largely on your earliest instruction and practices: The better the initial input, the better the eventual command of the media. This book focuses extensively on the fundamentals and refinements of architectural drawing, as well as on the essentials needed to raise architectural drafting to the realm of fine art.

Descriptive geometry, used to solve all problems of forms and their interrelationships, is the root of the language. Chapter 2, "Points, Lines, Planes, and Solids," presents the concepts of descriptive geometry along with its companion skill, spatial visualization. Here, you will develop the important skill of thinking in three dimensions, an ability that is crucial for rendering three-dimensional shapes and spaces two-dimensionally.

Chapter 3, "Applied Geometry," provides information on how to construct and calculate the areas of standard forms and shapes. Chapter 4, "Architectural Plans, Sections, and Elevations," covers the universal drawing types that architects employ, plus some construction particulars such as the typical thickness of walls and the height of doors. Chapter 5, "Paralines," includes the theoretical, practical, and pictorial aspects of this drawing type.

The graphic treatment of drawings is discussed in Chapter 6, "Shades and Shadows," and Chapter 7, "Presentation Graphics and Reproduction." The former explains the technical methods for casting shadows. The latter presents the design of the two-dimensional page in depth, as well as its duplication and manipulation through standard forms of reproduction.

Throughout the book, I have made an effort to show how a single drawing can be treated in different ways: understated, moody, tentative, finished, technical, humorous. While many of these drawings are imbued with my particular drawing style, others depict the historic techniques of the École des Beaux-Arts and the sensibilities of individual architects and artists. It is my hope, then, that in *The Principles of Architectural Drafting* you will find both a solid practical and mechanical basis for architectural drawing, as well as the inspiration you need to elevate your creations to fine art.

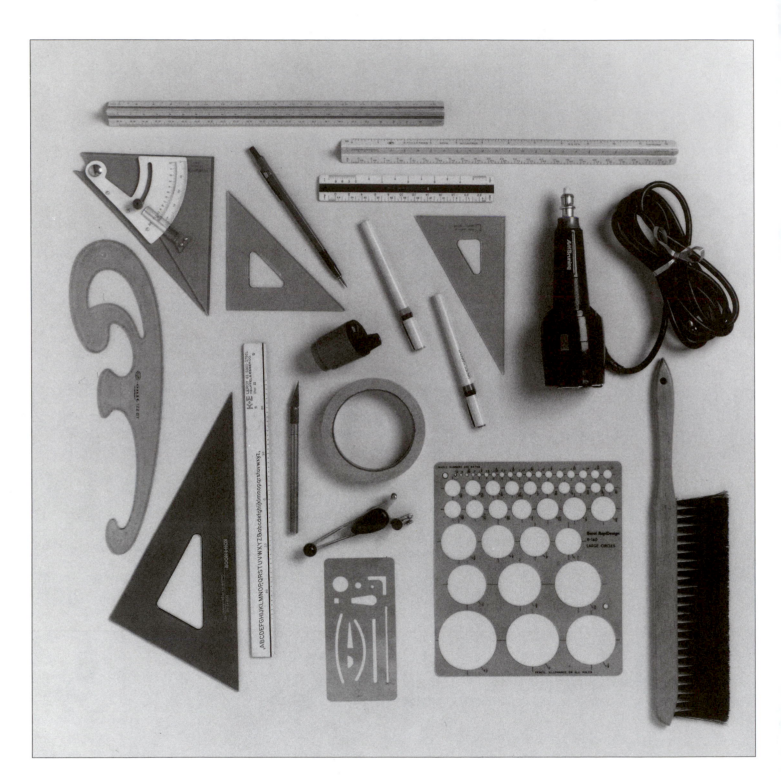

CHAPTER 1

TOOLS,
MATERIALS,
AND
THEIR USES

This chapter concentrates on tools, materials, and their uses as they apply to student work, rather than to drawings done in an office. Because this book addresses the basics of drafting—material that should be known before computer studies begin—no space has been allocated to computer hardware, software, or supplies.

Every architect, student, and drafter purchases tools and materials from local architectural or art supply stores. Unless one lives in a large metropolitan area, the selection can be limited. And even if one studies or works in a large city, stores will probably not carry a complete range of tools and materials. For a more complete selection, everyone should keep handy a catalog from a large supply house or store. The Charrette Corporation, 31 Olympic Ave., Woburn, Massachusetts, 01888-4010, is a good source. They have sold the most complete inventory of architectural supplies in the world for decades.

Conventional widsom says *buy the best tools you can afford.* Items such as drawing boards and instruments, for instance, should last a professional lifetime. For other items, such as scales and lead holders, less expensive ones work just as well, and they often get misplaced.

DRAFTING BOARDS

Chairs and drafting boards are obviously used in tandem. No person who is serious about architecture should buy a board less than 31" x 42" with a chair to match. The major criteria for selecting among the dozens of available boards is stability. Test a board by leaning on a corner. If it rocks, don't buy it, regardless of its expense or up-to-date appearance. The first major reason for excluding the rocker is that, although a bad habit, a coffee or tea cup is often rested on a board. If the board rocks, the drink will spill. Second, the drafter has to occasionally work from the sides of the board, and even the top edge. In these cases a person's body weight can easily tip the board over.

Three basic types of boards are available: drafting tables with the board fixed to a stand; boards without stands; and fold-up-against-the-wall boards. Drafting tables always have some method for adjusting the tilt and usually the height. There are high tables meant for near-vertical drawing with a drafting machine, but architects seldom use the arrangement. Architects normally set boards at a 10° to 20° tilt with the height close to the desktop height (28"). This tilt lessens the tendency for pencils and pens to roll down the board, and the height allows computers, phones, and reference tables to be conveniently used from a single chair height.

Boards without stands are cheaper than ones with stands, but they must be set on another table surface. These boards come with or without an adjustable-tilt mechanism. Like all boards, they are made of machine-finished softwood or plastic with either hardwood or metal side edges.

TRADITIONAL WOOD PEDESTAL   CENTRAL PEDESTAL

FIG. 1.1

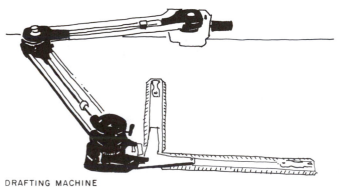

DRAFTING MACHINE

FIG. 1.2

Drafting boards that fold up against the wall are available but should only be purchased if space is at an absolute minimum. These boards are mounted on wall tracks with arms under the board that lock onto the tracks. Wall-mounted boards are inherently less stable than any drafting table.

Some inexpensive boards come with a laminated-sheet vinyl surface. Most architects prefer to attach a separate protective sheet to the wood surfaces. Two kinds are available: a cellulose acetate bonded to paper, and a thicker vinyl, available in two color combinations. Despite its higher cost, the vinyl is preferred because compass-point holes and light cuts from a knife heal instantly. Additionally, the surface can be replaced if severely damaged.

WALL – MOUNTED

FIG. 1.3

DRAFTING BOARD ACCESSORIES

The most economical approach is to make your own board from plywood and 2" x 8" pieces of wood cut at a 10° to 20° angle. This type of board can be set on a flush, solid core door supported by carpenter sawhorses or trestles. The door, which is longer than needed for a drafting board, serves as an ample reference board and place to set drafting tools. If the door is set at the right height, the board can be removed and the solid-core door used as a dining table.

Because student drawings are often large—up to 30" x 40"—the drafter has to lean over the board to draw at the top of the sheet. A Spiroll is a necessity for avoiding this tiring position. A slotted tube attached to the bottom edge of the board, it allows the sheet to be curled inside. The top is consequently moved down to a more convenient location.

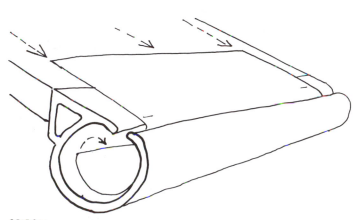

SPIROLL

FIG. 1.4

When a Spiroll is used, register marks—short, light lines—should be drawn at the edges of the paper. These marks ensure perfect realignment when the sheet is moved.

Boards are also used to build models on. For this purpose, a double-thick piece of inexpensive chipboard should always be on top of the board to protect its surface from deep knife cuts and spilled glue.

Should one live in a dusty location, a separate, thin plastic cover (available in architecture and design supply stores) should be placed over the board when it is not in use.

An eye hook screwed to the edge of a wooden drafting board is a convenient place to hang an electric eraser.

TYPICAL CHAIR   WITH ARMS

FIG. 1.5

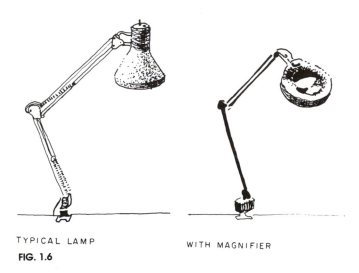

TYPICAL LAMP   WITH MAGNIFIER

FIG. 1.6

BAD   GOOD

FIG. 1.7

DRAFTING CHAIRS

A drafting chair must be comfortable. With armchairs, lounges, and sofas, design often conflicts with comfort. Many visually appealing chairs are very uncomfortable to sit on. By contrast, only a few drafting chairs present this dilemma, but if one does, there should be no question about preference. You must sit for many continuous hours in a drafting chair, so never buy one without seat padding. It is also advisable to purchase a chair with height adjustment (16" to 21" minimum) and casters. Chairs with arms are a questionable luxury as your arms rest on the board when drafting, anyway. Avoiding foot rests and arms allows more money to be spent on a better chair.

The most expensive chairs are made from stainless steel or cast aluminum. Less expensive chairs are painted or chrome-plated. If the latter two materials are cheaply applied, rust coming through the surface can show over a long period of time.

DRAFTING LIGHTS

A drafting lamp is the third absolute necessity for drawing. Like boards and chairs, there are literally dozens to choose from. Unless one uses a board without a base or a fold-up, buying a lamp that attaches to the board with a screw-clamp is the best choice. All clamp-lamps come with adjustable, spring-loaded arms. This allows the light to be moved to any board location and stay fixed until moved again. Every lamp with arms has a maximum reach determined by the length of the arms. Be sure the reach will be adequate for the given board.

Light sources are either incandescent, fluorescent, or a mixture of the two, and some lamps are balanced for natural daylight. The drafter needs as much light as possible, so select a lamp that will accept at least a 100-watt incandescent bulb. Be cautious about any lamp that only gives fluorescent light, as it may not provide enough illumination.

Incandescent lamps use more energy than fluorescent lights and subsequently cause more heat—unwelcome on a hot day or night. The heat, however, can be used for another purpose. Ink on a drawing takes time to dry. An incandescent lamp put a few inches away from the drawing will cut the drying time in half. Remember also that all lights cast shadows. Shadows should not fall over a line being drawn or a scale when measuring because inaccuracies can occur.

MOVABLE STORAGE

Taborets are convenient, movable storage units with shelves and usually drawers. Ideally, every workplace should have materials, instruments, and tools at arm's reach. A taboret helps.

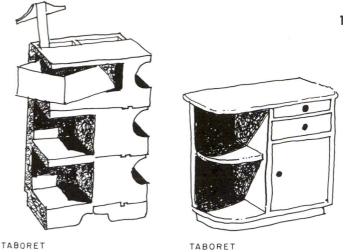

TABORET   TABORET

FIG. 1.8

DRAWING INSTRUMENTS

Purchasing inexpensive drawing instruments can be a waste of money since the good ones will last a professional lifetime. If at all possible buy a complete set or, at least, purchase a few necessary, high-quality pieces. All instruments are made of metal and their quality is determined by how finely the parts are machined. Some pieces have screw threads and must turn with absolute smoothness. Also, there should be no looseness, or "play," between parts.

Instrument sets usually contain at least two bow compasses, a short bow extension, a traditional ink ruling pen head, a pen barrel, and a divider.

COMPASSES

A compass allows the drafter to draw circles of exact radius, rather than being limited by the given sizes of circle templates. The large bow compass is used for circles up to a 6" radius, and the smaller one up to 3". Two different-size compasses are convenient for making larger or smaller circles. If cost is a factor, the larger size is more important to buy because it extends the radius of circles well beyond what is available on templates and can be used for all but the smallest circles. An accompanying template will provide satisfactory, but less accurate, results for smaller circles.

Compasses have two arms that are held apart by a small threaded rod and adjusted by a thumb screw. One of the arms takes a replaceable sharp pin for circle centers. The other arm accepts different drawing attachments: one for lead, another for an ink ruling pen head, as well as adapters for technical drawing pens. A universal adapter takes drawing pens, fiber-tipped pens, ball-point pens, or lead holders with a maximum diameter of 1/2".

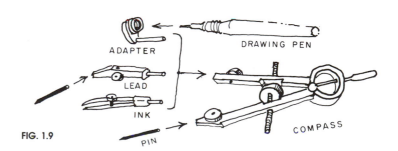

ADAPTER   DRAWING PEN

LEAD

INK

PIN   COMPASS

FIG. 1.9

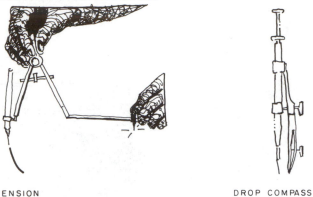

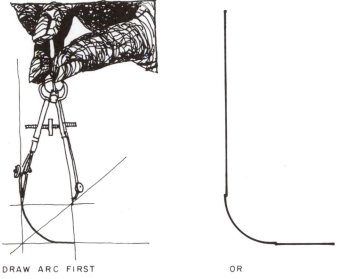

A short bow extension can be inserted into a compass to enlarge circle radii up to 10" or so. Extremely small circles cannot be made with a bow compass. For these sizes, a small drop compass can be purchased.

EXTENSION
FIG. 1.10

DROP COMPASS

With either a compass or circle template, always draw an arc between straight lines first, followed by the joining lines. Otherwise, there is a good chance that the combination will not have a smooth transition.

DRAW ARC FIRST   OR
FIG. 1.11

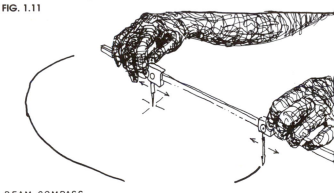

Beam compasses, with or without extension tubes, allow the drafter to draw large circles with up to 24" radii.

BEAM COMPASS
FIG. 1.12

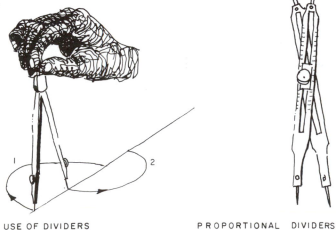

DIVIDERS

Dividers transfer dimensions from one drawing location to another or successively mark off a series of equal measurements. There is usually no threaded rod and thumb screw to hold the arms apart as exists in the compass; like the compass, the ends of the arms will accept different heads and points. Proportional divers convey enlarged or reduced dimensions.

Care must be taken when marking off a series of measurements. Should the initial measurement be slightly off, this error will accumulate.

USE OF DIVIDERS   PROPORTIONAL DIVIDERS
FIG. 1.13

Before the invention of technical drawing pens after World War II, ruling pens were the only way to ink straight lines. Ruling pen heads from an instrument set can be inserted into the provided barrel or other instruments. They can also be purchased with the head permanently attached to the barrel. Ink line thickness is established by turning the thumb screw on the side of the head.

Tempera paint can be loaded into a ruling pen for straight lines over watercolor, marker, tempera renderings, or even pencil drawings. The tempera (or other paint) is inserted with a brush and must have the right consistency. Add more water or paint to obtain a smooth but opaque flow.

LOADING WITH INK   LOADING WITH PAINT

FIG. 1.14

Ruling pens are inexpensive compared to drawing pens and do not have clogging problems. To work at all, they must be cleaned every time they're used. Among the four or five types available, the cross-jointed pen is the easiest to clean because one blade rotates free of the other. Unless you only occasionally ink a few lines, technical drawing pens are preferred.

Ruling pens should not be overloaded as the liquid will flow too freely. The result will be blobs and overruns at the ends of lines. Excess liquid is removed by stroking a paper towel against the side of the pen. To start the liquid flowing, run the loaded pen across the side of the first finger of the non-drafting hand. Then test the pen on a separate piece of drawing surface. This will indicate if there is too much or too little liquid in the pen, and whether the line thickness is correct.

STANDARD RULING PEN   CONTOUR

CROSS JOINTED

RAILROAD   CORRECT TOO LITTLE TOO MUCH

FIG. 1.15   **FIG. 1.16**

SPECIAL INSTRUMENTS

An ellipse machine, or ellipsograph, has the same advantages a compass has: it is exact and produces larger sizes than templates (up to a 7" axis). The ellipse dimensions are set by two concentric thumbscrews on a central mechanism that separates two plastic disks. A pencil or technical pen is inserted into the same mechanism, and then the two disks are rotated by a knob on the perimeter of one of the disks. Unless you specifically need to draw many accurate ellipses, the ellipse machine is a relatively expensive luxury.

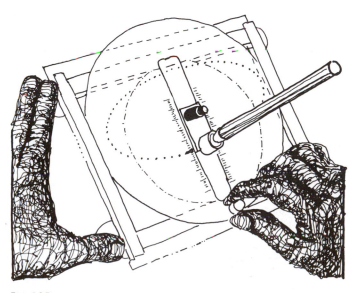

ELLIPSE MACHINE

FIG. 1.17

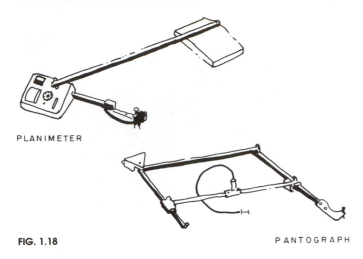

PLANIMETER

PANTOGRAPH

FIG. 1.18

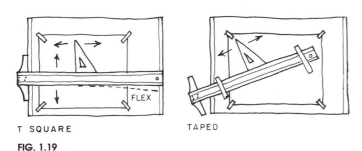

T SQUARE

FLEX

TAPED

FIG. 1.19

Planimeters and pantographs are also expensive, specialized instruments. The planimeter measures areas of a drawing or map, usually with a digital readout. The pantograph enlarges or reduces an original with the use of mechanical arms.

T-SQUARES

These tools are used to draw straight lines, either with pencil or ink. All are available in different sizes, materials, and costs. Besides being used for drawing, they can be employed in model making. For this purpose, metal ones are a must.

T-squares and parallel bars are meant for drawing horizontal lines (parallel to the longest edge of the drafting board). Both move up and down on the short edge of the board, and triangles are slid along the horizontal edge of the tool. T-squares are portable and considerably less expensive than parallel bars. Select a T-square that will cover the length of the drafting board. The best T-squares for drawing are made from hardwood with clear acrylic edges. The acrylic allows lines just below the edge to be visible. Adjustable head, calibrated, all-wood, stainless steel, and aluminum T-squares are available for particular uses. Attachable aluminum edges with screw clamps can be purchased for T-squares on do-it-yourself boards.

When a series of parallel lines are made with triangles, T-squares can be taped to the board. One of the T-square's major disadvantages, however, is that it will flex at the extremes of the long arm. To avoid this problem, locate the drawing as close to the head as possible.

PARALLEL BARS

While they are more expensive, parallel bars are preferable to T-squares because they are permanently attached to the board and have no "flex" problems. Parallel bars slide up and down on a cable that is attached to the bottom of the board. From there, the cable runs through the bar, up the sides of the board, and across the top. A thumbscrew/clamp allows the bar to be fixed at angles other than parallel to the bottom edge of the board.

Most parallel bars have a beveled top for easy gripping, and clear acrylic edges for visibility. The bar moves on steel rollers inserted into the bottom surface. Some bars have a thin metal tape adhered to the acrylic edges for cutting against. A few have a brake that locks the rule firmly into one position.

Always draw light register marks at the edges of the paper so the bar can realigned when it's changed back to the horizontal position. In fact, all drawings should have register marks. Drawings must often be taken off the board and later put back. Register marks provide the longest possible horizontal reference and, therefore, the most accurate.

CLAMP & ADJUSTMENT   SPRING

CABLE

REGISTER MARK

PARALLEL BAR

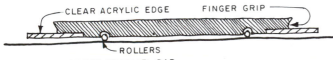

CLEAR ACRYLIC EDGE   FINGER GRIP

ROLLERS

SECTION THROUGH PARALLEL BAR

FIG. 1.20

Triangles (also known as set squares) are essential tools for constructing parallel and angled lines. Only three kinds exist: 30°/60°/90°, 45°/45°/90°, and adjustable.

The first two are absolutely necessary for drafting; the adjustable is very useful to have, unless you're on a limited budget and substitute a protractor. All triangles come in various sizes (their size is the length measured along the longest perpendicular side). As a general rule, the size of a triangle should correlate to the size of a drawing: small triangles for small drawings, and vice versa. (Practically all of the drawings in this book were done with 4" triangles). Six to 8" triangles are convenient sizes for beginners; 4" triangles are useful for hand lettering and small detail. As the beginner advances, the need for different sizes will become apparent.

Triangles with an inking edge prevent ink from bleeding (spreading) under the edge of the triangle. (If you have to ink with a triangle that does not have this edge, three small coins taped to the bottom surface of the triangle raise it above the drawing surface, thereby eliminating bleeding.) The centers of most triangles have triangles or circles cut out of them, and some of these inner figures also have finger lifts—thinner shaped portions—for convenience when picking the triangle up.

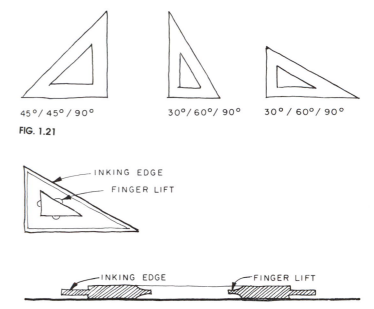

45°/45°/90°   30°/60°/90°   30°/60°/90°

FIG. 1.21

INKING EDGE
FINGER LIFT

INKING EDGE   FINGER LIFT

SECTION THROUGH TRIANGLE

FIG. 1.22

Transparent plastic triangles come in clear, smoky brown, green, or fluorescent orange. Generally, the smoked and green ones have stepped inking edges. The fluorescent triangles have no inking edges but provide better visibility through the plastic.

Besides being a tool for drawing angles and making parallel lines, 30°, 45°, 60°, and 90° triangles can be used together to construct any angle from 15° to 345° in 15° increments. Sliding one triangle against another allows parallel lines to be drawn without the aid of an adjustable triangle, T-square, or parallel bar. There are no set ways to perform this operation. Many combinations will work, and if one doesn't for one reason or another (the parallel bar is usually in the way), simply try another.

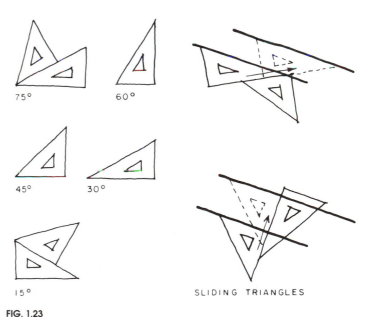

75°   60°

45°   30°

15°

SLIDING TRIANGLES

FIG. 1.23

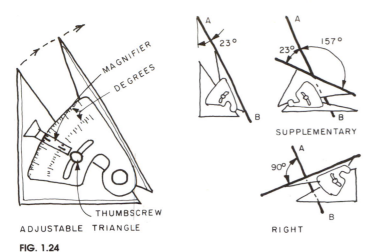

ADJUSTABLE TRIANGLE

FIG. 1.24

SUPPLEMENTARY

RIGHT

Adjustable triangles construct or measure exact angles and are used to make new lines parallel to an existing line. Any angle can be set by the thumbscrew on an adjustable triangle. The best adjustable triangles have an inking edge and a magnifying lens over the calibrations.

After drawing one line in a given direction, flip the adjustable triangle to another side against a parallel bar. This allows a supplementary angle to be made. Changing to the second side, a line at 90° to the original line can be drawn. In Figure 1.24, the initial line is 23° to the vertical, the second side produces a supplementary angle (180° - 23° = 157°), and the third side gives a line at right angles to initial line AB.

LEAD

There is no lead in "lead" pencils or drafting "lead"—only graphite and a binder. The more graphite in the combination, the softer the "lead"; the more binder, the harder. Drafting leads have seventeen specific combinations of graphite and binders: 9H is the hardest grade and 6B, the softest.

HARDEST

9H Very hard; used for extreme accuracy; difficult to erase;
8H nearly impossible to reproduce; limited availability
7H
6H
5H
4H

3H Medium hardness; general-purpose; 2H and F are a
2H popular combination for drafting
H
F
B

2B Soft; not used for drafting, but excellent for architectural
3B illustration; smudges; easy to erase; reproduces well
4B
5B
6B

SOFTEST

Drafters employ more than one grade of lead, and particular grades vary from one manufacturer to another. The best way to avoid this variation is to select one manufacturer's lead and then experiment to find personal preferences.

LEAD LINEWEIGHT

Chapters 2 and 3 offer instruction in the use of different lineweights to indicate spatial depth and the application of a standard lineweight code for drafting. Density, or darkness, and thickness are the two determinates for lineweight. Some drafters prefer three grades of medium-hard lead to achieve the needed variations in darkness. However, most drafters get the same, or better, results from just two grades. These drafters employ a sharp, medium-hard lead, such as

2H, for the lightest lines, and a sharp, medium-grade lead, like F, for slightly darker lines. The darkest lineweight is done with two strokes from a sharp F lead, or a single stroke with a slightly rounded F lead point.

One of the biggest mistakes a person can make when drafting is to not achieve maximum density. Press hard when drawing. Lines must be as dense as possible with any grade of lead or they will not reproduce well. To test for darkness, take the drawing off the board and look at a light source through the back of it. Lines that do not have maximum density will look gray instead of black. The following basic instructions should yield good results:

1. Hold any drafting pencil as close to vertical as is conveniently possible. With less of an angle, sharp points tend to snap off.
2. Rotating the pencil while drawing helps keep the point sharp and maintains uniform line thickness.
3. For general drafting, hold the lead tip away from straight edges, because a point held directly against a straight edge will dirty drafting equipment and drawing surfaces.
4. When extreme accuracy is required, reverse the above procedure: Draw directly against the corner of a straight edge, use harder leads to maintain a sharper point longer, and avoid triangles and parallel bars with an inking edge.
5. Most drafters have two mechanical or clutch pencils at their drafting board, both with medium-hard lead, one for lighter lineweight and the other for darker lines. Having two holders avoids frequent changes of graded leads.

LEADS, MECHANICAL PENCILS, AND LEAD HOLDERS

The vast majority of architects prefer mechanical pencils and lead holders over wood pencils. Both mechanical pencils and lead holders are available in a wide selection of gribs, pocket clips, and styles that accept different lead sizes. The major difference between these two types is that with a holder, the lead is held outside the end of the barrel. The holding mechanism in a mechanical pencil is inside the barrel.

Mechanical pencils take thinner leads—down to about 0.2 mm—in either round or flat sticks. They give a constant line thickness and never need sharpening. The downside is that these pencils cannot be used for lettering, shading, or sketching.

Lead holders are commonly called clutch pencils. Unlike mechanical pencils, clutch pencils are used for the complete range of drawing needs. Because the round, thicker 0.5 mm leads are longer than the leads for mechanical pencils, they don't have to be replaced as often. In addition, the lead allows for a sharp, wedge-shaped or rounded point. For these reasons, clutch pencils are purchased much more often than mechanical pencils. Standard-grade leads are always available, and a number of special leads are also made for the clutch pencil: color, nonreproducing blue, smearproof, washable leads for plastic drafting film, and more.

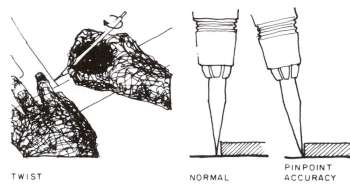

TWIST   NORMAL   PINPOINT ACCURACY

FIG. 1.25

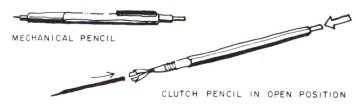

MECHANICAL PENCIL

CLUTCH PENCIL IN OPEN POSITION

FIG. 1.26

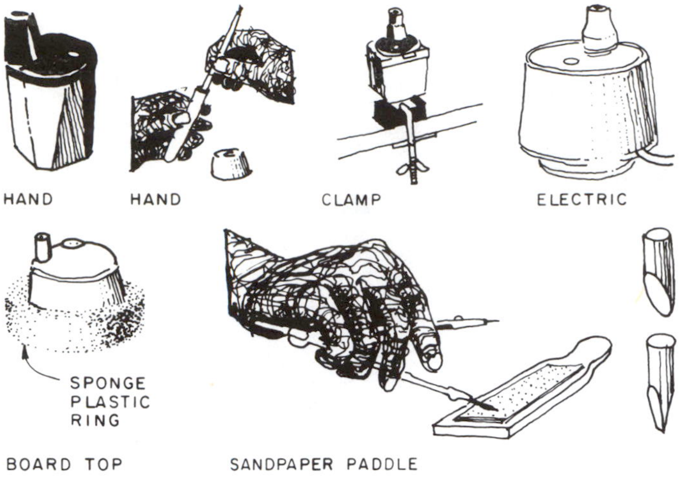

HAND   HAND   CLAMP   ELECTRIC

SPONGE
PLASTIC
RING

BOARD TOP   SANDPAPER PADDLE

FIG. 1.27

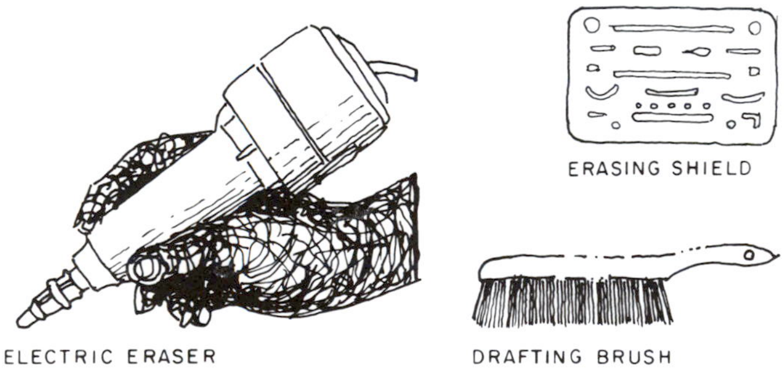

LEAD SHARPENING AND ERASING

The lead in a clutch pencil is sharpened in a pointer, which gives the best taper. One can select from the four basic types: hand-held; pointers that are clamped to the board; electric; and sharpeners that sit on the board. Sandpaper paddles have a number of fine sandpaper strips stapled to a small wood base. This type of sharpener is handy to sharpen lead in a compass or to give a variety of points to wood-pencil leads (useful for illustration).

After clutch pencil lead has been sharpened to a fine point, there is always a small amount of lead dust that clings to the point. This dust drops onto drawings and causes smudges. Some pointers have a small built-in cleaning pad on the top of the pointer, and a few have a sponge plastic collar that fits over the sharpener. Inserting the point into one of these materials takes the dust off the lead. Stroking the point on a paper towel or knocking the holder against the drafting board edge will accomplish the same goal.

The extremely fine points that sharpeners give often snap off when the first line stroke is made. This can be prevented by slightly rounding the point on a piece of paper.

There is an almost-true saying among people who do a lot of hand drafting on working drawings: "Never draw in the morning what you can't erase in the afternoon." Beginning students quickly learn to follow this advice after starting a drawing over again and again. Remember, though, that while lines must be completely erased, care should be taken not to damage the drawing sheet. This will either create a hole or irregularities in the surface. The latter defect changes evenness when pencil shading over the area. Also, regardless of the type, a dirty eraser should be cleaned on a scrap of paper, or it will add graphite to the drawing.

The sooner you can afford an electric eraser the better. Unlike an electric pointer, an electric eraser is a necessity because drafters erase frequently. Electric erasers come with batteries or a cord. Electric-cord erasers are somewhat inconvenient in that the cord has to move over the drawing, but battery-powered ones suffer from a common fault: the batteries run out at the wrong time, and recharging takes hours.

A clutch arrangement at the end of the electric eraser opens to accept 1/4"-round, 7"-long sticks of erasers. Many different kinds of erasers are available for special purposes, in gradations from hard to soft.

The number of hand-held erasers is almost endless: round sticks that fit into a holder; ones meant for plastic drafting film, ink, or charcoal; some that are hard and others that are soft. Pink Pearl erasers are good for general-purpose work. Some drafters shake or rub fine-grained art gum from an erasing pad onto a sheet before drawing to help keep the surface clean. When used after drawing, the art-gum crumbs help remove smudges. Although primarily used by

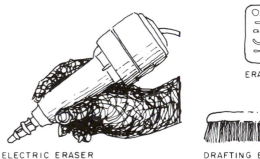

ERASING SHIELD

ELECTRIC ERASER   DRAFTING BRUSH

FIG. 1.28

artists, a kneaded rubber eraser is invaluable for architects, particularly for pencil illustration. It is made from a soft, pliable material which will knead into any shape, absorbs but never deposits graphite, and is excellent for making highlights and removing smudges. The kneaded eraser, however, will not erase hard linework. When heavy lead lines are erased, the original strokes may have caused graphite to be picked up on the back of the paper from a dirty board. Because this ghosted image will reproduce, always erase the back of the paper to remove graphite. A kneaded eraser works well for this purpose. Kneaded erasers become hard if unused for more than a couple of weeks. Pliability and erasability can be restored by a few seconds of folding and stretching.

A metal erasing shield is inexpensive and allows lines to be removed without disturbing others nearby. Slightly bending the corner of a shield makes it easier to pick up off the drafting board.

A dusting brush is another useful tool, used for sweeping eraser crumbs off the drafting board. As you erase, either blow the crumbs off the drawing or use a dusting brush. Otherwise, these particles will be ground into the paper surface and will erase parts you want to keep.

LEAD AND WOOD PENCILS

Although a couple of manufacturers make a series of graded pencils for drafting, few architects use them, except for illustration. However, purchasing softer B-grade wood pencils for illustration is less expensive than buying separate packages of lead for clutch pencils.

Grease, charcoal, and carpenter's pencils are often overlooked for architectural illustration. Grease pencils used on pebble board (a rough-surfaced mounting board) produce a very grainy drawing. Charcoal-pencil drawings done on charcoal paper give soft-looking illustrations. Carpenter's pencils (often called sketching pencils) come with wide B leads and, due to the lead size, can cover large drawing areas quickly. They must be sharpened with a knife.

Shading with wood pencils has a long history in architectural illustration, and thus never goes out of style for long. How the lead is or is not sharpened, whether the drawing surface is rough or smooth, and which stroke is used all affect one another and the final appearance of the drawing. Many art and architectural illustration books have been written on pencil shading. Study, practice, and experimentation are essential for developing skill.

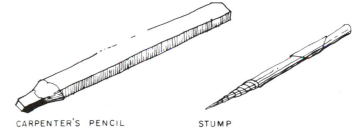

CARPENTER'S PENCIL   STUMP

FIG. 1.29

Shading can be used to literally depict materials or build up values in abstract patterns. Many illustrations contain both. Wedge-shaped leads, either in a clutch or wood pencil, give a good rendition of brick if used in short strokes. Underlining each stroke on two sides produces shades and further heightens the literal representation. Grass is depicted with a round point, and lead dust from a lead pointer can be used for clouds (see page 133). As mentioned above, the carpenter's pencil covers large areas quickly. With one particular stroke it can create an abstract pattern that gives a graphic consistency to a drawing. Multiple strokes generate compositionally related textures.

To achieve smoothness, a stump can be rubbed over an already shaded area. Note that this will slightly darken the tone. A stump, made of tightly wound gray paper, can be sharpened with a sandpaper paddle. Cotton balls and chamois are materials that will blend larger shaded areas.

Despite its popularity, colored pencil shading is beyond the scope of this book. Nevertheless, a few useful suggestions are worthwhile. First, the same methods for obtaining smoothness in black-and-white shading can be used with colored pencils. Limiting these techniques to a few areas creates textural play in a drawing. Second, know that the values (range of tones from black to white) are limited with colored pencils, and the chroma (brightness of color) can be too brilliant. One way to alleviate both characteristics is to apply color after having rendered the illustration with a full range of gray and black shading. This restricts the color to a tight, subtle, appealing understatement while extending values to give graphic punch.

With all shading, try to avoid erasing as much as possible, as the paper surface can change, causing uneven areas of shading. At all costs, avoid fingerprints on an area to be shaded; the grease from a print will cause noticeable variations. A piece of paper over a drawing will give you a place to rest your hands when shading. After a shaded drawing is finished, always spray a fixative over it to eliminate smudging. Some fixatives are labeled "workable," meaning drawings can be erased once fixed. Nevertheless, the drawing's ability to be erased will be limited to some extent.

WEDGE SHAPED

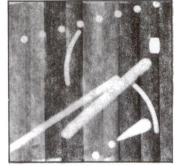

CARPENTER'S

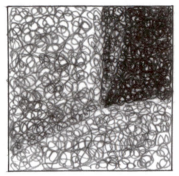

ONE TEXTURE

MULTITEXTURAL

WITH STUMP

FIG. 1.30

FREEHAND DRAWING WITH PENCIL

The art of sketching is all too often limited to early design explorations. The charm of these "thinking" drawings lies in their imperfection. Yet there is a compromise between the looseness of a sketch and precision of a hard-line drawing (one done with straight edges). With this type of freehand drawing, lines are carefully done at a slower speed than a sketch, but the human eye still makes accommodations for lines not touching or crossing and equal distances not being exactly equal. In this case, the "imperfections" are psychologically overlooked.

Tentative sketching, done with a series of scratchy strokes, looks . . . well, tentative. Either draw with a positive line and accept the approximation or erase and start over. Another option is to draw lightly at first, then firm up all or some lines. When drawing a straight, freehand line, keeping your eye on the end point produces a straighter line than following the point of the pencil.

The line drawings in this chapter use some incomplete lines, and their continuation is implied by dots or dashes. This gives these drawings a certain incompleteness without making them tentative. Also, the toned drawings in this chapter and in Chapter 7 were first made slowly and carefully, while the tones were built up with quick, almost random linework. The speed of the two types of lines created a distinctive character.

HAND LETTERING

Practically all hand lettering is done in pencil. Becoming proficient in this art takes many hours of practice. Vertical-style lettering with all capitals is the standard method adopted by most drafters, but there are also some other options: mixing capitals with lower-case letters; using only lower-case letters; or slanting letters. For presentation drawings, you can even use script or calligraphy, if well done. No matter what style is employed, it should not pull the eye away from the drawing and should be compatible with the architectural design.

All lettering should be done within lightly drawn guidelines. The space between lines of lettering is measured with a scale or Ames lettering guide. The letter width should be less than letter height. The Ames guide has three different systems for both the height of letters and the space between lines.

Unlike the distance between lines and letter heights, the space from letter to letter is determined by eye, rather than by measurement. If this space were equally measured, some pairs of letters would appear too close to one another while others would be too far apart.

Some drafters letter with straight vertical strokes using the back of a small triangle slid along the bottom edge of a parallel bar. Other strokes are drawn freehand. The awkward hand positions take getting used to, but once practiced, the method is fast and gives a consistent style.

Figure 1.34 shows the individual strokes that make up each letter. Note the preferred oblong proportions of most letters.

AMES LETTER GUIDE

FIG. 1.31

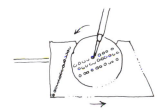

SPACING BY MEASUREMENT

FIG. 1.32

BY EYE

BACKHAND LETTERING

FIG. 1.33

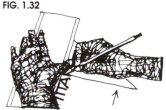

STROKES

FIG. 1.34

DRAFTING SURFACES

PAPER

Both opaque and transparent papers come in assorted types and are generally graded according to weight (thickness) and tooth (roughness). Each type works best with particular drawing techniques and tools. Personal choices will develop with experimentation. A word of caution: All paper shrinks, more or less, with changing humidity, sometimes as much as 1/16" in 40". This may or may not be important.

Newsprint is an opaque, inexpensive wood pulp paper best used for sketching. Hard drawing on newsprint is not recommended, as the surface is easily destroyed. Butcher's paper (a heavy brown wrapping paper) has more body and consequent toughness. Newsprint comes in different-sized pads, and both papers are available in rolls.

Heavier, opaque layout and sketch paper weighs 30 pounds or more. Watercolor papers, by comparison, start at 100 pounds and are as heavy as 300 pounds. Some papers are intended for sketching with soft lead or charcoal (they have more tooth), while others are smoother and meant for hard-line drawing. The assortment, cost, and available sizes of sketch paper are almost unlimited.

Inexpensive, thin, 8- to 11-pound transparent paper is available in both white and yellow. This cheap paper is known simply as "trace," "flimsy," or "bum wad," and comes only in rolls measuring 8" to 48" in width. It is literally used by the yard in the design stage of projects when one piece is placed over an already-drawn one. Transparency allows for a number of different reproduction methods. (This applies to vellum and Mylar as well.)

Vellum paper is usually made from 100% cotton rag and is standard for technical drawing with pencil. It is smooth, transparent, much tougher than trace, and erases well. Because of its wide usage, vellum is available in rolls, pads, and individual sheets. Rolls are made up to 48" wide by 50 yards, pads up to 18" x 24", and sheets up to 30" x 42".

Cutting vellum sheets or trace from rolls is time-consuming. To quickly achieve a straight edge without scissors or a knife with a short-width roll, lay a scale or other straight edge between the roll and the paper, then tear off the desired length. For wider rolls, or even with the shorter ones, the paper can be slipped under the parallel bar and torn. With just a little practice, straight edges are easily obtainable.

Paper must be attached to a drafting board by tape—never with thumbtacks. Masking tape looks the same as drafting tape but works less well. Round circular drafting "dots" can also be easily applied to the corners of drawings. These are slightly more adhesive than drafting tape.

TEARING

FIG. 1.35

Despite the wide availability of paper sizes, there are standard international sheet sizes in metric measurements. These different sizes have a constant ratio and no matter how any sheet is folded, the ratio remains the same. The following list is related to Imperial measurements (in feet and inches).

SIZE	MILLIMETERS	INCHES
A0	841 x 1189	33 1/8 x 46 7/8
A1	594 x 841	23 3/8 x 33 1/8
A2	420 x 594	16 1/2 x 23 3/8
A3	297 x 420	11 3/4 x 16 1/2
A4	210 x 297	8 1/4 x 11 3/4
A5	148 x 210	5 7/8 x 8 1/4
A6	105 x 148	4 1/8 x 5 7/8
A7	74 x 105	2 7/8 x 4 1/8

These sized sheets are not readily available in the United States. However, sheet sizes in the United States are sometimes referred to by letter. The chart below lists sizes.

A. 8 1/2" x 11"
   9" x 12"

B. 11" x 17"
   12" x 18"

C. 17" x 22"
   18" x 24"

D. 22" x 34"
   24" x 36"

Although the chart above is sometimes used, there really is no universal standard. Sizes 30" x 40" and 20" x 30", for instance, are popular presentation drawing sizes, but neither the international system nor the A,B,C,D system accommodates these dimensions.

BOARD

Boards are available for illustration, drafting, model making, matting, and framing. Surface, thickness, size, and cost vary within these general types. Illustration boards are made from 100% rag paper bonded to a cardboard backing. They are manufactured with three different surfaces: a rough, uneven texture; smooth (called cold-pressed); and fine-toothed (called hot press). Fine-toothed board is much the same as vellum and is suitable for either ink or pencil drafting.

Opaque drawing paper, maps, and photographs are usually mounted on boards with spray adhesives. Wet mounting, dry mounting, and mounting with rubber cement are three other alternatives. Temporary wet mounting is often used with watercolor paper and sometimes with other drawing surfaces. With watercolor paper, the paper is thoroughly sponged with water, taped with gum-strip tape (not drafting tape) to a board (not the drafting board). The wet paper stretches when wet and shrinks when dry to an absolutely flat surface. After the watercolors have dried, the sheet is cut off the board and the final drawing remains flat. (If watercolors are directly applied to paper without the above-described "stretching," the paper will buckle.)

SLIP SHEET

SLIP-SHEET MOUNTING

TACK
BACK

TACK
FRONT

DRY MOUNTING

FIG. 1.36

Another technique for wet mounting is to paint a mixture of casein glue and water onto masonite, place the paper or photograph onto the board, and let dry. The combination will curl, which can be neutralized by wet mounting craft or butcher's paper to the back of the masonite at the same time as the finished side is done.

With dry mounting, an adhesive sheet is placed between what is to be mounted and the board. The adhesive sheet is first "tacked" (spot-adhered) at the corners of the original with a tacking iron, and then the combination is next tacked to the mounting board. The three are pressed together in a hot mounting press.

At some point, most people have used rubber cement to glue something to something else, either with the one- or permanent two-coat method. Slip mounting is a special, two-coat process. Like the two-coat technique, both surfaces are coated with rubber cement and allowed to dry. Another sheet of cheap paper—any kind—is laid over the board with just a fraction of an inch not covered by the cheap paper. What is to be mounted is then aligned with this small portion and the cheap paper is slowly slipped out from between the two other materials, smoothing the original down in the process. (With a large original, the technique is more easily done with two people).

To avoid slips while trimming or cutting boards, use a rubber or cork-backed rule. Changing knife blades often prevents ragged edges. If they do occur, however, a sandpaper paddle can be used to smooth edges.

PLASTIC DRAFTING FILM

Plastic drafting film (commonly known by the trade name Mylar™) is very tough and close to 100% transparent. If you don't bear down too hard when erasing, Mylar™ can be erased an endless number of times without changing the surface. Its transparency also allows for the very best reproductions. The plastic is initially "frosted" (treated with chemicals) to achieve a fine-tooth suitable for drawing. Rolls, individual sheets, and pads come in two thicknesses with either one or two surfaces frosted.

Although the tooth of plastic drafting film is slightly too fine for normal lead, special leads are available. Even these, however, do not quite equal the results of standard leads on paper. The latter surface allows for easier application and shading, yet the reproduction of linework on Mylar™ is far superior.

Ink is nearly 100% opaque and plastic drafting film is close to 100% transparent. When ink is combined with the other positive characteristics of plastic drafting film, there is no equal for drafting linework. Anyone who has inked on paper and then does just one drawing on plastic drafting film never goes back.

Inks are either water soluble or waterproof. The former, often called India Ink, is used in fountain pens and for washes with a brush, but not for technical drawing. The latter is employed for drafting, varies in blackness (transparency) from 90% to 95%, has medium to fast drying times, and erases either well or excellently. Every ink manufacturer makes ink for both paper and plastic drafting film, plus special-purpose inks. When an ink is labeled non-clogging for a technical drawing pen, the phrase only means that it will clog less often than other inks.

Technical drawing pens are the best drawing tools for inking, whether used on paper or plastic drafting film. They are good for sketching, but most architects, students, and drafters find them less suitable for hand lettering, where some type of mechanical or applied lettering is preferable. A cap, barrel, sealed head unit, and ink container are the four basic parts of a technical drawing pen. The ink container has two threaded collars; one screws into the barrel and the head screws into the other. Ink from the plastic tube or cartridge flows by gravity and capillary action into the sealed head. To aid the flow of ink or to undo temporary clogs, shake the pen. The point, or nib, within the sealed head is made of steel, tungsten, or jewels, each meant for different drawing surfaces. In addition, points are available in various diameters—from .13 mm. (.005 inch) to 2 mm. (.079 inch). The following information will help you in the use and maintenance of your pen:

1. Points wear down over time, causing thicker lines or complete failure. Cheaper steel points are intended for paper, and if used on plastic drafting film—a much harder surface—will wear down quickly. Though they are more expensive, jeweled and tungsten points are tougher than steel, draw well on any surface, and outlast steel by tenfold. Considering their extended life, these types are well worth the additional cost.
2. Koh-I-Noor, one of the best pen manufacturers, makes Rapidograph pens and has a service policy: For a fraction of the cost of a new head, the company will replace the nib and thoroughly clean the pen.
3. When ink in the pen head dries out, shaking will not start the ink flowing. Always store pens in an upright position and cap them when not in use. A humidified storage unit can also be purchased. The humidifier and vertical storage lessen clogging.
4. Sooner or later every pen needs cleaning, and the time between cleanings depends on the particular ink used, the weather, and the size of the point—ink in smaller-sized nibs dries faster than larger-sized ones. If a pen is used

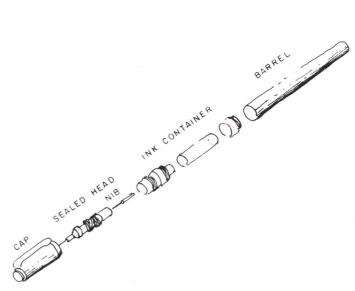

TECHNICAL DRAWING PEN

FIG. 1.37

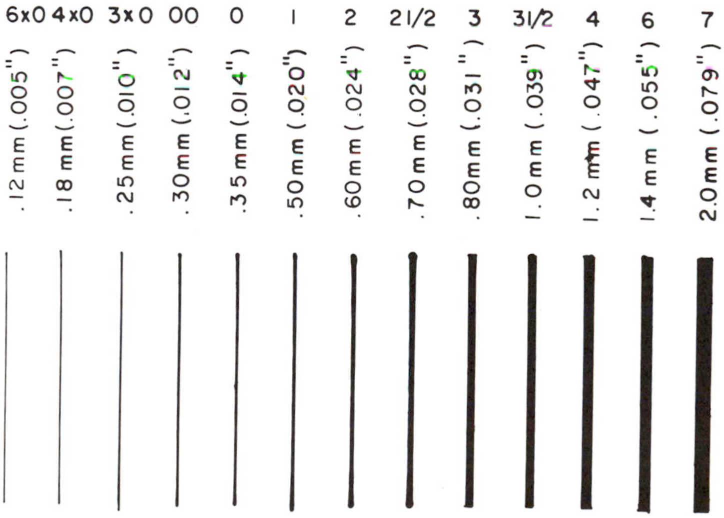

6x0	4x0	3x0	00	0	1	2	2 1/2	3	3 1/2	4	6	7
.12 mm (.005")	.18 mm (.007")	.25 mm (.010")	.30 mm (.012")	.35 mm (.014")	.50 mm (.020")	.60 mm (.024")	.70 mm (.028")	.80 mm (.031")	1.0 mm (.039")	1.2 mm (.047")	1.4 mm (.055")	2.0 mm (.079")

LINE SIZES FROM TECHNICAL DRAWING PENS

FIG. 1.38

every day, it will not clog. In fact, smaller-nibbed pens can usually be left for a few days without clogging and larger-sized nibs will last even longer. Regular cleaning eliminates the guesswork. Once a pen has clogged, flushing it under a faucet may or may not remove the dry ink. An inexpensive pressure-bulb cleaner with a threaded coupler for the pen head is effective for loosening the point up. In addition, the heads can be soaked in cleaner. An expensive ultrasonic cleaner with a special fluid lessens cleaning time and will always unclog a pen.

5. Erasing ink, even on plastic drafting film, should be done carefully or the drawing surface can become marred. New ink-line thickness on such an area will never match the original unerased line. Erasers meant for ink, particularly when used in an electric eraser, can easily burn a hole in both paper and film. A better safeguard is to forego a hard eraser and instead use a special, chemically treated eraser; a soft vinyl eraser with a special liquid eraser; or a soft eraser meant for paper with a wet tip. The last method allows for only one eraser for both ink and lead on all surfaces. Sticks for electric erasers can be bought individually, and purchasing a couple of different kinds and experimenting will establish personal preferences.

6. If an original is intended for opaque reproduction (see Chapter 7), white-out made for ink eliminates most erasing on paper. Lineweight over treated areas usually matches existing linework. Again, trial and error is recommended.

7. Small ink mistakes on film can be scratched off with a razor blade or sharp knife.

Disposable pens are an inexpensive substitute for technical drawing pens. They come with a variety of point diameters, and the quality of lines produced is nearly the same as with technical pens. The advantage to using disposable pens is that they never clog or need cleaning, and the ink inside them takes a long time to run out. Their disadvantage, however, is that the drafter must purchase more than one in a particular point size (once the pen runs out of ink, it's useless), the variety of point sizes is less than with technical pens, and their cost quickly exceeds that of technical pens when a lot of inking is done.

Felt-tipped pens are sometimes used for quick presentation drawings and frequently for sketches. The ink absorbs deeper into paper, takes longer to dry, and is difficult to erase. Felt-tipped pen ink does not stick to drafting film.

Markers are used for illustration but not drafting because their ink bleeds or spreads. Special marker paper lessens these characteristics and is available in pads up to 18" x 24" dimensions.

Large areas of black on a drawing give graphic impact but will buckle lightweight papers. This is not the case with board or plastic drafting film. On these surfaces, the area to be inked is first outlined with pen and then filled in with a brush.

The art of freehand drawing has a long history in China and Japan, and the brush technique takes years to master. Nevertheless, a little practice pulling and pushing stiff and soft brushes can produce textures for use in architectural illustration.

MECHANICAL LETTERING

Stencils, templates, guides, and lettering machines make up the inventory for mechanical lettering. With the exception of the machines, these tools can be used with either ink or pencil, but ink is the option of choice.

Stencils are used in warehouses for labeling packing cases and cartons. They have been adopted by architects for their high graphic impact. "Corbu" stencils, named after the famous architect Le Corbusier, have been popular among architects. Stencils are placed directly on a surface with indivual letters traced to be later filled in with ink, or inked directly with a brush. Because stencils are made from opaque material—usually metal or cardboard—spacing between letters is hard to judge. It's therefore best to lightly outline letters in pencil first.

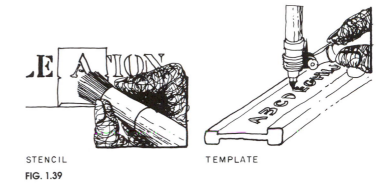

STENCIL

FIG. 1.39

TEMPLATE

Unlike stencils, most lettering templates have raised, transparent plastic for tracing. Although they are used with standard drafting pens, a few require a proprietary pen.

Lettering guide systems have two basic parts: a scriber, or "buggey," and the guide itself. One point of the scriber slides back and forth in a groove in the guide when it's moved from letter to letter. A second point traces the letter on the guide while the inserted pen forms the particular letter. A separate tool adjusts the height and slant when a guide is used. Guides come in eleven letter heights and thirty-two different letterfaces, including metric; guides with accent marks for Spanish, French, and German; slanted letters for isometric drawing (see Chapter 5); and Hebrew and Russian. Leroy, made by Keuffel and Esser, is the best manufacturer of lettering guide systems. (Keuffel and Esser refer to Leroy guides as templates. The author prefers the term guide. A template implies a cutout.) They aren't cheap, but will last a lifetime and produce more uniform letters than templates. The initial high cost of a Leroy set is, in just a short time, much less expensive than press-on letter sheets. Because Leroy is a permanent investment, the drafter will be restricted to the letterface initially selected. A neutral, conservative choice is advisable. All titles in this book were made with Leroy.

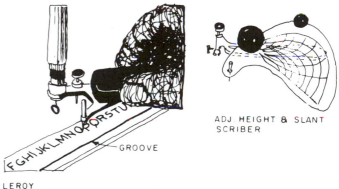

ADJ HEIGHT & SLANT SCRIBER

GROOVE

LEROY

FIG. 1.40

Although rarely useful in student work, a number of lettering machines are available. Kroy manufactures desktop machines that print letters onto adhesive tape as well as high-resolution thermal printers. Also, there are many computerized signage and lettering machines.

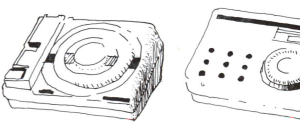

KROY – TAPE

FIG. 1.41

KROY – THERMAL

LINEAR MEASUREMENT

The meter was established by the French in 1791 and is equal to one ten-millionth of the distance from the equator to the pole of the Earth. The metric system is a decimal system similar to the United States' system of dollars and cents. The U.S. is one of the few countries in the world that still uses the Imperial system of measurements (feet-inches, or sometimes called inch-pound). The British, Australians, South Africans, and Canadians converted to metric since the 1970s. Thankfully, the U.S. is slowly moving in this direction.

The major difficulty with the Imperial system comes when adding fractional dimensions—the problem of finding the lowest common denominator. This is an inconvenience, to say the least. Metric measurements are based on units of ten and suffer none of the Imperial measurement potentials for mistakes.

1 mm. is 1 millimeter	=	1/1000 of a meter
1 cm. is 1 centimeter	=	1/100 of a meter
1 dm. is 1 decimeter	=	1/10 of a meter
1 km. is 1 kilometer	=	1000 meters
100,000 centimeters	=	1,000,000 millimeters

CONVERSIONS

IMPERIAL TO METRIC	METRIC TO IMPERIAL
1 inch (1") = 2.540 cm.	1 mm. = .039"
1 foot (1') = .305 m.	1 cm. = .394"
1 yard (1 yd.) = .914 m.	1 m. = 3.281' or 1.094 yds.
1 mile (1 mi.) = 1.609 km.	1 km. = .621 mi.

Architectural and engineering drawings are normally done at less than full size, and the reduction is expressed as a fraction or ratio of real size. A scale is a tool that has different ratios printed on it and is used for drawing measurement.

IMPERIAL	APPROXIMATE METRIC
1/16" = 1'0"	1:200
1/8" = 1'0'	1:100
1/4" = 1'0"	1:50
1/2" = 1'0"	1:20
1" = 1'0"	1:10
3" = 1'0"	1:5

The Imperial system also has fractions of 6"=1'0" (one-half full size), 3/4"=1'0", 3/8"=1'0", 3/16"=1'0" and 3/32" = 1'0". Imperial fractions are on architectural scales, and usually have two on each scale edge running in opposite directions. These scales come in 6", 12", and 24" lengths. The twelve-inch is a must for beginners, and 6" is very convenient. Scales have a triangular shape (six different scales), or are flat with beveled edges (four different scales). At the end of each individual scale are inch measurements. When measurements are made, keeping your eye at right angles to the board and scale helps accuracy.

TRIANGULAR METRIC

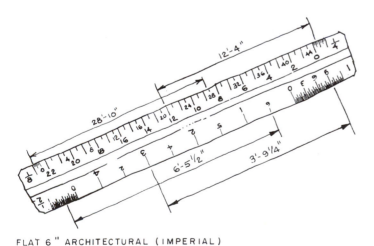

FLAT 6" ARCHITECTURAL (IMPERIAL)

FIG. 1.42

Engineers have accommodated the fractional problem of the Imperial system by using decimal fractions of a foot on scales. The subdivisions between feet are consequently marked off in units of ten and the scales are similarly expressed in units of ten: 1"=10', 1"=20', 1"=30', 1"=40', and so on. These divisions can also be employed for 1"=1', 1"=2', 1"=3', etc. Unlike architectural scales, there is only one scale per edge.

Surveyors' drawings, necessary for architectural work, are made with engineering scales. These scales are handy when transferring dimensions from one drawing location to another. Because an engineer's scale has only one scale per edge, there is no confusion caused by two scales running in opposite directions.

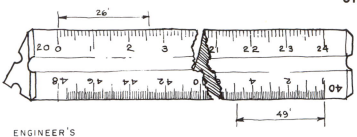

ENGINEER'S

FIG. 1.43

ANGULAR MEASUREMENT

A drafting machine and adjustable triangle allow an angle to be set, then moved without resetting to draw parallel lines. With protractors, only an angle is marked off. They are available as either full circles with 360° or half-circles with 180°.

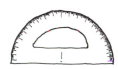

PROTRACTORS

FIG. 1.44

TEMPLATES

There are dozens of non-lettering templates available to the architect. A circle template is a must for drawing, and a standard 7" x 8" template with forty-five different-sized circles is good to have. A lavatory/kitchen planning template is the next template you should purchase. After you have these two, your particular needs will dictate what to buy. Among the many other templates available are general ones with different geometric shapes, ellipse templates, furniture templates, landscape templates, and a host of others. Non-lettering templates do not have inking edges but can be raised off the drawing surface by temporarily resting them on two triangles or other straight edges.

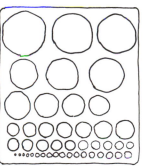

CIRCLE TEMPLATE

PORTION OF BATHROOM + KITCHEN TEMPLATE

FIG. 1.45

CURVES

Irregular curves can only be drawn mechanically with the aid of French curves. Consequently, every student must sooner or later buy these tools. It is advisable to purchase at least two of them, one with slow curvature and another that changes curvature quickly. They can be purchased with or without inking edges.

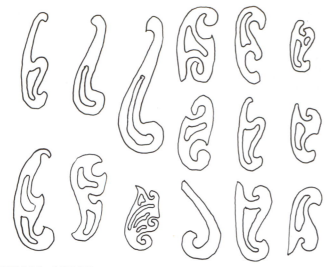

FRENCH CURVES

FIG. 1.46

ONE CURVE WITH ONE FRENCH CURVE

FIG. 1.47

More likely than not, one edge of a French curve will not make the complete shape desired. Various segments of the curve will need to be used, or even parts of another French curve. The final product should have smooth transitions from one portion to another.

SPLINE WITH WEIGHTS   LEAD–FILLED SPLINE

FIG. 1.48

For longer, more regular curves, a thick plastic spline held in place with weights can be purchased. A flexible curve rule that has a lead core allows the spline to be fixed for a particular curve

Dry-transfer sheets have letters or symbols printed on the back of transparent plastic sheets covered with a light adhesive. The printed material is rubbed with a dull pencil or burnisher and transferred to the drawing surface. When all letters or symbols have been transferred, trace is placed over the final product and rubbed down again.

Many different letter faces are available (390 typestyles alone from Letraset), in letter heights from 8-point to 96-point. The transparency of the sheet helps letter spacing.

Although dry transfer manufacturers print greater numbers of certain letters than others, inevitably some letters are used up before others. This bothersome fact makes dry-transfer lettering sheets even more expensive than their high initial cost.

LETTER SIZES

FIG. 1.49

STICKY-BACKED TRANSFER SHEETS

The same manufacturers that make dry-transfer sheets also produce sticky-backed transfer sheets. Tones, patterns, and textures are printed onto nearly-transparent, sticky, thin plastic sheets that have a backup sheet of tough plastic or paper. The two are placed over a drawing area to receive the printed material and roughly cut freehand. (It is easy to cut through drawing paper when trimming sticky-backed material. A light hand is required.) The cut sticky-backed area is then lifted off the backup sheet, positioned over the appropriate drawing area, and cut to exact size. Excess material is then removed, and what remains is rubbed down with a burnisher or small triangle.

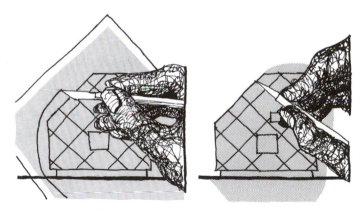

CUTTING STICKY-BACKED TRANSFER TONE

FIG. 1.50

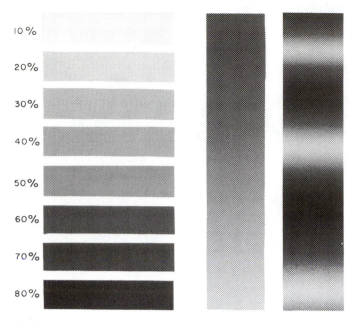

10 %
20%
30%
40%
50%
60%
70%
80%

STICKY - BACKED TRANSFER TONES

FIG. 1.51

Sticky-backed sheets come in percentages of gray at various line screens (dots per inch), as well as graded tones. Abstract textures, line patterns, literal representations, or architectural materials, cars, people, trees, and bushes are also available. Sheet size is limited to 9" x 12". Abutting sheets to cover large areas will always produce a noticeable seam.

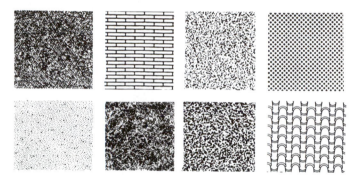

STICKY - BACKED TRANSFER TEXTURES AND PATTERNS

FIG. 1.52

CLEANING AND CLEANLINESS

Tools should be clean before use, particularly with lead on paper, or reproducible smudges will occur. Regular cleaning is a good idea, but if time or a lack of compulsion does not allow this, triangles and T-squares need cleaning more frequently than any other tools as they slide directly on the drawing surface. Parallel bars, or more specifically, the rollers, are the next biggest offenders for dirty drawings. Lead ghost images from the drafting board can be another problem. Tools such as scales, pens, clutch pencils, and the like only need cleaning if you feel compelled to do so.

It should go without saying that your hands should always be clean. Since some drawings take a long time to complete, experienced drafters will cover all areas of the drawing, except the immediate area being worked on, with tissue. It's also a good idea to rest your hands on a piece of paper when lettering or shading in order to prevent smudging.

DRAWING STORAGE

Finished drawings should be protected at all times. Large, flat, often fireproof file cabinets are the permanent home for originals in offices. Student drawings should be stored in a flat container of some sort. For instance, a number of cheap portfolio cases are made in cardboard, and more expensive ones come with handles and zippers. Rolling the drawings up in a cardboard or plastic tube is another alternative. When rolling a paper original or print, always roll with the finish surface on the outside. Unrolled drawings have a residual curl. This is easier to manage when the finish surface is on the outside. Drawings that have already been rolled have a residual curl. This is easier to manage when the finish surface is on the outside. Original drawings never leave a professional office unless they are to be reproduced. When you do take them in to be reproduced, use a tube.

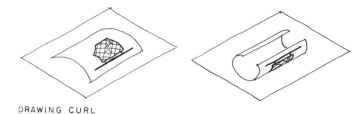

DRAWING CURL

FIG. 1.53

NEVERS

1. Never fill a pen with ink over a drawing.
2. Never shake a pen over a drawing.
3. Never leave an ink bottle uncapped.
4. Never use a knife against the plastic edge of a triangle, T-square, parallel bar, or scale.
5. Never use a scale as a straight edge.
6. Never draw horizontal lines with the lower edge of a T- square or parallel bar.
7. Never draft without taping a drawing to the drafting board.
8. Never use thumbtacks to fix a drawing to the board.
9. Never fold an original drawing.
10. Never put a drink anywhere near an original drawing.

HEALTH

We now know that spending many hours at a computer can cause eye and hand problems, so standing up and stretching every twenty minutes is advisable. Drafters who spend a lot of time drawing by hand are prone to severe posture strain, because they naturally hunch over the drafting board, forcing the spine into abnormal curvature. Standing up and stretching can also help this condition, but an even better corrective excercise is to regularly sit up straight. If you are far-sighted, wearing bifocal glasses will force your head to more correctly align with your spine.

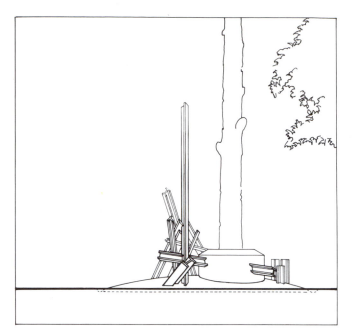

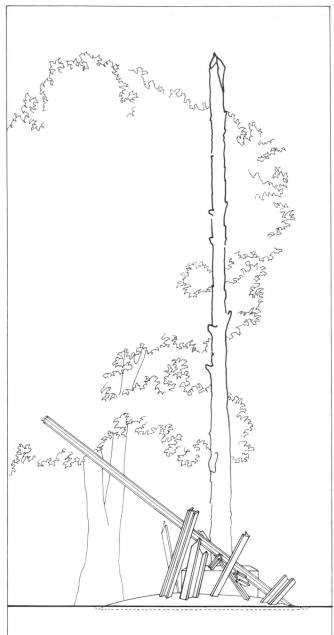

CHAPTER 2

POINTS, LINES, PLANES, AND SOLIDS

PLAN

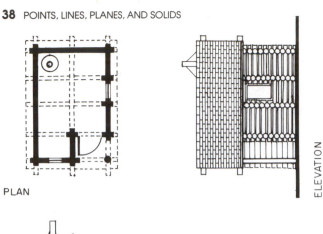

ELEVATION

SECTION

ELEVATION

MULTIVIEWS

FIG. 2.1

PARALINE

PERSPECTIVE

FIG. 2.2

Prior to the late eighteenth century, there was no standardized method for making architectural drawings. Although some ways of drawing corresponded to our current usage of drafting, most did not. In the 1790s, Gaspard Monge, a French physicist and engineer, developed Descriptive Geometry—the technique for relating a series of drawings to completely describe any three-dimensional object. His technical process became the universal standard for engineering and architectural drawing.

In this chapter, descriptive geometry has been selectively adapted for architectural purposes. The methods explained form the abstract basis of architectural drawing, and practical demonstrations of principles can be seen by following the cross references to actual building designs in chapters that follow. This chapter also includes "spacial observations" to help develop the all-important facility of seeing in three dimensions, and an introduction to three-dimensional graphic theory.

Today, all architects draw multiviews—multiple views of plans, sections, and elevations—using descriptive geometry. Each of these multiviews presents a two-dimensional image. When enough plans, sections, and elevations are combined, the building can be envisioned.

Architects also draw perspectives and paralines—illustrations that present a single, three-dimensional resemblance of a building. Perspectives and paralines are easier to grasp visually, more time-consuming to draw, and always hide some views. Multiviews, by comparison, require a person to look at more than one drawing for visual understanding. It is the completeness of multiviews that makes them the predominate drawing type during all phases of the architect's work.

Multiview drawings enlist the parallel projection of imaginary lines from an object or building onto transparent planes with a viewer outside looking at the resultant picture. This method of producing a drawing, called orthographic projection, does not match human seeing; there is no convergence of parallel lines into space. The transparent planes, or image planes, can be horizontal, vertical, or sloping in space. If the plane is horizontal, the multiview is called a plan and describes a view looking up or down but always parallel to the horizon. A plan shows length and width but not height. Vertical image planes are elevations and indicate length and height or width and height, but not both. Plans and elevations are flat in nature and have many advantages over paralines and perspectives: Right angles of the original object remain right angles, horizontal lines are horizontal, and all lines parallel to their original counterparts are directly measurable. A multiview that is projected onto a sloping image plane is an inclined view.

By definition, what is constant in orthographic projection is that all projection lines must be parallel and strike the image plane at right angles.

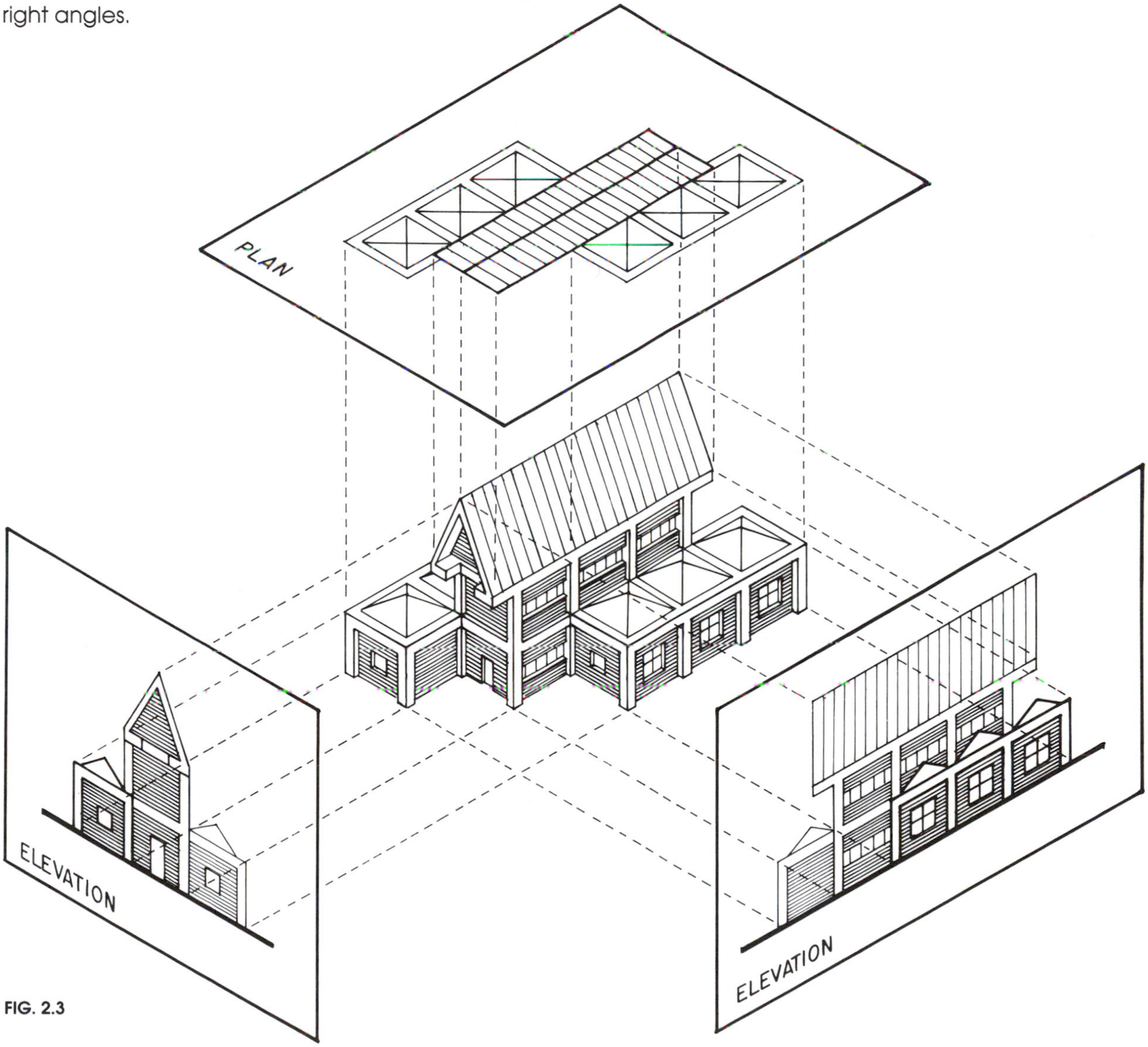

PLAN

ELEVATION

ELEVATION

FIG. 2.3

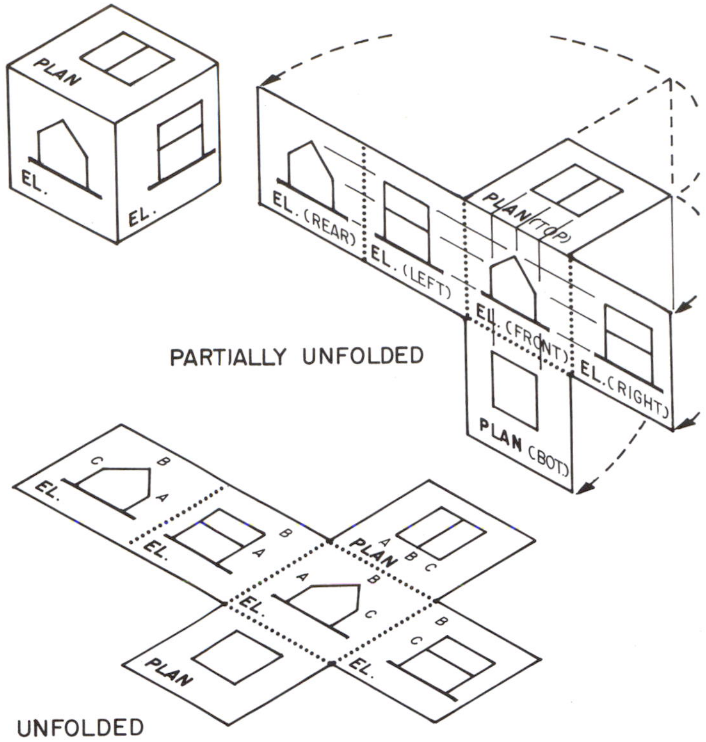

THE THEORETICAL BOX

The majority of plans and elevations assume a conventional six-sided theoretical box surrounding an object. When the drawing is done, the sides of the box are unfolded into a flat plane (the drawing paper) where there is a new set of parallel lines showing commonness of height, length, and width from view to view. The most typical method of unfolding the box is illustrated in Fig. 2.4.

Six views are seldom required with descriptive geometry problems. The reason for this is that lines and planes usually need only two views for spatial definition. The other four only show mirrored information: The top plan is the reverse of the bottom plan, and an elevation from the left is a reverse of the right. Three or more views are needed with solids, particularly in architectural drawing.

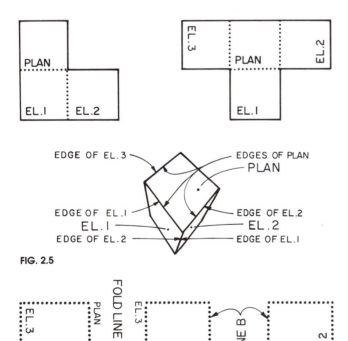

FIG. 2.4

PARTIALLY UNFOLDED

UNFOLDED

Fig. 2.5 shows one arrangement of less than six views derived from the unfolding technique described above. To its right is another arrangement obtained from a different unfolding method. The latter requires the viewer to turn his or her head for reading. Both methods are used in this chapter. Note that regardless of the unfolding technique, elevations are on vertical image planes and are at 90° to the plan.

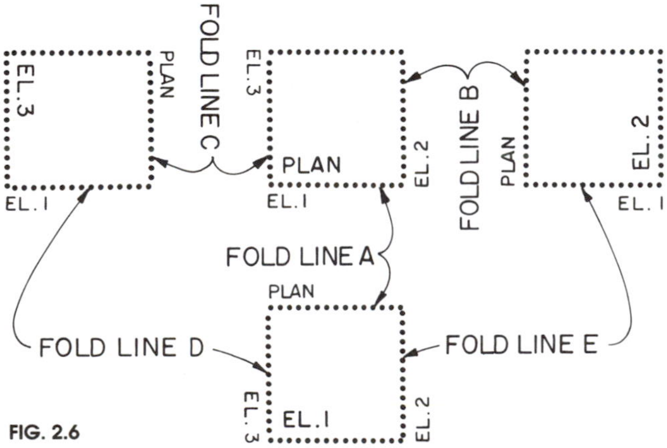

FIG. 2.5

Multiview drawings should be thought of as both a group of unfolded views and as separate views obtained by the viewer moving around and over an object, stopping in front of each image plane, and taking a picture at right angles to that image plane. At each location the photograph shows other views as edges.

Lines A,B,C,D, and E, in Fig. 2.6 are the edges of the unfolded box, and consequently are named fold lines. Each fold line is common to another view. For example, when looking at Elevation 1, the vertical fold lines are the edges of two other elevations, and the top fold line is the edge of the Plan.

FIG. 2.6

POINTS AND DIMENSIONS

Any two points within the theoretical box have three dimensions (two horizontal and one vertical) parallel to image planes. These dimensions define the spatial relationship between the two points. When points and dimensions are orthographically projected onto horizontal or vertical image planes, only two of the three dimensions can be seen in any one view. For example, a plan shows length and width but not height; an elevation shows height but not both length and width. Also, horizontal and vertical dimensions must be the same from view to view. The height between points must be the same in all elevations; a width in one view must be the same in another, etc. (This chapter uses slashes to show dimensional limits rather than arrows. The slash is preferred by most architects. Also, although most authors of descriptive geometry textbooks reference dimensions to fold lines, this chapter uses dimensions between points. Either dimensioning system produces the same orthographic results.)

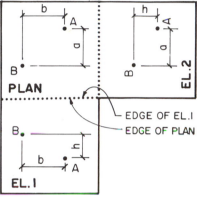

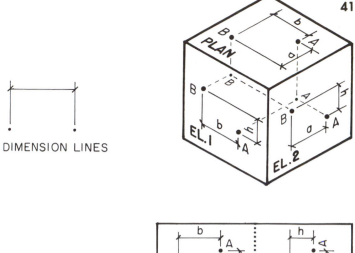

DIMENSION LINES

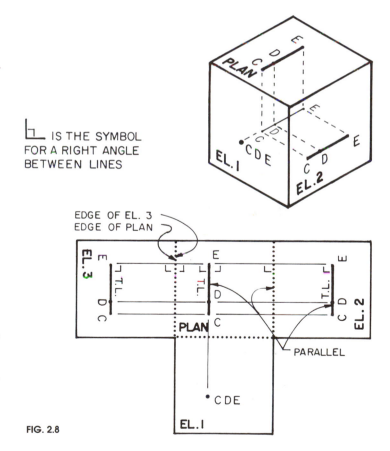

FIG. 2.7

POINTS, LINES, AND TRUE LENGTH

When a horizontal line is perpendicular to an elevation, the elevation will show the line as a point. Likewise, a vertical line will appear as a point in plan. Any point on a line can be projected into other views of the line. For instance, in Fig. 2.8, point D in Plan is projected into Elevation 2 and 3.

The true length of a line only appears on an image plane that is parallel to the original line inside the theoretical box. A true length line (T.L. in drawings) is exactly the same length as the original line—it cannot be shorter or longer. When a line is in true length, the projection lines from the original line must be at 90° to the original, as well as by definition of an orthographic view, 90° to the image plane.

The identification of points in descriptive geometry illustrations starts with an arbitrary selection of one view (in Fig. 2.8, Plan). Then the closest point to another view with a letter is labeled (point C is the closest point to Elevation 1). Other points can then be identified as they either get successively higher or lower, ahead or behind of the initial selection (point E is behind C in Plan). Finally, the same points in other views are labeled (Elevation 1, 2, and 3).

⌐ IS THE SYMBOL FOR A RIGHT ANGLE BETWEEN LINES

FIG. 2.8

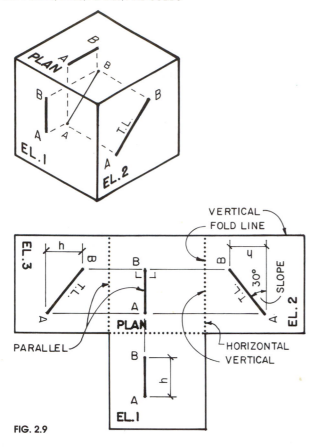

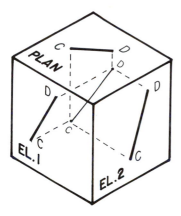

FIG. 2.9

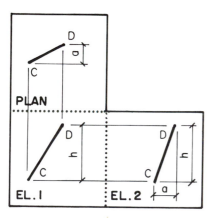

FIG. 2.10

SLOPING LINES

A sloping line is neither horizontal nor vertical but is parallel to two elevation image planes of the conventional six-sided box. In Fig. 2.9, the sloping line AB is in true length in Elevation 2 and 3. All other views will illustrate the sloping line in foreshortened or less than true length.

Fold lines, as discussed earlier, are the edges of other views; any fold line in plan is the edge of an elevation and represents verticality in plan. The fold lines in Elevation 2 show horizontality on two edges and verticality in the other two. The slope of a line, also shown in Elevation 2, is defined as the angle formed between a true length line and a horizontal line drawn from the lowest point of the given line.

All titles and labeling of points are horizontal in elevations. By custom, titles in elevations are always at the bottom of a drawing. This location makes them parallel to the fold line between plan and elevation.

OBLIQUE LINES

An oblique line is not parallel to any side of the theoretical six-sided box. All conventional views will show foreshortening and none will indicate true length.

SPATIAL OBSERVATION: *In Fig. 2.10, point D is "a" distance behind C and appears as such in both Plan and Elevation 2.*

TRUE LENGTH OF OBLIQUE LINES

Finding the true length of an oblique line involves changing the shape of the theoretical box. For example, the true length of line CD from Fig. 2.10 on the previous page is constructed by drawing Elevation 5 in Fig. 2.11, a new view parallel to the original line, and unfolding the box in a different way. To accomplish this, a line is drawn parallel to CD in Plan. This is the edge view of Elevation 5. When unfolded, line CD appears in true length. Elevation 5 is parallel to CD inside the box and, for practical purposes, made an oblique line into a sloping line.

Note that all elevations are at 90° to the plan, but not necessarily at 90° to other elevations. Elevation 5 in Fig. 2.11 is at 90° to the plan, but not at 90° to adjacent Elevation 2 or Elevation 4. An elevation not at 90° to the other elevations is technically called an auxiliary elevation.

In all descriptive geometry problems, dimensions have to be taken from one view to another. A lightly drawn line serves for direct projections. When scaling dimensions and transferring them to another drawing, using dividers is most dependable. Marking the given dimensions on the edge of a separate piece of paper, moving the paper to the new location, and remarking is the next most precise. While a scale can be accurate if used carefully, it is nevertheless subject to mistakes (e.g. a 4'-6" dimension ends up as 4'-8" or 5'-6").

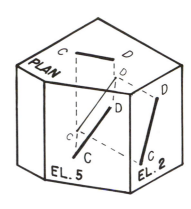

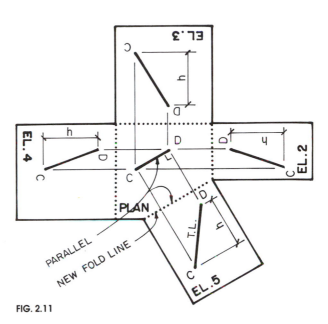

FIG. 2.11

ELIMINATING THE THEORETICAL BOX

Because countless elevations can be projected from a plan, representing the many unfolded sides of the theoretical box can become confusing. In architectural work, the sides of the box are never shown. For these two reasons, the sides will not be shown for the remainder of this chapter.

When the sides of the box are eliminated, remember that the title of an elevation is horizontal and parallel to the now imaginary fold line between plan and elevation. Projections from the plan are therefore perpendicular to the title "Elevation" or "El".

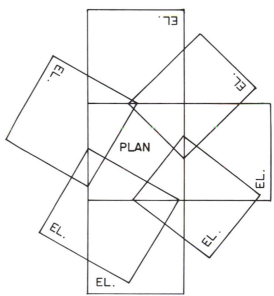

FIG. 2.12

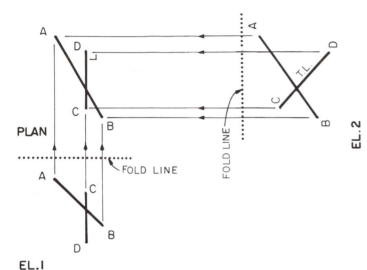

PLAN

EL.1 (Given)

COMMON
FOLD LINE
VERTICAL
EDGE VIEW OF
EL.2

EL.2 (Given)

PLAN

FOLD LINE

FOLD LINE

EL.1

EL.2

FIG. 2.13

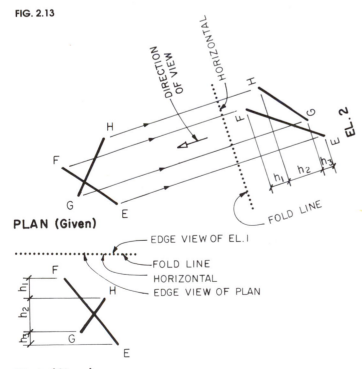

DIRECTION
OF VIEW

HORIZONTAL

PLAN (Given)

FOLD LINE

EDGE VIEW OF EL.1
FOLD LINE
HORIZONTAL
EDGE VIEW OF PLAN

EL.2

EL.1 (Given)

FIG. 2.14

DRAWING A THIRD VIEW OF LINES

The first step when drawing a new multiview from two given views is to label common points and then examine both drawings before continuing. In Fig. 2.13, the closest point to Plan is labeled A in the elevations, and the other end of the line is designated B. Line CD is likewise labeled. When examining the two given elevations, imagine the common vertical fold line between the two elevations. This line is also an edge view of the other elevation. In Elevation 1, line CD is parallel to the edge view of Elevation 2. Line CD is therefore a true length line in Elevation 2.

Once points have been identified and two given views analyzed, projection lines are drawn from the two elevations (at right angles from the title "EL.") to locate individual points in Plan. Point A is found, point B next, etc. Points are then connected to form lines. In complicated problems, points should be located in a new view one at a time, rather than projecting all points from one view and then doing the same from a second drawing. The latter technique can cause confusion or mistakes. Projection lines in orthographic drawing must be at right angles to edge views and image planes of other views. In Fig. 2.13, sloping Line CD in Plan is parallel to the fold line between Plan and Elevation 2, confirming that CD is a true length line in Elevation 2.

In Fig. 2.13, two elevations were given and a plan was constructed. In Fig. 2.14, Plan and Elevation 1 are given and a second elevation is drawn. The solution to Fig. 2.13 was resolved by projection only, while Fig. 2.14 is solved by projection *plus* measuring dimensions in one drawing (EL.1), and remeasuring them in another view (EL.2).

The point closest to Elevation 1 has been labeled E in Plan. This makes point F in Elevation 1 the closest to the image plane of Plan and E the furthest. The height dimensions are vertical and, consequently, at right angles to the horizontal in all elevations.

The open arrow indicates the direction of the view from Elevation 2 (an auxiliary). This direction is horizontal in Plan and, by nature of orthographic projection, in the opposite direction from projections.

SPATIAL OBSERVATION: *There are no true length lines present in Fig. 2.14. All lines are oblique.*

DIMENSION TRANSFER LINES

A 45° line (marked XY in Figs. 2.15 and 2.16) drawn across projection lines is a construction aid for transferring dimensions at right angles from one view to another. This alternative to scaling and rescaling dimensions is based on the two sides of a 45° triangle being equal. This technique lessens mistakes associated with measuring and re-measuring dimensions.

In Fig. 2.15, the height dimension from given Elevation 1 is transferred to the new Elevation 2. In Fig. 2.16, Plan dimension "a" is transferred to Elevation 2.

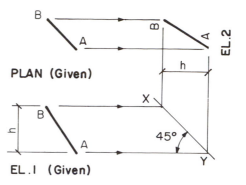

FIG. 2.15

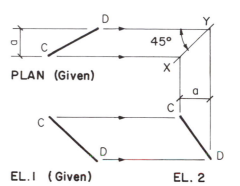

FIG. 2.16

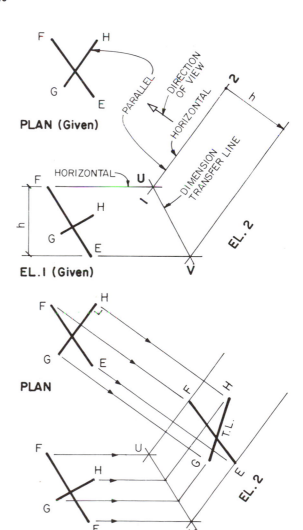

Any number of auxiliary elevations can be drawn from a plan. In Fig. 2.17, a dimension transfer line is used to construct an auxiliary elevation not at 90° to others. If, for instance, an elevation showing oblique line GH in true length were required, line 1,2 would first be drawn parallel to GH. This line is horizontal and is parallel to the imaginary fold line between the two views. Next, the height dimension "h", which must be the same in all elevations, is measured from Elevation 1 and rescaled downward from the line just drawn. This establishes the horizontal and common height. After this, the four lines defining maximum height are extended from the two elevations until they intersect. The two points of intersection are connected to form the dimension transfer line UV. (The viewing direction determines the horizontal, angle of the dimension transfer line, and whether or not there are any true length lines.)

Elevation 2 is completed by drawing projection lines from Plan at right angles to line GH into Elevation 2, and by then transferring dimensions from Elevation 1 (Fig. 2.17).

Dimension transfer lines can also be used to transmit dimensions from plan to inclined views (shown later). For an architectural example of dimension transfer lines, see page 118.

SPATIAL OBSERVATION: *In Fig. 2.17, line GH in Elevation 1 slopes away from the image plane with point G closest to the elevation. This observation comes from looking at both Plan and Elevation 1 simultaneously.*

FIG. 2.17

INCLINED VIEWS

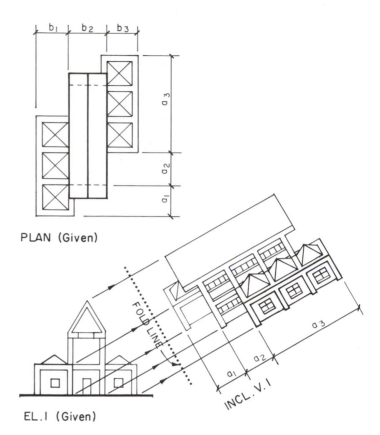

PLAN (Given)

EL.I (Given)

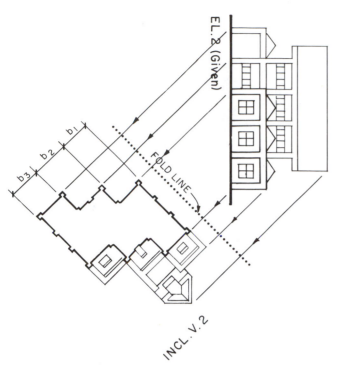

FIG. 2.18

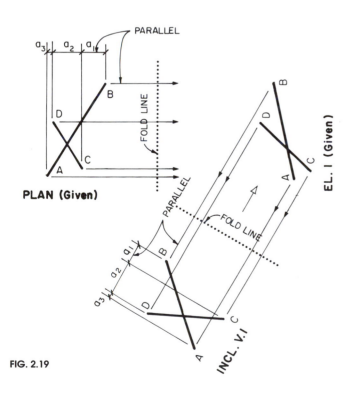

PLAN (Given)

FIG. 2.19

Inclined views ("Incl.V." in drawings) are multiview drawings that use orthographic projections in sloping or oblique image planes. These views can only be unfolded from an elevation or other inclined view. Unlike the inclined views above, right angles in the original object do not necessarily end up as right angles in an inclined view.

In Fig. 2.19, (bottom) Inclined View 1 is projected from given Elevation 1. The location of points along projection lines in this new view have the same relationship to each other and the new fold line as the corresponding points in Plan: Point B is the closest to the fold line, Point A is the furthest. The dimensions a_1, a_2, and a_3 in both views are parallel to projection lines and at right angles to their respective fold lines. (Note that there are no true length lines in this example.) In other words, the relationship of points in an inclined view is found by skipping a view backwards. In Fig. 2.19, Inclined View 1 was unfolded from Elevation 1 and Elevation 1, in turn, was unfolded from Plan. Elevation 1 was the view skipped over.

SPATIAL OBSERVATIONS: *Inclined View 1 in Figs. 2.18 and 2.19 look at an angle to the top of the illustration. Inclined View 2 in Fig. 2.18 shows a tipped bottom view.*

True length lines can be found by drawing inclined views. In Fig. 2.20, Inclined View 1 depicts the true length of line AB (projections from Elevation 1 are at 90° from the line). Inclined View 1 was unfolded downward and Inclined View 2 upwards. Therefore, Inclined View 1 shows the underside of the line, while Inclined View 2 shows the top.

If necessary, inclined views can be projected from another inclined view. Inclined View 3 was taken from Inclined View 2 (dimensions were obtained by skipping a view backwards to Elevation 1).

Titles for all inclined views in this chapter are parallel to the projection lines for Inclined View 1, and at right angles to projection lines for Inclined View 2. Unlike elevations, titles for inclined views are not necessarily related to the horizontal.

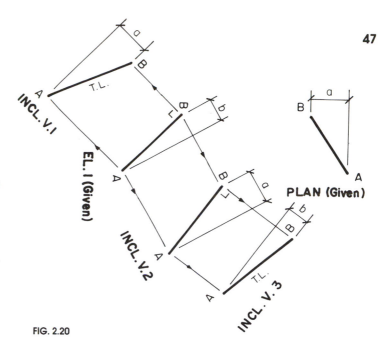

FIG. 2.20

INTERSECTING LINES

When two lines intersect, their crossing point (C.P.) must be the same in all multiviews. The test for whether two given lines intersect or are separate is made by simply projecting from one crossing point into an adjacent view. This will show if the two crossing points are on the same projection line. If they are, the lines intersect. If not, the lines are separate.

For example, the crossing points in Plan and Elevation 1 are on the same projection line in Fig. 2.21. Auxiliary Elevation 2 in Fig. 2.21 confirms intersection (line CD appears as a point on line EF).

In Fig. 2.22, lines GH and IJ are proven separate since the crossing points are not on a common projection line. But once this has been realized, the important question of which line is in front of which still needs to be answered.

Displaying what is ahead or behind of what can and can't be seen is called visibility. Frequently, these features can be understood by inspecting given views. However, Fig. 2.21 does not reveal visibility. In this case, a mechanical process must be used for determination.

For visual clarification, the two lines in the bottom of Fig. 2.22 have been changed to thin planes. To find whether plane IJ is ahead or behind of GH in Elevation 1, the crossing point is projected into Plan where it hits plane IJ before striking plane GH. Because the Plan shows relative closeness to the image plane of the elevation, IJ is ahead of GH in Elevation 1. In a like manner, projecting the crossing point of Plan into Elevation 1 tells the viewer that GH is higher than IJ in Plan.

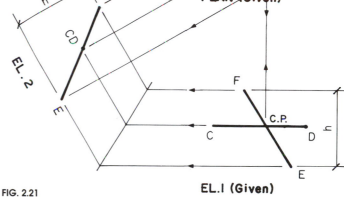

FIG. 2.21

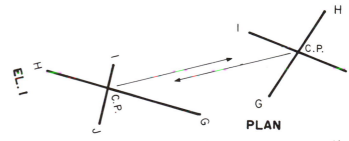

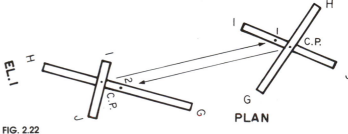

FIG. 2.22

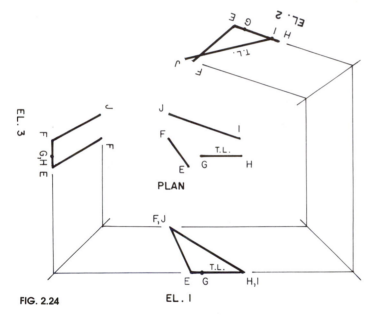

FIG. 2.23

POINTS AND LINES: SOME EXAMPLES TO NOTE

This section provides a few graphic applications of the mechanical projection techniques, types of multiviews, and principles previously described in this chapter. In the following pages, the basic material so far presented is expanded into more architectural elements of planes and solids. A thorough absorption of this early material is not only useful, but essential for understanding what follows.

Fig. 2.23 shows two lines parallel in space. They will always be parallel unless they appear as a single line (Elevation 1 and 3) or as points (Inclined View 2). Lines that appear as points are always projections from a view showing the lines as true length (points in Inclined View 2, true length in Inclined View 1).

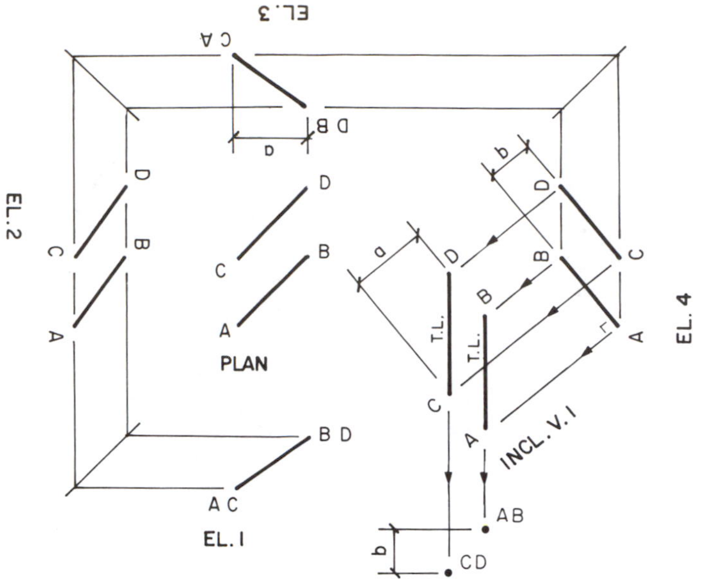

FIG. 2.24

As stated earlier, all views must be examined in descriptive geometry problems to determine spatial relationships. Elevation 1 in Fig. 2.24 suggests a plane is formed, but what appears as a triangle is actually composed of three non-intersecting lines (revealed in Plan). Individual lines or portions of lines within this illustration appear as true length lines in certain views and not in others. For example, GH is true length in Plan and Elevation 1; IJ is true length in Elevation 2.

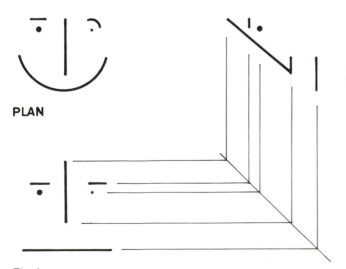

FIG. 2.25

A straight line in one view may be a curve in reality. The curved mouth in Fig. 2.25 is visible as a straight line in Elevation 1, which tells the viewer that the mouth is in true length and shape in Plan. The nose is two lines and Elevation 2 depicts true shape. Also, the eyes, which appear as circles in two views, must be spheres.

Usually, any two views will graphically describe a pattern of lines. In this example, Plan and Elevation 1, however, do not describe the nose.

A curve in only one plane is called a two-dimensional curve. One that is not in a single plane is called a three-dimensional curve. A single curve can also be both two- and three-dimensional (see page 155 for an example).

If two views of a curve are given, other drawings can be made by projecting common points into the new view. In Fig. 2.26, a semi-ellipse combined with a straight line are given in Plan and Elevation 1. A series of points are marked off in Elevation 1 and projected to Plan. The points from both these views were then taken into Elevation 2, originating the true sized (T.S.) curve/straight line. Any other views, such as Elevation 3, can be drawn by similarly using common points from any two adjacent views.

The curve in Fig. 2.26 is on one plane (plan shows a straight line). Other curves may not be in one plane, therefore no single drawing can indicate true shape, size, or length.

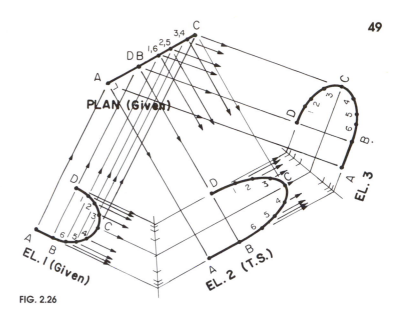

FIG. 2.26

Many descriptive geometry problems must be resolved by projecting from given views, finding a solution, and projecting back to modify preceding views. Additionally, some problems involve more than simply constructing a new view, particularly when descriptive geometry is applied to architectural work.

In Fig. 2.27, the problem is to draw line FH perpendicular to GFE in the direction shown in the given Plan. The solution requires knowing two principles in advance. First, perpendicularity can only be established in a view that shows the original line in true length (Inclined View 1). Second, the true length of a line perpendicular to another can only be measured in a view that displays the original line (EFG) as a point (Inclined View 2).

The first step is to establish the direction of line FH in all four views. Any point (x) on the direction line in Plan is projected into Inclined View 1, where FH must be perpendicular to GE, and then into Elevation 1. The direction is then found in Inclined View 2 by projecting from Inclined View 1 and using the "b" dimension from Elevation 1. EH can then be measured along this direction in Inclined View 2 and projected back to previous views (shown lightly dashed for clarity).

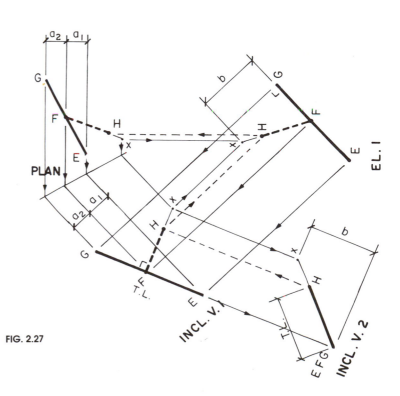

FIG. 2.27

FLAT PLANES

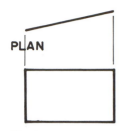

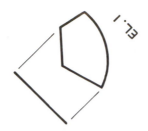

PLAN

EL. I

FIG. 2.28

PLAN

Planes can be flat, curved, or warped (warped planes are discussed in Chapter 3). Triangles are always flat planes, if the corners are connected by straight lines. If one view of any plane is a straight line, the plane is flat (Fig. 2.28).

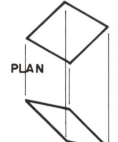

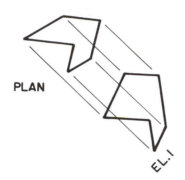

PLAN

EL. I

FIG. 2.29

PLAN

Any plane that has an even number of sides with opposite sides parallel in two views and in which all points project from view to view is a flat plane (Fig. 2.29).

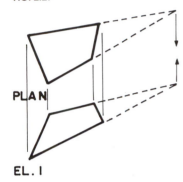

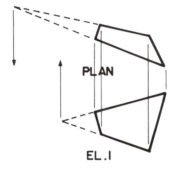

PLAN

PLAN

EL. I

EL. I

FIG. 2.30

Quadrilaterals may or may not be flat. If two opposite sides of a figure can be extended to form two matching triangles (all points must project from one view to another), the plane is flat (Fig. 2.30). If points do not project, the plane is not flat.

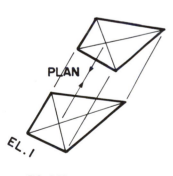

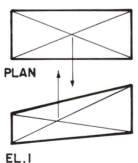

PLAN

PLAN

EL. I

EL. I

FIG. 2.31

A second test for the flatness of a quadrilateral is much the same as the test for intersecting lines: The centers, found by connecting corners, must be on a common projection line for the plane to be flat (Fig. 2.31). Given one view, an entirely new architectural view can be created by employing this test for the flatness of a quadrilateral. For instance, if a roof plan were given, the center of this plane, along with the corners, would be projected into an elevation. These lines would serve as control elements for any desired heights.

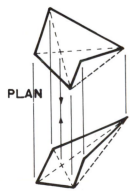

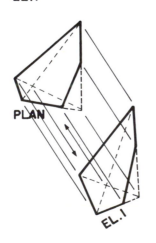

PLAN

PLAN

EL. I

EL. I

FIG. 2.32

A five-sided plane can be made into a quadrilateral by connecting two points or by extending two sides (Fig. 2.32). In either case, testing the imaginary quadrilateral for flatness will determine if the original five-sided figure is flat.

If a plane with more than five sides does not appear as a straight line in a given view, the plane may still be flat. To determine flatness, an edge view (a straight line) must be drawn (see page 55).

Flat planes can be generated within imaginary flat planes. If the corners of a plane touch the sides of an imaginary flat plane and project from view to view, the real plane is flat.

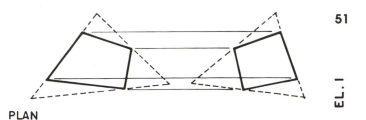

PLAN

FIG. 2.33

THE THIRD VIEW OF PLANES

Given two views of a plane, a third view is drawn by projecting points from the given views until the projections intersect, and then connecting points to form lines. Once all lines are connected, a third view is complete.

Fig. 2.34 is a sloping flat plane (line AB in Elevation 1 is parallel to Plan).

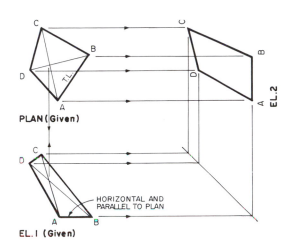

FIG. 2.34

The triangle is an oblique plane: it has no side parallel to the conventional six-sided box.

> SPATIAL OBSERVATION: *After Elevation 2 is obtained, it can be visualized that, from looking at Plan, point F is behind point E. Elevation 2, despite its unfolded location, is a "side" elevation and shows point F in the same "behind" relationship to point E.*

If you cannot visually grasp a particular geometric configuration immediately, follow mechanical projection. You will find that spatial visualization improves with experience.

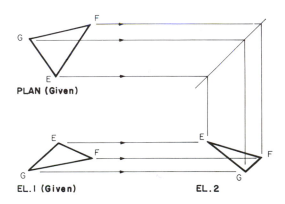

FIG. 2.35

Fig. 2.36 demonstrates the construction of a third view of a warped plane. This figure is a hyperbolic paraboloid (see Chapter 3, page 94. The building on page 98 has a hyperbolic paraboloid as a roof.

> SPATIAL OBSERVATIONS: *In Figs. 2.34 and 2.36, Elevations 1 look at an angle to the top of the figure. Elevation 1 in Fig. 2.35, on the other hand, shows the underside of the triangle.*

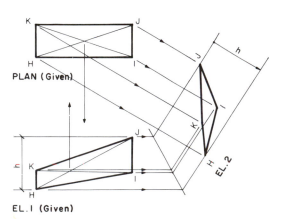

FIG. 2.36

IMAGINARY LINES ON PLANES

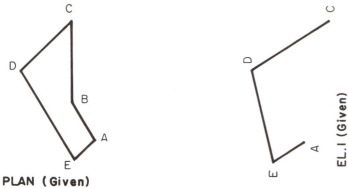

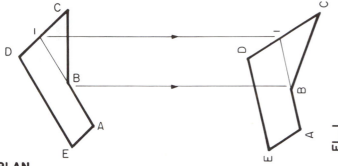

PLAN

FIG. 2.37

Similar to testing for the flatness of a plane, drawing imaginary lines has many uses in descriptive geometry. One is to complete the shape of a plane if certain lines are missing.

In Fig. 2.37, an extension of line AB in Plan originates point 1. After the new line A1 is projected into Elevation 1, point B can be transferred to Elevation 1. B, in Elevation 1, is then connected to C, thereby completing the shape in both views.

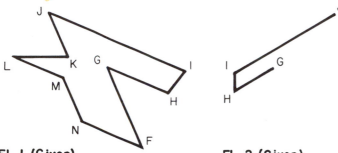

EL.1 (Given)   EL.2 (Given)

The more complex example in Fig. 2.38 employs the same kinds of imaginary lines, starting with a line at point 1, going through G to find F in Elevation 2; 2 through G to locate M; etc.

There is no set order or starting point for the usage of imaginary lines to complete a figure. In fact, lines do not even have to be entirely on the plane. Line 3,4,5 to find N, and F through 7 to locate I are examples of this fact.

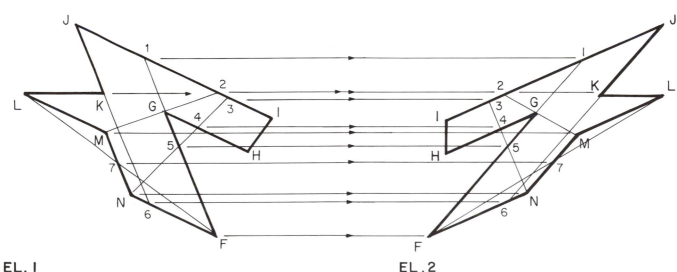

EL.1   EL.2

FIG. 2.38

Creating a true length line on a plane where none exists is another use of imaginary lines. This is necessary when drafting the true size of an oblique plane, explained later in this chapter.

It was previously demonstrated that the true length of a line can only be seen in a view parallel to the original line. To construct a true length line in one view, an imaginary line is first drawn in an adjacent view. This new line must be parallel to the view in which the true length is desired. Next, this new line is projected into the other view, where it will be true length.

Line C1 in Fig. 2.39 is drawn in Plan parallel to Elevation 1. Therefore, when line C1 is projected into Elevation 1, it is true length.

Fig. 2.40 shows how, given any two views, true length lines can be produced in both drawings.

In Fig. 2.41, line 1,2 in Elevation 1 is parallel to the image plane of Plan and the imaginary fold line. Line 1,2 is in its true length in Plan. In addition, imaginary line 3,4 is generated in Elevation 1 and in true length in Inclined View 1.

Many examples that follow require a true length line to be established in one view or another. The exact location of the initial imaginary line can be anywhere, as long as it is parallel to a fold line. For example, line 1,2 in Fig. 2.41 could have been higher or lower in Elevation 1, as long as it was horizontal.

Transferring a given point from one drawing to a second view is a third use of imaginary lines. In Fig. 2.42, point a is located in the given Plan (note test for flatness), but not in given Elevation 1. To locate this point in Elevation 1, a line—any line—is drawn through point a in Plan, and line 1,2, along with point a, are projected into Elevation 1.

SPATIAL OBSERVATION: *In Fig. 2.39, point A is the highest point of the triangle (as seen in Elevation 1).*

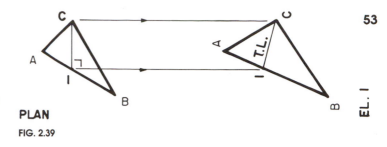

PLAN
FIG. 2.39

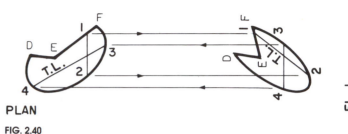

PLAN
FIG. 2.40

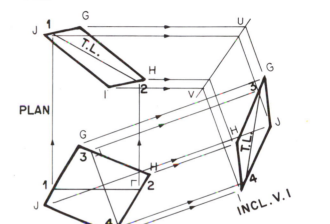

PLAN

EL. 1

FIG. 2.41

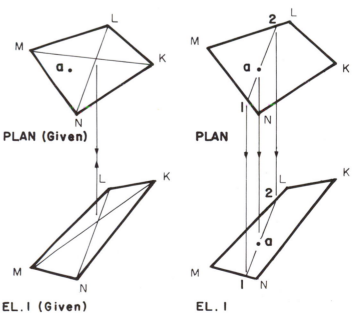

PLAN (Given)   PLAN

EL.1 (Given)   EL.1

FIG. 2.42

DRAWING TRUE SIZE PLANES

The true size of any flat plane, whether horizontal, vertical, sloping, or oblique, must be a projection from a view in which the plane appears as an edge view (an edge view of a flat plane is, by definition, a straight line).

An edge view of a plane will have all lines on it represented either as points or lines, some of which may be in true length. The true-sized view of a plane will have all lines on the plane in true length.

Similar to the drawing of a third view of lines, given drawings must be examined before constructing a new view. In Fig. 2.43, lines AD and BC appear as points in Plan; the two lines are therefore true length lines in given Elevation 1. In addition, lines AB and DC in given Elevation 1 are horizontal and consequently parallel to the imaginary fold line between Elevation 1 and Plan; AB and DC are in true length in Plan.

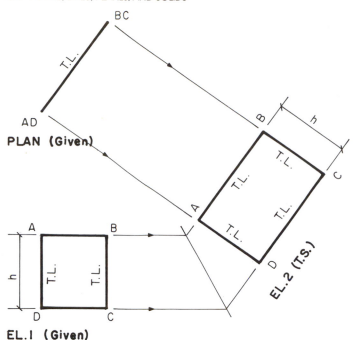

FIG. 2.43

A flat plane can appear as an edge view in more than one view. However, it would be impossible for any flat plane to be an edge view in plan and elevation.

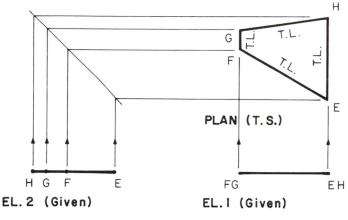

FIG. 2.44

Flat planes can be circular or even irregular in shape. However, it would be impossible for any flat plane to be an edge view in plan and elevation. Circles are circles when an image plane is parallel to the shape. Only two other representations of a circle are possible: a straight line or an ellipse.

Consequently, a cylinder when cut at an angle not at 90° to the central axis will produce an ellipse.

SPATIAL OBSERVATION: *The three planes on this page are either vertical or horizontal.*

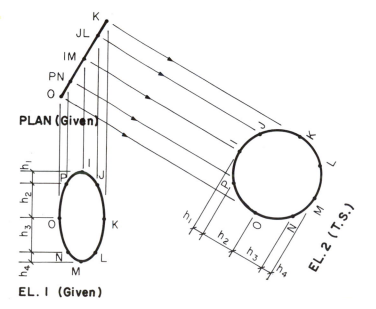

FIG. 2.45

A sloping plane is neither horizontal nor vertical, but has at least one line horizontal (AB in Elevation 1 in Fig. 2.46). The standard six views of the theoretical box will often not show an edge view.

On the previous page, edge views were given. On this page, they are not. The construction of an edge view requires an understanding of the following logic: When a line in one view appears as a point, the line is in its true length in the view from which it was projected. Conversely, when the direction of a view is parallel to a line and the view looks at the end of the line, the line will appear as a point. To construct an edge view, draw a view in which a true length line appears as a point.

In Fig. 2.46, line AB is horizontal and consequently parallel to the imaginary fold line between Elevation 1 and Plan. Line AB is therefore true length in Plan. Elevation 2 is drawn by looking at the end of true length line AB, and Inclined View 1 is the true sized view of the triangle. (See page 106, where a sloping triangular skylight has been drawn. The true length of one side of the triangle appears in the roof plan, and the true size of the skylight is projected from the edge view (Section CC).

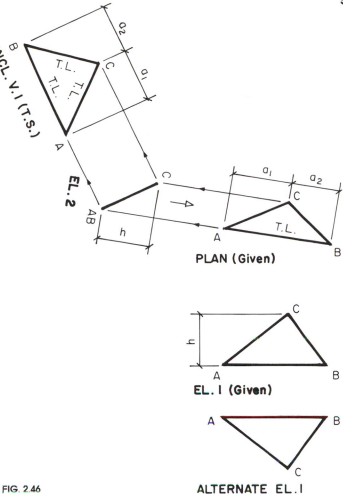

FIG. 2.46

In Fig. 2.47 the edge view requires Inclined View 1 to be drawn by looking at the end of true length line DE in given Elevation 1. Inclined View 2 produces the true shape and size of the plane. In this example, a dimension transfer line conveys dimensions b_1, b_2, and b_3 into Inclined View 2.

SPATIAL OBSERVATIONS: *In Fig. 2.46, Inclined View 1 displays the underside of the true sized plane. Elevation 1 in both illustrations on this page presents the tops of the planes in an angled view. If an alternative Elevation 1 had been given in Fig. 2.46 the view would have shown an angled bottom view of the triangle.*

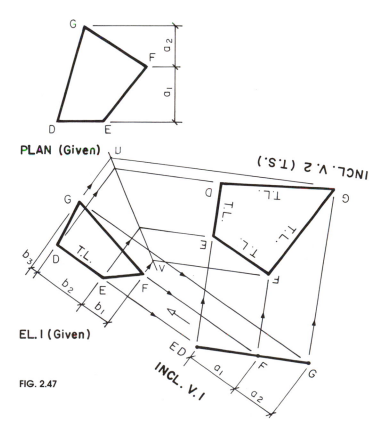

FIG. 2.47

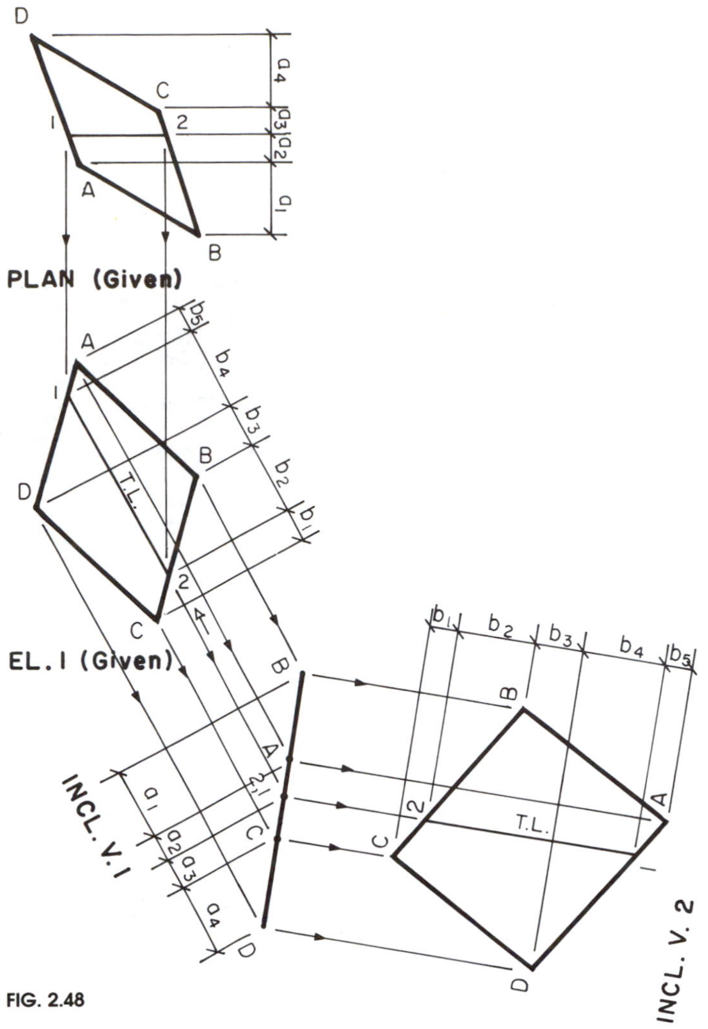

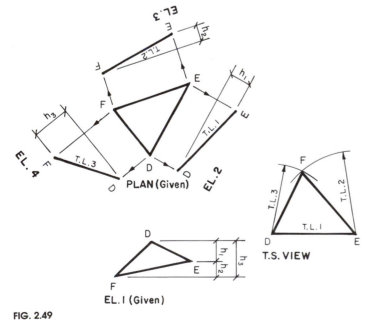

PLAN (Given)

EL. I (Given)

INCL. V. I

INCL. V. 2

FIG. 2.48

PLAN (Given)

EL. I (Given)

T.S. VIEW

FIG. 2.49

TRUE SIZE OF OBLIQUE PLANES

An oblique plane is similar to any oblique line: it has no side parallel to any view of the conventional six-sided box. To draw the true size of such a plane, an imaginary true length line must be constructed first. (The plane in Fig. 2.48 is a parallelogram in two views and projects from view to view, therefore the figure is flat.) An edge view is drawn next followed by the true sized view.

Transferring dimensions in a complex problem can become overwhelming. Remembering to skip a view backwards to find relationships (page 46) and dimensions at right angles to fold lines is paramount. Even if these principles are partially forgotten, another method of reasoning can be applied. When looking for dimensions to draw the edge view of plane ABCD, the imaginary line 1,2 will appear as a point in the edge view. Therefore, dimensions are scaled in Plan to accomplish that. Likewise, in the true-sized view (Inclined View 2), line 1,2 must be in its true length. Dimensions in Elevation 1 are measured parallel to line 1,2.

The only time you don't need the edge view of a plane is when you want to find the true size of triangles. In this case, a true-size elevation can be drawn of each edge, and the consequent dimensions used as radii to construct the true size.

SPATIAL OBSERVATION: *Given elevation 1 shows the underside of the figure in Figs. 2.48 and 2.49.*

POINTS AND LINES WITH PLANES

The shortest distance between a point and a line can be found by constructing a view that shows the given line as a point, and then drawing a true-sized view of the connecting line (see page 49). Another solution, shown in Fig. 2.50, is to draw an imaginary oblique triangle by connecting given point C with A and B. A true-sized view of the triangle was then drawn, and, in this view (Inclined View 2), all lines on the plane are in their true length. Therefore, a line drawn perpendicular to AB, which connects with point C, is the shortest distance between C and AB.

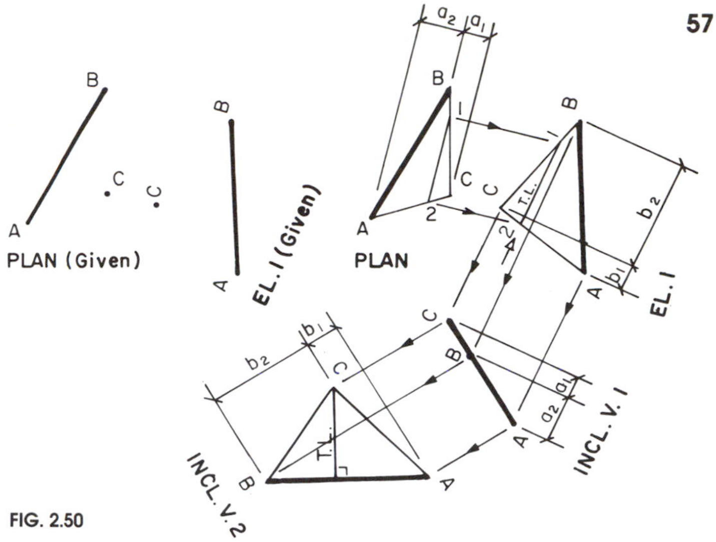

FIG. 2.50

The problem in Fig. 2.51 is to find and draw the shortest distance between point F on the circular plane and line DE. The direction of the shortest distance must be at right angles to the true length of line DE (seen in Inclined View 1). However, this view shows only direction and not true length. Inclined View 2 does show true length. Line FG is then projected back to Plan (shown dashed). Neither Elevation 1 nor Plan will show GF in true length. The back projection of the shortest distance could have been applied to the first illustration to show the new line in given views.

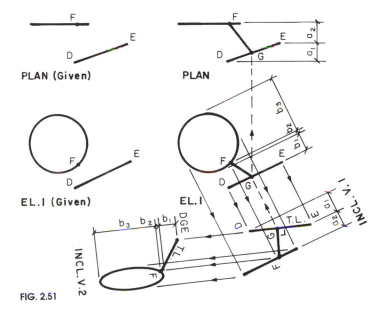

FIG. 2.51

Any line perpendicular to a plane is perpendicular to any true length line contained on the plane. The plane in Fig. 2.52 is flat (see page 50). To find the direction of a line perpendicular to the given Plan from point M, line 1,2 must first be projected into Elevation 1. Line 1,2 is then in true length, and establishes the location of point M. An arbitrary length line MX is drawn perpendicular to 1,2; the direction has been established in Elevation 1. The same process is reversed by using 3,4 in Elevation 1 to find the direction in Plan.

Note that line XM could have been in the opposite direction in both views but would have been hidden beneath the plane (Elevation 1 looks at an angle to the top of the plane).

On page 123, there is an 8"-thick triangular solid in Elevation 2. The direction of thickness was established by using true length lines in two views, and then drawing the 8" thickness in a true-sized view of the direction.

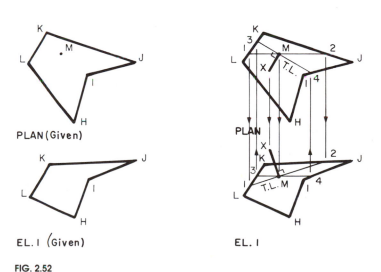

FIG. 2.52

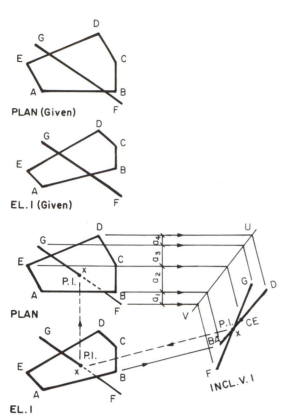

PLAN (Given)

EL. I (Given)

PLAN

EL. I

FIG. 2.53

LINES PENETRATING PLANES

There are two methods for finding where a line intersects a plane. In the first, an edge view of the plane is constructed and the point of intersection (P.I.) appears in this view. The P.I. is then projected back to the preceding drawing (long dashed lines).

The edge view of plane ABCDE in Fig. 2.53 is drawn by looking at the end of true length line AB from Elevation 1. The point of intersection x can be seen in the new view—Inclined View 1—and x is projected back to the two given views. (Note the use of line UV to transfer "a" dimensions from Plan to Inclined View 1. See page 45.) What part of the line is ahead of or behind the plane is determined in Inclined View 1: the Gx portion of the line is ahead of the plane, and xF is partially hidden by the plane (indicated by short dashed lines in Elevation 1 and Plan).

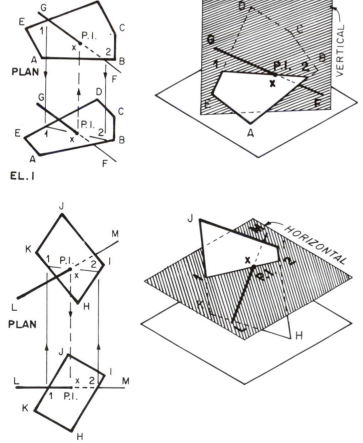

PLAN

EL. I

PLAN

EL. I

FIG. 2.54

The second method uses only two given views and an imaginary plane that cuts through the given plane. For example, line GF in Fig. 2.54 is imagined to be on a vertical cutting plane that slices through the given plane, intersecting the given plane along line 1,2 in Plan. These points are then projected into Elevation 1. The place where line GF crosses 1,2 in Elevation 1 marks the point of intersection, which is then projected back into Plan.

With this cutting plane method, visibility is automatically accomplished. The projection of point 1 from Plan hits line GF in Elevation before line ED, meaning that Gx is higher than ED in Plan. Likewise, the projection of point 2 from Plan strikes AB before GF. Fx is therefore lower than AB in Plan.

Cutting planes can be horizontal if a horizontal line is present in the given elevations. Fig. 2.55 shows the cutting plane concurrent with horizontal line LM in Elevation 1. The projections are the reverse from the vertical cutting plane example in Fig. 2.54. The point of intersection is found in Plan and projected back into Elevation 1. This means that Lx is ahead of KJ in Elevation 1, and xM is behind HI in Elevation 1.

The same construction procedures and test for visibility apply when a sloping cutting plane is used to find where a line penetrates a plane.

All three types of cutting planes utilize the establishment of an imaginary plane in one view concurrent with a given line, the projection to an adjacent view for solution, and the projection back to preceding views. (See page 123. The intersection of a chimney with a sloping plane—a roof—is found by using a vertical cutting plane.)

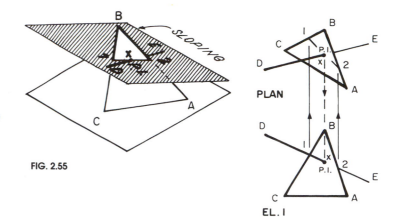

FIG. 2.55

SHAPES ON PLANES

Any shape can be drawn on a given plane by first constructing it in a true-sized view. To execute this in Fig. 2.57, we must draw a circle with a given radius (RAD.) on the six-sided plane tangent to lines FG and FK.

The true-sized view of the six-sided figure is found by drawing 90° projections from the Plan. Next, you must locate the center of the circle before actually drawing it. Two lines are drawn parallel to GF and FK at a distance equal to the radius of the circle. The center of the circle is where these two lines intersect. Now, you're ready to draw the circle.

In Elevation 2 (T.S.) in Fig. 2.57, the circumference is divided into equal parts, projections are made into Plan, and taken into Elevation 1, forming an ellipse.

FIG. 2.56

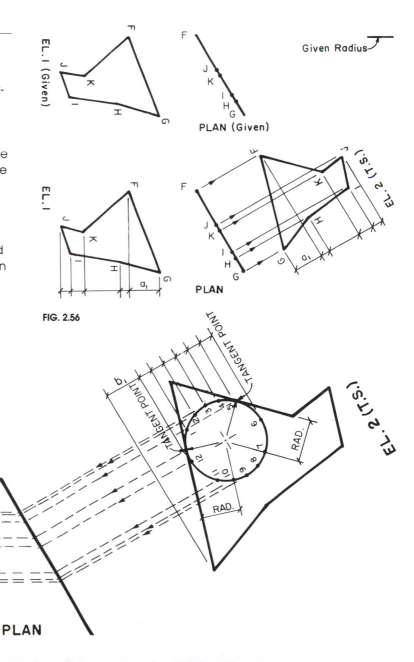

FIG. 2.57

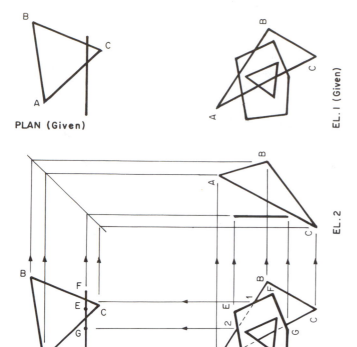

PLAN (Given)

EL. 1 (Given)

EL. 2

PLAN

EL. 1

FIG. 2.58

OVERLAPPING PLANES

Planes overlap planes frequently in architectural drawing. In descriptive geometry problems, it is often difficult to determine whether planes overlap or intersect, particularly when the drawings do not immediately reveal visibility.

Although the two views in the top of Fig. 2.58 do not reveal intersection or separateness, a visual analysis does indicate that there are only two planes present. Elevation 1 suggests three planes, but Plan indicates only two. This means the equilateral triangle must be a hole in the five-sided polygon.

Visibility (displaying what is ahead of or behind what can be seen and what cannot) is determined by two methods in Fig. 2.58. First, Elevation 2 is drawn, indicating two separate planes. Second, mechanical projection is used: Point 1 in Elevation 1, when projected into Plan, strikes line EF before AB. Therefore, EF is ahead of AB in Elevation 1. Point 2 is also ahead of AB in Elevation 1. Further testing of similar points (not shown) would reveal that EFGHI is ahead of, and separate from, ABC. (Descriptive geometry problems in this chapter show all lines defining planes continuous. Short dashed lines in solutions to problems indicate lines hidden behind planes.)

SPATIAL DEPTH

Spatial depth can be implied by making lines closer to the viewer darker than lines that are further back in space. This technique relates to human vision: Distant objects, planes, and lines are less distinct and contrasty than nearer ones. Although it's time consuming to darken lines closer to the image plane on a computer, it's easy to do when drawing by hand. Darkening should be done in all architectural plans, sections, and elevations.

The use of tones can also imply spatial depth, and even the *amount* of depth. Depending on the graphic arrangement of abstract planes, lighter planes can recede in relation to darker planes (the distant hills phenomenon). Or, lighter-toned planes, when foiled against darker ones, can come forward towards the viewer. The amount of contrast implies the amount of depth or the degree of movement in space: the greater the contrast, the greater the spatial movement.

The tones in Fig. 2.60 range from black to white, providing maximum spatial movement and consequent graphic impact. In the lower right corner, the tonal range has been compressed into grays; there is no black or white. There is therefore less spatial movement in the latter example.

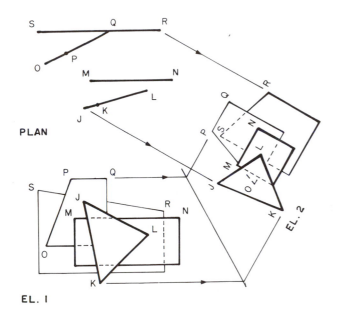

PLAN

EL. 1

FIG. 2.59

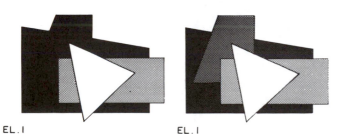

EL. 1

EL. 1

FIG. 2.60

SLOPING PLANES INTERSECTING OBLIQUE PLANES

When two flat planes intersect, there is one line of intersection (L.I. in drawing) common to both planes. The method for finding this line involves only two techniques: edge views and cutting planes.

In the upper portion of Fig. 2.61, ABCD slopes downward from line AD to BC. These two lines are also parallel to the mutual fold line between the two given views; therefore, they are true length in both views.

Once these visual observations have been made, Elevation 2, the edge view, can be drawn by looking at the end of AD and BC. Elevation 2 shows where line EH and GH intersect the other plane. The points of intersection x and y are then projected back to the two given views, and the line of intersection is drawn by connecting x and y in these two views. Visibility is apparent in Elevation 2.

The edge view method for resolving the intersection of planes is essentially the same as that for the resolution of intersection of lines and planes (see page 58). In other words, the edge view is treated as a line intersecting a plane.

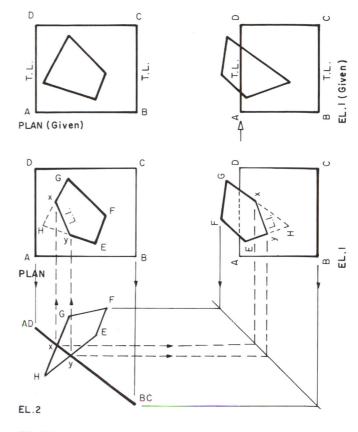

FIG. 2.61

The solution for Fig. 2.62 is obtained in the same manner as above, but the initial scan of the two given views does not reveal that an edge view can be constructed in Plan. Consequently, a true-length line must be generated in one of the given views. Then, as in the above illustration, an edge view can be drawn, the line of intersection found, and projections made back to the two given views.

SPATIAL OBSERVATIONS: *Two planes in both illustrations on this page could have been solids. The third view is necessary not only to find the line of intersection, but to reveal that all figures were planes.*

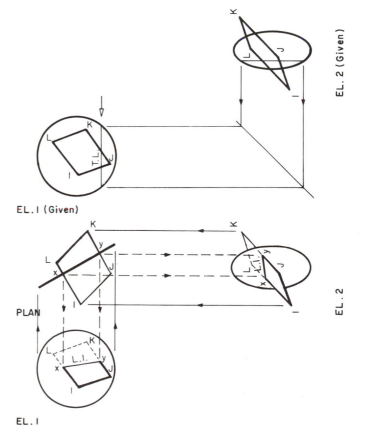

FIG. 2.62

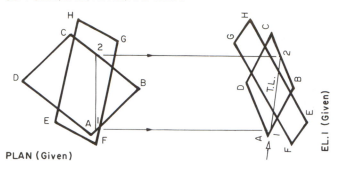

PLAN (Given)

EL. I (Given)

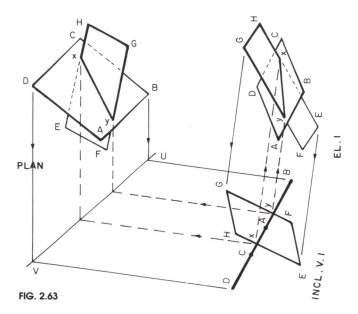

FIG. 2.63

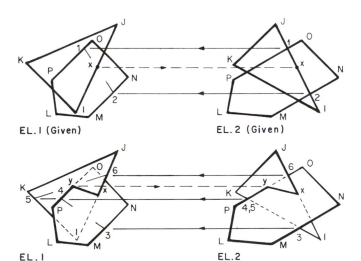

EL. I (Given)   EL. 2 (Given)

EL. I   EL.2

FIG. 2.64

EL. 2   EL. 2

FIG. 2.65

INTERSECTIONS OF OBLIQUE PLANES

On the previous page, the intersection of sloping planes with oblique planes was found by constructing the edge view of the sloping plane. When two oblique planes intersect, neither Plan nor any elevation will provide an edge view. To use the edge-view method for determining intersections, the edge view must be drawn by looking at the end of an imaginary true-length line. In this edge view, the points of intersection can be found, projected back to given views, and connected to form the line of intersection.

In Fig. 2.63, points xy in Inclined View 1—the edge view of plane ABCD—can be found, projected back to the given views, and connected to form the line of intersection. Inclined View 1 looks at an angle to the top of Elevation 1; the GH portion of plane EFGH is above the other plane, with the EF portion below.

The second way of solving intersections, the Cutting Plane method, has two advantages: The solution can be drawn by using only two drawings; and a check for visibility is made at the same time. However, trial and error is involved.

In Fig. 2.64, sloping cutting plane 1,2 is assumed in given Elevation 2. The reason for this cutting plane is to determine if line IJ penetrates plane LMNOP, so the projections of 1,2 into Elevation 1 are drawn to lines MN and OP. The answer here is that Line IJ does intersect at point x. This projection provides a visibility check: It shows that Jx is ahead of OP in Elevation 2. In the projection of point 2, MN is ahead of JI in Elevation 2.

Cutting plane 3,4—also originated in Elevation 2—poses the question of whether IK penetrates the other plane. The answer is no, but MN is ahead or in front of the triangle in Elevation 2. Cutting plane 5, 6 makes us ask whether OP penetrates the triangle. In this case, yes, at point y. The line of intersection xy has now been established and the visibility has been determined.

Spatial depth has been implied in Fig. 2.65. On the left, tones are compressed toward the dark side; on the right, they are compressed toward the light. Each creates a different abstract mood.

TRUE ANGLE BETWEEN INTERSECTING PLANES

When two planes intersect, the true angle between them can be measured in a drawing that depicts both planes as edge views. The line of intersection between the planes (Inclined View 3 in Fig. 2.66) will be a point and come from a previous drawing that showed the line of intersection in true length (Inclined View 2).

The given Plan and Elevation reveal that the planes are flat; the opposite sides of a six-side figure can be extended to form parallelograms. Triangles are always flat. Lines DI and FG are in true length in both given views. Consequently, no imaginary true length line needs to be constructed, and the edge view of EFGH can be immediately drawn (Inclined View 1). The true length of intersection line xy constructed in Inclined View 2 and Inclined View 3 displays the true angle between planes.

SPATIAL OBSERVATION: *In Elevation 1, the view shows the topside of the triangle, even though part of the triangle is behind the six-sided figure.*

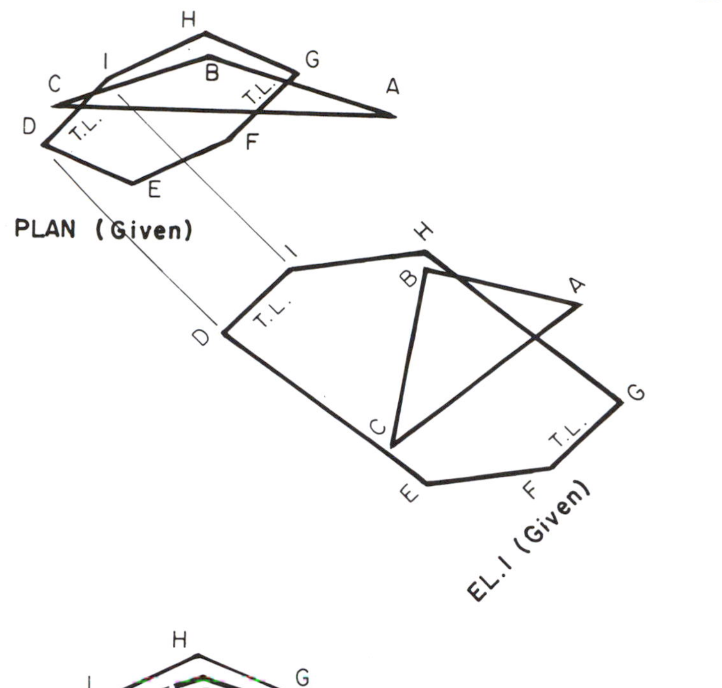

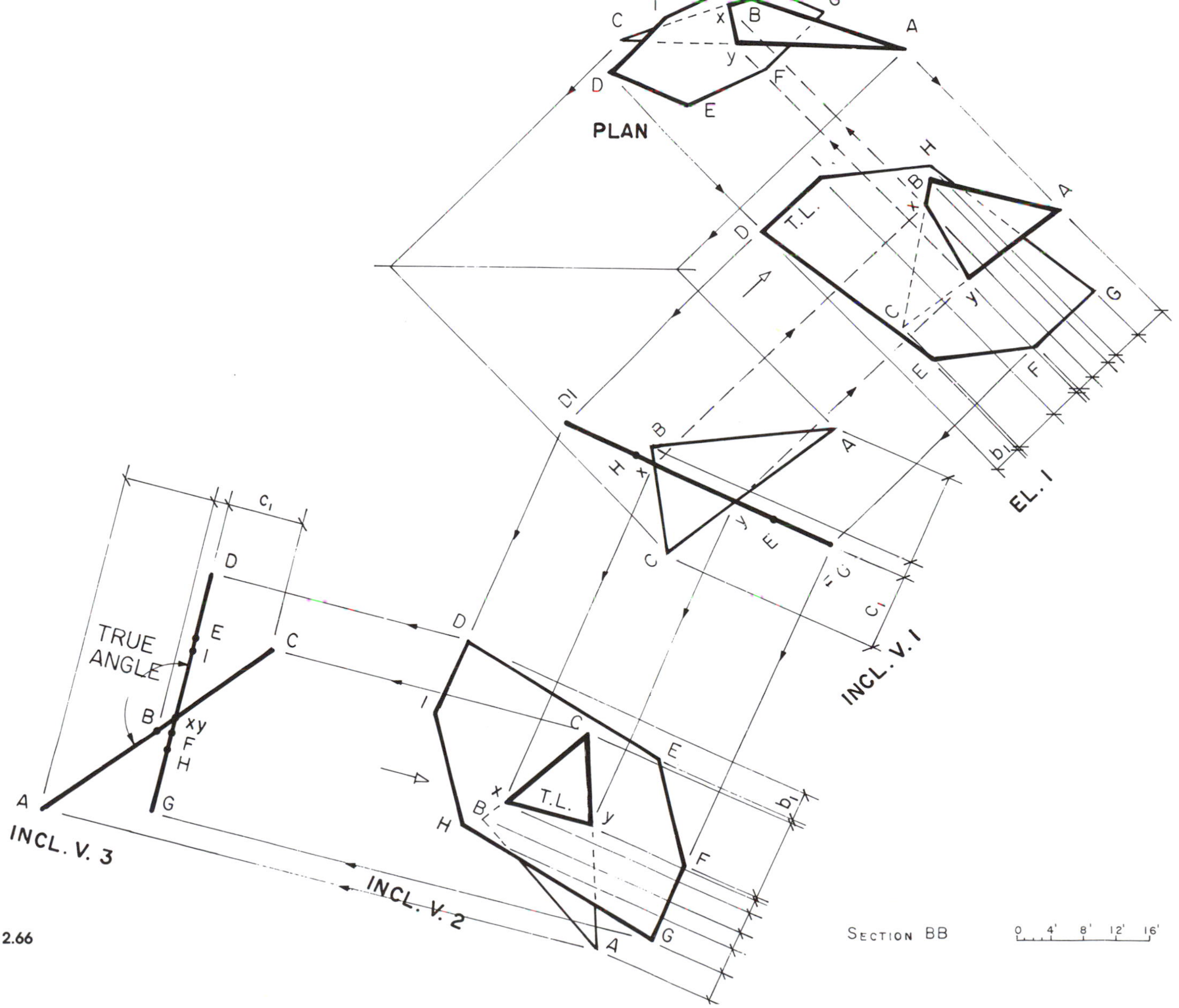

PLAN (Given)

EL. I (Given)

PLAN

EL. I

INCL. V. I

INCL. V. 2

INCL. V. 3

TRUE ANGLE

T.L.

FIG. 2.66

Section BB   0 4' 8' 12' 16'

PLANES: SOME EXAMPLES TO NOTE

The two examples on this page and the next are compound—they have more than one intersection—involving curves. The solution to these problems, as well as other complex examples, requires a systematic approach, starting with a spatial analysis of the givens. Next, drawing the most apparent or easiest elements can make clear what might have been unclear at first glance.

In Fig. 2.67, the problem is to draw Elevation 2 at right angles to Elevation 1. The first step in the spatial analysis is to determine that three planes are present. The first plane, ABCD, is a sloping plane with an edge view shown in Elevation 1; the second, EF, is a vertical plane; and the third is composed of two vertical semicircular planes connected by a short tangential plane, HI. All three planes intersect each other.

First, we draw the most obvious element, sloping plane ABCD, in the new view. Next, to solve the problem, find the intersection of plane EF with the sloping plane. Because an edge view of the sloping plane is present (Elevation 1), the points of intersection, w and x, are found in this view and projected into Elevation 2. (Frequently, there are two methods for resolving any descriptive geometry problem. An alternate solution to this intersection problem is to use vertical cutting plane 1,2 established in Plan and project it into Elevation 2).

The easiest intersection is complete and shown in the second set of drawings. What is yet to be resolved is the intersection of sloping plane ABCD with the semicircular/tangent plane GHIJ.

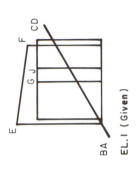

PLAN (Given)

EL. I (Given)

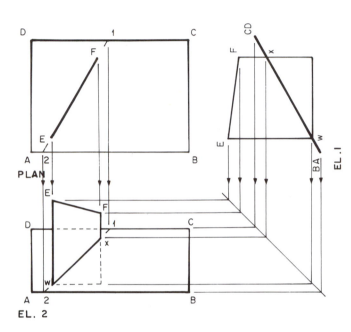

PLAN

EL. 2

The heights of GHIJ can be projected from Elevation 1 into Elevation 2, but the line of intersection with the sloping plane requires a return to the theory of points and lines: Any vertical line will appear as a point in Plan. By reversing this fact, points can be laid out along GHIJ in Plan and projected into both elevations, where they become lines. Elevation 1 indicates the intersection of each of these lines with the sloping plane (only y and z are shown as examples), and the points of intersection projected into Elevation 2. When enough points and lines are taken into Elevation 2, the line of intersection becomes two semi-ellipses. (In actual drafting, knowing that the two semicircles in Plan will appear as two semi-ellipses in Elevation 2 limits the number of projections to the few necessary to construct an ellipse with a template or other means. An architectural example of a curved surface intersecting a flat plane is illustrated on page 119. In this illustration a curved roof meets the vertical face of a building.

PLAN

EL. 2

FIG. 2.67

The second example is more complex than the first, but the strategy for solving the problem is the same. Beginning the spatial analysis, we see that the straight/curved plane slopes upward from E to F (F is the point of tangency), and then around to G. This plane is intersected by the folded triangular plane ABCD with line AD lower than BC (partially hidden by ABC in Plan). By looking at the Plan, we see that line AB is the closest line to Elevation 1 and does not intersect EFG. Finally, EFG appears as an edge view in Plan.

Solving the easiest starts with locating a number of intersection points in the edge view of EFG: Line AC penetrates EFG at point t; line AD, also seen in Plan, cuts through EFG at u and v. These three intersection points are projected into Elevation 1. The question now remains: Does line EF penetrate ABC, ACD, or both? To find out, cutting plane 1,2 is established in Plan and finds line EF intersecting ACD at point w. Similarly, cutting plane 3,4 in Elevation 1 finds intersection point x in Plan, which is then projected back to Elevation 1. Intersection points v and w occur on the flat part of the EFG, so they can be connected by a straight line.

If you find it difficult to visualize what lines are ahead of or behind plane EFG, the mechanical method described on page 47 can be applied.

The results of the above procedures are shown in Fig. 2.68 (the second set of drawings.) At this point in solving the intersections, what may have been unclear at first glance should start to be more apparent.

The remaining problem to resolve is the meeting of EFG with the folded plane between x and t. From point x to F (the point of tangency), the intersection occurs on the flat part of plane EFG. When two flat planes meet, the line of intersection must be a straight line, so cutting plane 5,6 is taken through F in Plan (y and F are the same in Plan). When this cutting plane and y are projected into Elevation 1, a portion of the intersection line can be drawn by connecting x and y. Last, a series of cutting planes, starting with 7,8 in Plan, are projected to the Elevation, locating points along the curved intersection between y and t.

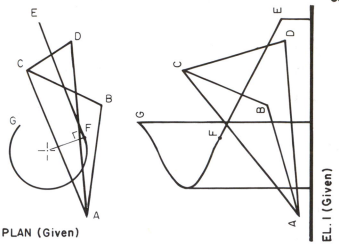

PLAN (Given)   EL. I (Given)

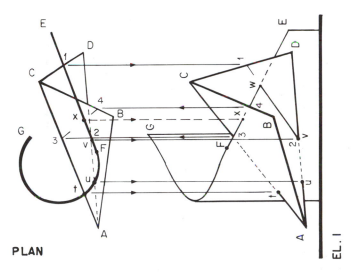

PLAN   EL. I

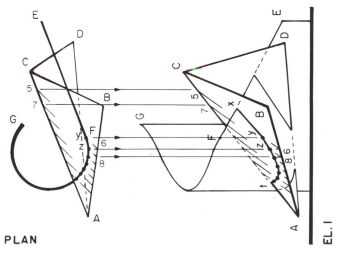

PLAN   EL. I

FIG. 2.68

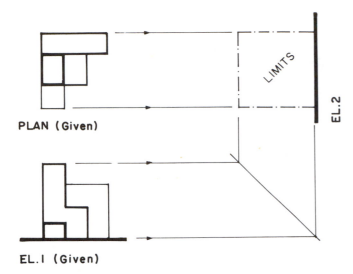

PLAN (Given)

EL.I (Given)

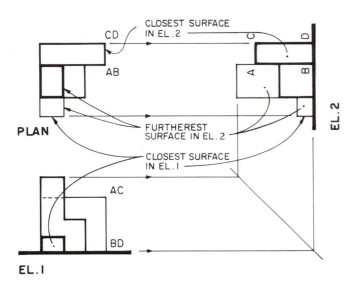

PLAN

EL.I

CD — CLOSEST SURFACE IN EL.2

AB

FURTHEREST SURFACE IN EL.2

CLOSEST SURFACE IN EL.I

AC

BD

EL.2

THE THIRD VIEW OF SOLIDS

Drawing a third view of solids when given two views is similar to drawing the third view of lines or planes. Usually, simple projection is the solution.

Seeing darker lines coming toward the image plane and lighter ones receding can be a help identifying a solid. However, if the form cannot be immediately visualized, a systematic approach is a necessary starting point, rather than spending further mental energy. At some point in this process, the shape of the object will become apparent.

The first logical step for drafting a third view is to define the limits of the object by projecting from the two given views. Nothing can exceed these limits. Next, in the second, the surface closest to Elevation 2 (ABCD) is drawn, followed by the next closest plane, and so on. Not all hidden lines need to be drawn; only those that are essential for understanding. This approach is called analysis by surfaces. An equally valid strategy would be to start with the tallest component making up the solid.

SPATIAL OBSERVATION: *Architectural elevations assume the cutting of a plane—the ground—in front of an object or building. The consequent intersection line is on the vertical image plane. It is drawn with the darkest line weight.*

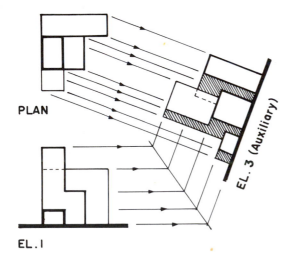

PLAN

EL.I

EL. 3 (Auxiliary)

Elevation 3 in the third drawing is traditionally called an auxiliary elevation. An auxiliary elevation is any elevation not at right angles to the four primary elevations of the theoretical box. This type of multiview has the advantage of showing more than one side of an object, giving a clear presentation of three dimensionality, despite horizontal lines not being true length. (See page 111 for an architectural example of an auxiliary elevation.)

FIG. 2.69

SOLIDS ON HORIZONTAL PLANES

Certain forms presented on this page may be difficult to grasp at first glance.

Fundamental shapes—spheres, cylinders, pyramids, prisms, and cubes—become recognizable once seen and used. Traditional architectural forms, such as roofs, also become apparent when they are used.

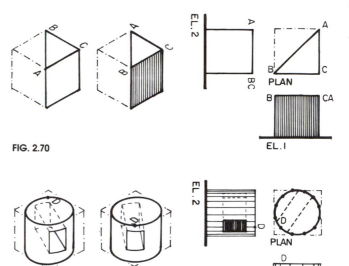

FIG. 2.70

In Fig. 2.70—a right triangular prism—the Plan could not have been drawn from the two elevations unless points were labelled. Without this identification, the Plan could have been a cube.

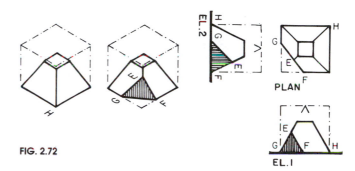

FIG. 2.71

The cylinder in Fig. 2.71 has a slot cut out of it. Any third view can be drawn from the other two without labelling points. Projecting the subdivisions of the circle in Plan to Elevations in this figure also gives the feeling of roundness. Elevation 1 uses technically correct projections, while Elevation 2, although technically incorrect, generates a more believable curvature. This subjective exaggeration becomes a visual necessity when the curvature is small. (See page 112 for an architectural example.)

Pure geometric forms can be transformed by eroding portions from the shape shown in Fig. 2.72. Recognition of the basic original figure—in this case a right triangular pyramid—is a significant aid in drafting.

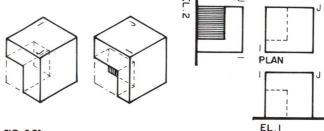

FIG. 2.72

The cube in Fig. 2.73 has been deformed by undercutting. Both Plan and Elevation 1 show hidden lines. Elevation 2, on the other hand, shows none, making it more informative. Generally, a drawing with fewer hidden lines is more demonstrative, if a choice is possible.

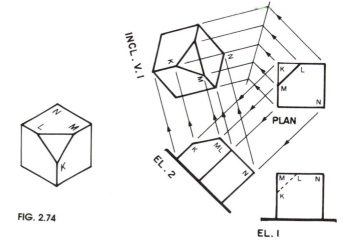

FIG. 2.73

INCLINED VIEWS OF SOLIDS

Inclined views of solids are the theoretical basis for paralines (see Chapter 5). Inclined views of solids are used in architectural work to show the true size of planes that make up solids.

Since elevations are projections from plans, the dimensions for Inclined View 1 in Fig. 2.74 are taken from Plan and not Elevation 1. (This form is an abstraction of Building A at the beginning of the next chapter. The true size of the triangular skylight of Building A is drawn on page 106.)

FIG. 2.74

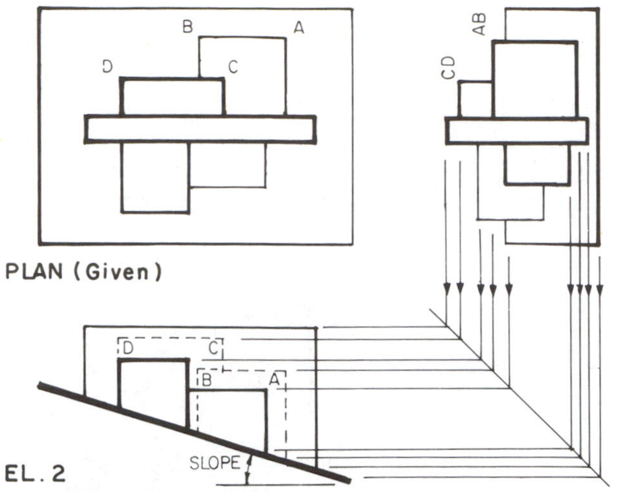

PLAN (Given)

EL. 1 (Given)

EL. 2

SLOPE

FIG. 2.75

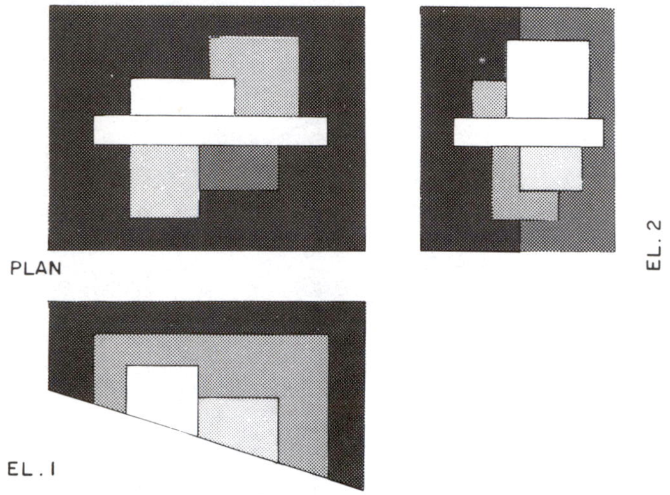

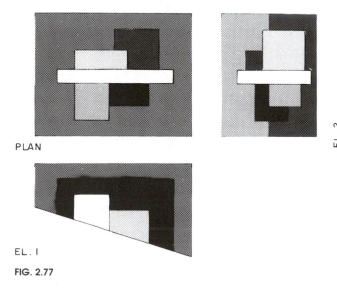

PLAN

EL. 1

EL. 2

FIG. 2.76

PLAN

EL. 1

EL. 2

FIG. 2.77

SOLIDS ON SLOPING PLANES

The third view of this group of solids (Elevation 2) was obtained by projecting from the two given views. Labelling of points was limited to the tops of hidden solids that might be difficult to visualize.

The slope of any plane is the angle between a horizontal line and the edge view of the plane.

SPATIAL MOVEMENT

Fig. 2.76 has no blacks but does have whites. Consequently, the spatial movement is less than in Fig. 2.60 (the left hand example) on page 60, but slightly more than in the other example on the same page.

Fig. 2.77 displays a different strategy for three-dimensional graphics. In these three drawings, a middle gray is used for the background while darker tones recede and lighter ones come forward. The spatial movement is only a little greater than in the drawings above, but less than in Fig. 2.60 (the left hand example) on page 60.

Fig. 2.78 takes yet another strategy. The object has all components toned, which makes it recede into the white background. The tones have a dark-to-light sequence that, when combined together, create less spatial movement than in the other two examples on this page. (These forms are the basis for the architectural design shown on pages 125 and 126. They also appear in Chapter 5 and 6.)

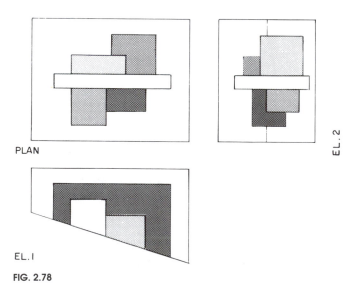

PLAN

EL. 1

EL. 2

FIG. 2.78

Two cutting planes define the intersection of the solid with the plane—both originated in Plan. Cutting planes 1,2 and 3,4 construct two edges of the solid in Elevation 1; the other two edges of the solid must be parallel (two lines parallel in space must be parallel in another view).

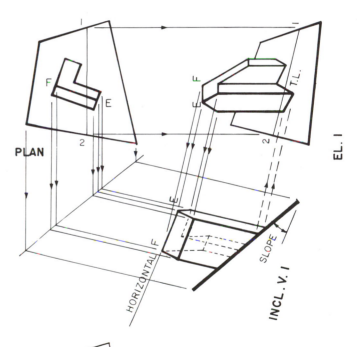

The slope of the oblique plane in Fig. 2.79 is found in the edge view (Inclined View 1) of the plane. Line EF is horizontal in Elevation 1 and remains horizontal in the edge view. (Should a horizontal line be required in any inclined view, an arbitrary horizontal line can be drawn in plan and one elevation, then transferred to the inclined view. Also, an inclined view does not necessarily duplicate right angles of the original figure.)

The illustrations in Fig. 2.79 are another example of using line weight—including wedge-shaped ones—to depict spatial depth.

Titles for plans, by architectural custom, are horizontal on the drawing page and at the bottom of the illustration. With architectural elevations, titles are also located at the bottom of the drawing, but parallel to the horizon of the drawing rather than to the page.

Additionally, architectural titles should be visually less important than the drawing itself. The viewer's eye should be attracted to the drawing first.

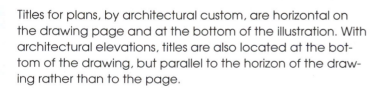

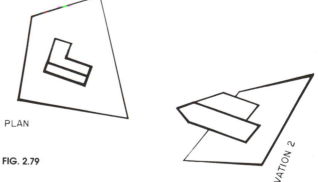

FIG. 2.79

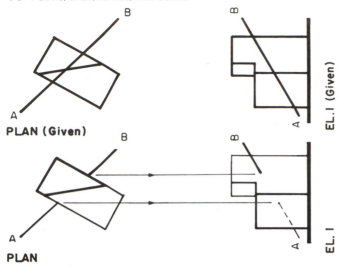

PLAN (Given)

PLAN

FIG. 2.80

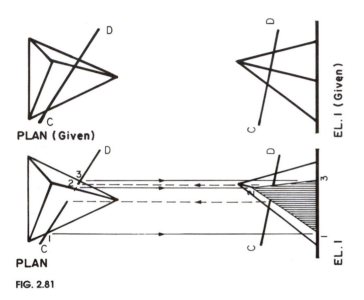

PLAN (Given)

PLAN

FIG. 2.81

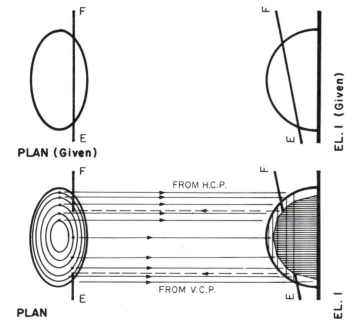

PLAN (Given)

FROM H.C.P.

FROM V.C.P.

PLAN

FIG. 2.82

LINES INTERSECTING SOLIDS

The techniques for obtaining the intersection of lines and solids are the same as lines penetrating planes: using edge views and cutting planes. Edge views are the easiest to see in given drawings and, if present, should be the first method applied. For solutions, each surface of a solid is treated as a plane, the point of intersection is found, and then the next possible plane is considered in the same manner. (Keep in mind that in descriptive geometry, neither lines nor planes are drawn within a solid.)

A visual examination of the solid in Fig. 2.80 reveals that, in Plan, all surfaces of the solid are edge views. The intersection of AB with the solid can be seen in Plan and projected into Elevation 1.

No edge views are present in the offset pyramid in Fig. 2.81. Therefore, a cutting plane is used to find the intersection. The vertical cutting plane is assumed in Plan concurrent with line CD. This cutting plane and line CD are projected into Elevation 1, where the points of intersection can be seen and projected back to Plan. The hatched area in Elevation 1 is the vertical cutting plane.

Like the illustrations in Fig. 2.81, no edge views are present in this elliptical solid. The solution involves both a series of horizontal planes (H.C.P) and a vertical cutting plane (V.C.P.). All cutting planes for this problem are originated in Plan.

The horizontal series of cutting planes originated in Plan are projected into Elevation 1, where they become horizontal lines. Next, a vertical cutting plane, on which line EF is located, generates another set of projections from Plan. This set intersects the horizontal planes in Elevation 1 and shows what the cutting plane looks like when it cuts through the solid (the hatched area) and the points of intersection. (If enough cutting planes had been used, the shape of the hatched area would have been a smooth curve.)

A combination of serial, sloping cutting planes and a vertical plane containing the given line yields this intersection of a line and an offset cone. Although the intersection could have been found with only the two given views, Elevation 2 more clearly shows the resolution.

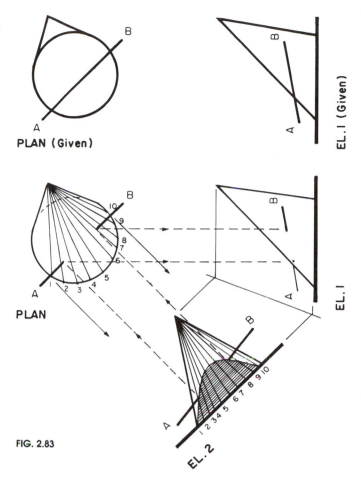

FIG. 2.83

LINES INTERSECTING SOLIDS: SOME EXAMPLES TO NOTE

Lines do not always cut through a solid. In this example, a variation of the pyramid from the previous page, the vertical cutting plane is below the line, meaning that the line is separate. The use of visibility checks would have given the same conclusion.

Lines can penetrate a solid in more than one location and even be hidden in certain views.

SPATIAL OBSERVATION: *The angular undercutting of the solid (seen in Elevation 1) causes a dashed line in Plan.*

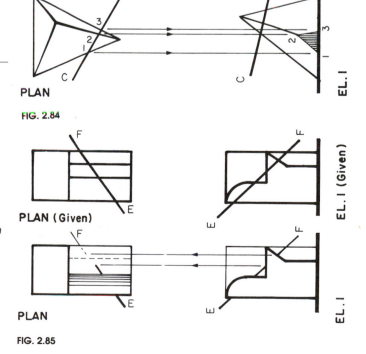

FIG. 2.84

FIG. 2.85

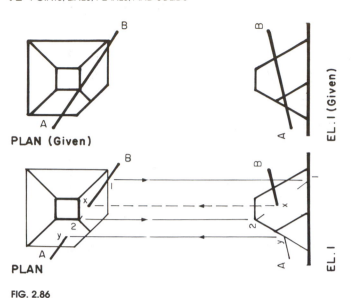

PLAN (Given)

PLAN

FIG. 2.86

Many intersection problems need to be resolved by more than one method. The edge view method is the easiest to see and execute.

In Fig. 2.86, two edge views of the truncated pyramid are present in Elevation 1. The point of intersection y can be seen in one edge view and projected into Plan. This tells the viewer there must be another point where the line exits the solid. Vertical cutting plane 1,2 is assumed in Plan, projected into Elevation, and identifies point x, the other intersection point. It is then projected back to Plan.

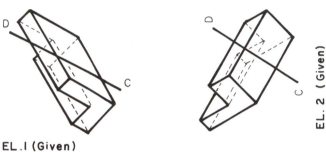

EL.I (Given)

Unlike the last example, the given drawings of the solid in Fig. 2.87 do not show any edge views, so the intersections must be found by cutting planes alone. Before trial projections are made, certain sides of the object can be eliminated by logic: A line that does not cross the side of a solid in two views cannot penetrate that side. Consequently, planes EFGHIJ and IJKP need not be tested for intersection.

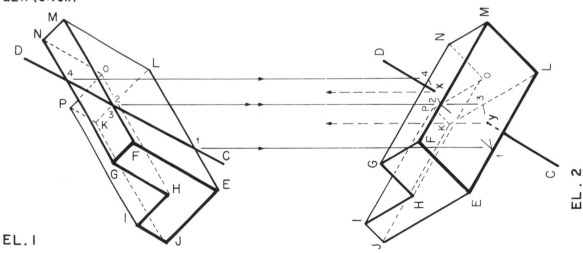

EL.I

In the first trial, 1,2, originated in Elevation 1, shows that CD does not penetrate EFML (Line CD does not cross 1,2 in Elevation 2). In the second trial, 1,3 from Elevation 1 identifies point of intersection y. Third, 2,4 finds point x as the other point of intersection.

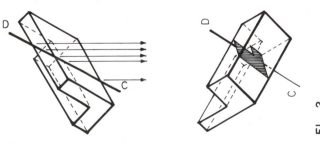

EL. I

FIG. 2.87

If all possible points from Elevation 1 were taken into Elevation 2, the full cutting plane would appear in Elevation 2 (shown hatched). Line CD would be on this plane, but in descriptive geometry problems, lines within solids are not drawn.

HORIZONTAL PLANES INTERSECTING SOLIDS

When a horizontal plane intersects a solid, the plane becomes an image plane with the portion of the solid above it removed. What is left on the plane is the profile of the cut object (shown hatched) and the projections of the object beyond. This new type of multiview is a plan, although it differs from what has been considered a plan up to this point in the chapter. Previously, a plan was the projection onto a horizontal plane floating above an object. Architects refer to this view as a roof plan.

Architectural plans and their graphic treatment differ from descriptive geometry plans in a number of other important ways. First, an architectural plan cuts through a building and shows wall/floor thicknesses and interior volumes. Second, dashed lines in descriptive geometry indicate a line covered up by a plane and below, or beyond, the cut of the image plane. Architects reverse this graphic code: Dashed lines usually represent something above the image plane or something behind the viewer. In such instances, the dashed line is usually described in a note. Third, architectural plans can be a view either looking up or down. Fourth, the image plane itself is never shown in architectural drawing.

The three examples on this page are a mixture of architectural and descriptive geometry conventions: No wall thicknesses or interior volumes are shown, the lines above the image plane are indicated dashed, and the cut area on the image plane is cross hatched (never done with architectural plans).

In Fig. 2.88, the dashed lines, marked above, are the intersections of planes that form the portion of the roof above. (See page 38, where the dashed lines in Plan are the roof overhang and the logs above.)

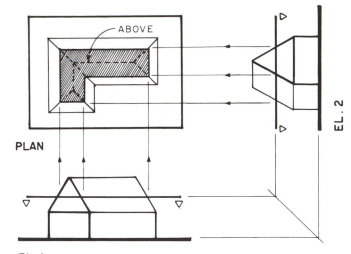

FIG. 2.88

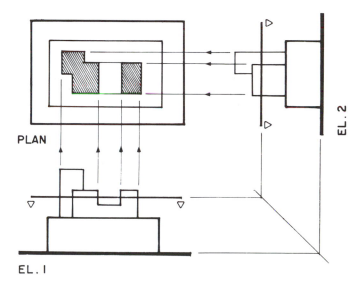

FIG. 2.89

With any plan, the height of the horizontal image plane above the lowest point of the solid determines the plan configuration. If the image plane in Fig. 2.89 had been slightly higher, it would have only cut the highest element.

The points in the more complex Fig. 2.90 are labelled in order to avoid confusion when projecting.

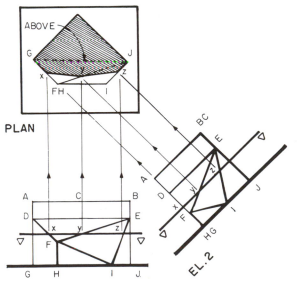

FIG. 2.90

VERTICAL PLANES INTERSECTING SOLIDS (SECTIONS)

Vertical image planes intersecting solids—sections in architectural drawing—are similar to the horizontal planes intersecting solids shown on the previous page. Unlike those drawings, the direction of view for a section is indicated by arrows at the ends of the line representing the image plane. Because more than one section is made for architectural work, sections are labelled by numerals or numbers.

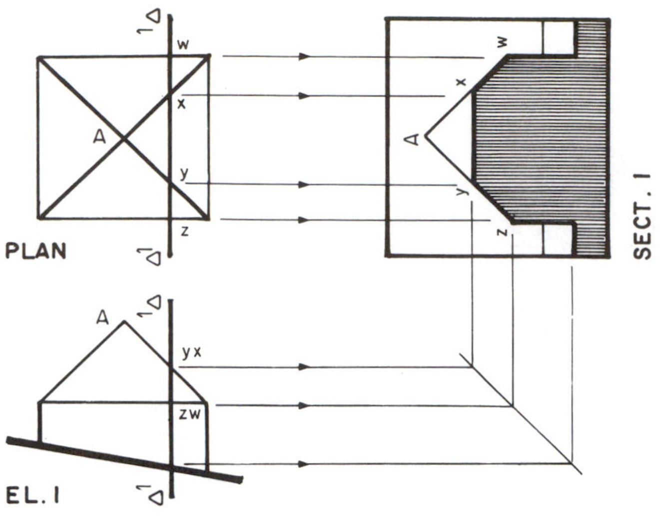

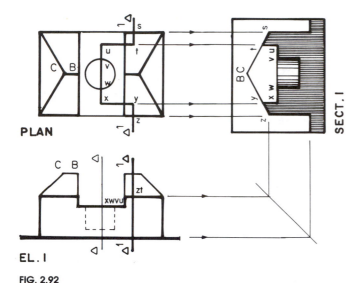

FIG. 2.91

Fig. 2.92 shows how sections can be offset or broken. (Plans can also be broken or offset. See page 114.) The purpose of this type of section is to provide a more informative description of an object or building in a section. (See pages 124 and 130 for architectural examples.)

In Fig. 2.93, an image plane cuts through the object at an angle, and two entirely different sections are projected. Although not drawn in section, the dotted lines are the portions of the object removed or behind the viewer.

FIG. 2.92

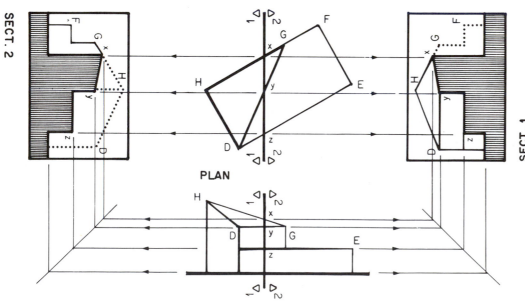

FIG. 2.93

SLOPING AND OBLIQUE PLANES INTERSECTING SOLIDS

The edge-view method can be employed to find where sloping and oblique planes intersect solids, but the construction is tedious. It is simpler to instead use cutting planes.

The easiest intersection to find in Fig. 2.94 is the straight line intersection of the plane with the solid. Three cutting planes in Plan intersect the solid at points u,v, and x. The planes and points are projected into Elevation 1 to establish the straight line intersections.

These same cutting planes hit the circular portion of the solid at x,y, and z, and they are likewise projected into Elevation 1. The resultant shape (shown dashed) in Elevation 1 is an ellipse. Only points x,y, and z were projected, enough to draw the ellipse with a template. (See page 123, where the intersection of a chimney with a sloping plane—a roof—is found by using a vertical cutting plane.)

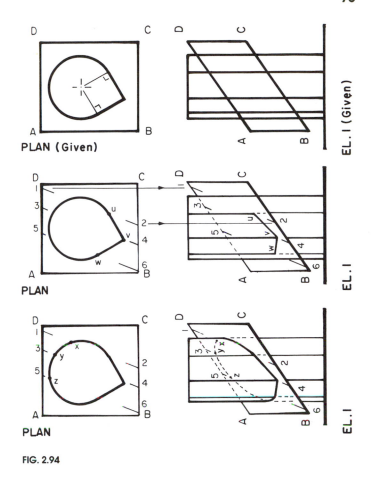

FIG. 2.94

In Fig. 2.95, a series of trial cutting planes, all originated in Plan, are used to determine the lines of intersection. The first trial shows cutting plane 1,2 in Plan finding line OP intersecting plane EFJK at point v. In the second trial, 3,4 tests whether MN penetrates plane EFJK. (The answer is no, it doesn't.) Third, 4,5 tests the same line for penetration of HIJE. (Again, no, it doesn't.) Fourth, 6,7 finds EJ penetrating MNOP at w. And last, 8,9 finds HI penetrating MNOP at x. The same trial process is used to find intersection points y and z, but for clarity, the cutting planes are not shown.

Problems of oblique planes intersecting solids are resolved by the methods of trial and error cutting planes.

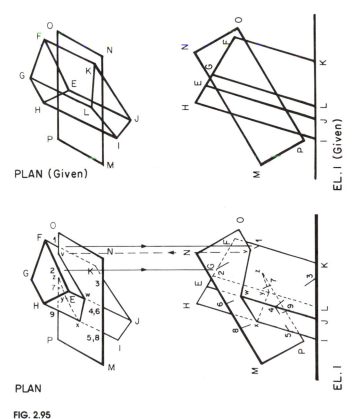

FIG. 2.95

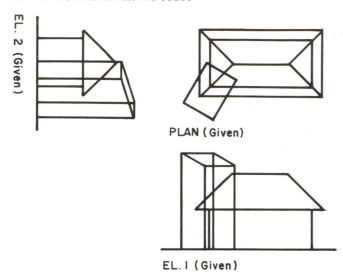

EL. 2 (Given)

PLAN (Given)

EL. I (Given)

INTERSECTING SOLIDS

Both the edge-view and cutting-plane methods are used when solving the intersections of solids, but the edge-view method is the easiest to see and use. In addition, edge views occur most often in plans (most architectural solids and buildings have vertical edges or walls—edge views, in other words).

By their very nature, intersecting solids are compound problems. Visualization is the starting point. Questions such as What form is higher or lower than another?, Which lines or planes are hidden?, Which lines are sloping, vertical, or horizontal? should be answered before drawing.

On this page, a rectilinear block intersects a solid with a hipped roof. The block is both taller than and partially in front of the other solid. The roof overhangs the other solid.

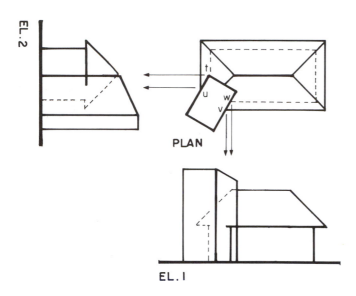

EL. 2

PLAN

EL. I

Once the three-dimensional features have been realized (Fig. 2.96, middle), intersection points u, t, v, and w can be seen in Plan and projected into the two elevations. Point x can also be seen in Plan, if careful attention is paid to the drawings.

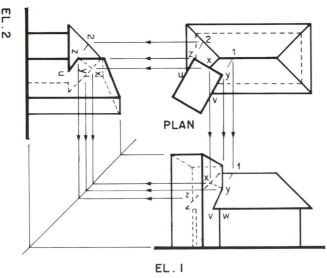

EL. 2

PLAN

EL. I

FIG. 2.96

The remaining intersection points y and z can be found in two ways: Point y can be located on cutting plane v1 and projected into Elevation 2; or, the same intersection point can be found in an edge view in Elevation 2 and projected into Elevation 1. Intersection point z can also be found in two similar ways.

INTERSECTING SOLIDS: SOME EXAMPLES TO NOTE

An analysis of the configuration in the upper portion of Fig. 2.97 informs the viewer that there are two intersecting solids with one higher than the other. The top of the lower solid has a horizontal line AC drawn diagonally with two triangular planes sloping downward from this line.

Once visualized, the simplest method for finding intersections in intersecting solids—edge views—is employed.

In Fig. 2.98, a cylinder intersects a hemisphere. A series of horizontal cutting planes are generated in Plan. These planes and their intersections with the cylinder are projected to Elevation 1, thereby creating the curved intersection.

To find the intersections in Fig. 2.99, a series of radial, vertical cutting planes are utilized.

The location of cutting planes in Figs. 2.98 and 2.99 (the last two examples) need not be evenly spaced. They only need to be projected accurately from the initial view.

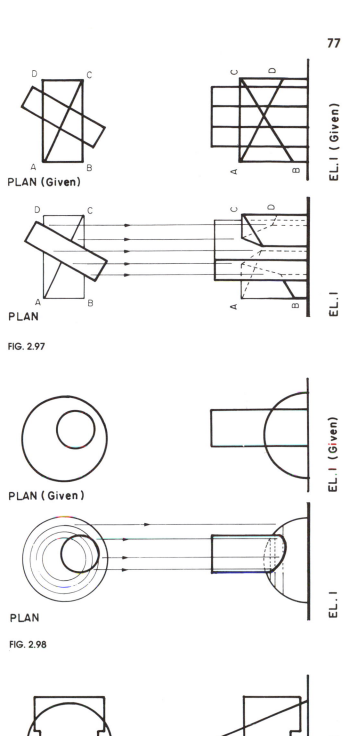

FIG. 2.97

FIG. 2.98

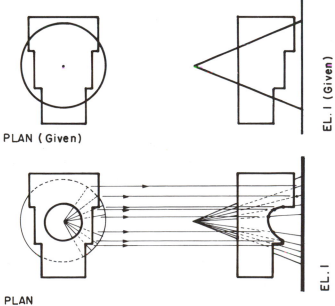

FIG. 2.99

The strategy for resolving the intersection of solids (particularly in difficult examples) depends on visualization. Fig. 2.100 has two forms: a solid with an oblique top, and an oblique rectilinear prism. Further, all three drawings show edge views: the vertical edges of plane ABCD in Plan; plane ABCD in Elevation 2; and EFGH in Elevation 1. This last edge view does not intersect the solid with the oblique top.

Plan is the first drawing to examine for edge view intersections. In this problem, intersection points z, y, and x are found in Plan (Fig. 2.100). Elevation 2 contains the other useful edge view, and w is there. No other intersection points can be found by the edge-view method, so cutting planes are used. Systematically going back to Plan, a vertical cutting plane concurrent with x1 finds point v in Elevation 1. A second vertical cutting plane concurrent with z2 in Plan locates point u in Elevation 2. Finally, cutting plane 3,4 in Elevation 1 establishes point t, the final intersection point in Elevation 2.

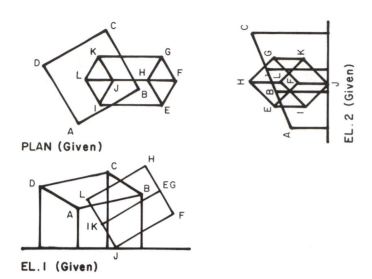

PLAN (Given)

EL. 2 (Given)

EL. I (Given)

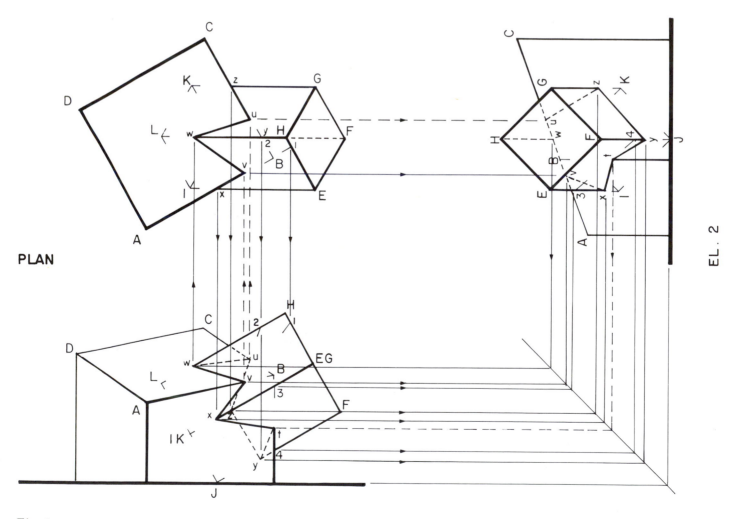

PLAN

EL. 2

EL. I

FIG. 2.100

SPATIAL MOVEMENT AND MOOD

The amount of blacks, whites, and grays in a drawing can generate a psychological mood, something linework cannot accomplish. The tonal range and consequent spatial movement for the drawings in Fig. 2.101 have been compressed and the mood is powerful. Although personal sensibilities may not match what is implied in the drawings, they are gloomy, heavy, disturbing, and brooding. Yet while all three drawings express the same mood, that mood is generated in different ways. Plan and Elevation 2 display a lighter object against a darker background; Elevation 1 reverses the object/background relationship.

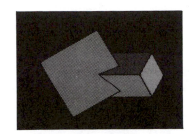

PLAN

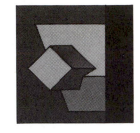

EL. 2

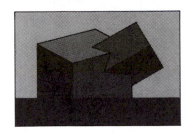

EL. 1

FIG. 2.101

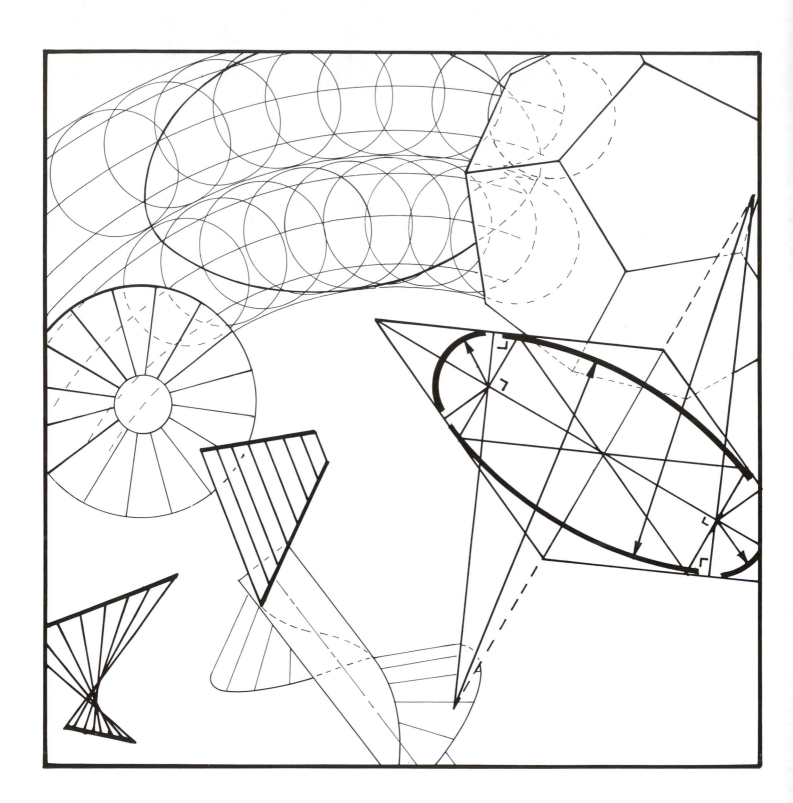

CHAPTER 3

APPLIED GEOMETRY

In this chapter, plane and solid geometry are applied to points, lines, planes, and solids using both classical and practical means. Technical systems for spatial description, names of geometric figures, and a few mathematical formulas are given. The material reviewed here concentrates on information that is pertinent to architectural work, leaving a fuller treatment of less architectural elements to other sources.

Classical geometry, inherited from the Greeks and other early cultures, uses only a straight edge and compass; no measuring tools, such as a protractor or scale, and no T-squares, parallel bars, or triangles. These methods set limitations for drawing. For example, there is no way to trisect an angle using classical geometry. Despite the limitations, classical geometry has practical applications, particularly when laying out large-scale work at a construction site, if surveyor's instruments are not available and drawing tools would be far too small.

Some of the material presented in this section is approximate, suitable for pictorial rather than construction drawings. Exactness and perfection, even when using computers, is relative. The area of a circle, for example, is dependent upon pi, and there is no "exact" value for pi.

POINTS

Points are located by referencing one to another, as used in this chapter, or to an abstract set of three axes at right angles to one other. This coordinate system is mathematical in origin and often used when drawing with computers. In this system, any point is identified by its relationship to X,Y, Z axes. (In the example, point A is one unit along the X axis, 4 units along the Y axis, and 3 units up the Z axis).

On a larger scale, the combination of longitudes and latitudes locate coordinates of points in relationship to the Earth. Longitudes fix points east or west of a semicircle running north/south through Greenwich, England. The east or west departure from 0° longitude through Greenwich is expressed in degress (°), minutes (') and seconds ("), or in decimal percentages of a degree using the metric system.

Latitudes are full circles circumventing the Earth parallel to the equator. They are identified by the angle between the center of the Earth and the diameter of a particular latitude.

Longitudes cannot exceed 180° and latitudes cannot exceed 90°. (The point shown at 45°E Longitude and 30°S Latitude is in the Indian Ocean, just south of Madagascar.)

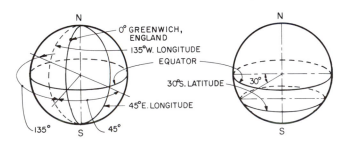

COORDINATES OF POINTS

FIG. 3.1

The needle of a compass always points north. The direction or bearing of a line is measured in degrees, minutes, and seconds east or west of true north, or translated into an angle from south (it is impossible for a bearing to be greater than 90°). The needle points to magnetic north, rather than true north, and readings can be corrected for localized deviations from true north by consulting special maps.

Surveys identify the direction or bearings of property lines by giving corrected compass readings. In the process of making a survey, the surveyor starts at the intersection of two boundaries (point A in the example), takes a reading, proceeds to the next intersection (point B), takes another reading, and so on. (All external angles formed between boundaries in a survey must add up to 360°.)

Azimuths are another method for measuring the direction of a line. Azimuths are angles usually measured clockwise from true north (the United States geodetic survey uses south) and cannot exceed 360°.

An altitude is the solar angle of a sun's ray in relation to the horizontal, a bearing, and a particular location on Earth at a given hour of the year.

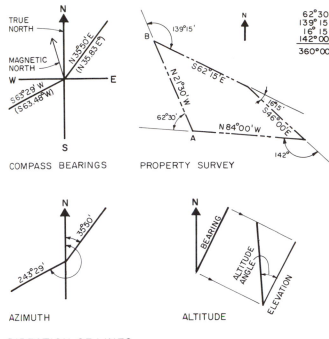

COMPASS BEARINGS   PROPERTY SURVEY

AZIMUTH   ALTITUDE

DIRECTION OF LINES

FIG. 3.2

LINES AND SUBDIVISIONS

There are many cases in architectural drawing where a line of given length must be subdivided into a number of equal parts. If, for instance, a 10'9" line must be subdivided into eight equal parts of 1'4-⅛", the successive measuring out of the eight parts will never come out to exactly 10'-9". A better method is to draw a new line of any length at any angle to one end of the given line, mark off eight equal spaces at any scale along this new line, connect the eighth point with the end of the given line, and draw parallels from the points on the new line back to the given line.

If two parallel lines are given, the distance between them can be accurately subdivided by laying a scale between them, matching the numbers on the scale to the desired number of subdivisions, and marking off points.

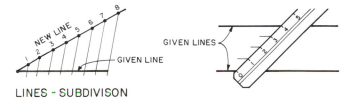

LINES - SUBDIVISON

FIG. 3.3

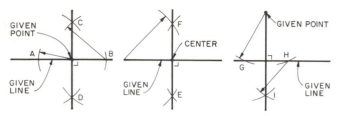

LINES PERPENDICULAR TO LINES

FIG. 3.4

LINES PERPENDICULAR TO LINES

To draw a line perpendicular to a another line at a given point by using classical methods (Fig. 3.4, left), two arcs of equal radius are swung from the given point until they intersect the given line at points A and B; from A and B, two other arcs are swung until they intersect; and the intersection points C and D are connected to form the line perpendicular to the given line at the given point.

For the classical method of drawing a line perpendicular to another line at the midpoint of the first line (Fig. 3.4, center), swing two arcs of equal radius from each end of the given line; and connects the intersection points E and F with a line.

For the classical method of drawing a line perpendicular to a given line from a given point not on the line (Fig. 3.4, right), swing an arc from the given point until it intersects the given line at points G and H; from G and H, swing two other arcs until they intersect at point I; and connect the given point with I.

The practical means for drawing all three of these problems is to use a scale, parallel bar, T-square, or triangle.

ANGLES AND SUBDIVISIONS

A right angle has 90° between the two lines forming the angle; an obtuse angle, more than 90°; and an acute angle, less than 90°. Two angles are complementary if they add up to 90° and supplementary if their angles add up to 180°.

There are three methods for bisecting an angle. In the first, (left and middle above), an arc is drawn from the junction of the two lines that form the angle to originate points A and B; and another two arcs are drawn from A and B to locate C and the bisector of the angle.

The second and third methods are practical and involve measuring tools. In the second (right), equal distances are measured along the two lines forming the angle; right angles are made using an adjustable triangle; and where the two right angles intersect is the point that the bisector passes through.

In the third method a protractor is used to measure the given angle. Then the angle is mathematically subdivided.

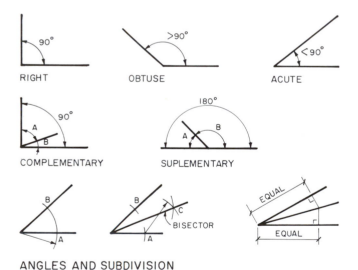

ANGLES AND SUBDIVISION

FIG. 3.5

CURVED LINES (TWO-DIMENSIONAL)

A curve that lies on one plane is a two-dimensional curve. A curve not on one plane is a three-dimensional curve.

Cycloids, epicycloids, hypocycloids, involutes, and spirals, are curved lines called roulettes.

A cycloid is a two-dimensional curve created by the movement of a fixed point on the circumference of a circle rolling along a straight line. Similarly, an epicycloid is the path of a point rolling along the outside of an arc, and a hypocycloid along the inside of an arc.

To construct a cycloid, divide the circumference of a circle into any number of equal parts; calculate the length of the circumference and lay it out as a straight line; divide this line into the same number of subdivisions as the circle; draw a series of equally sized circles, using each subdivision of the line as a center; and project the subdivision of the original circle to the corresponding circle along the straight line. The intersection points are connected to form the cycloid. The drawing process can, alternatively, start by assuming the straight line length, treating this length as the circumference, calculating the radius of the circle, and following the above procedure.

Drawing the epicycloid and hypocycloid is done in a similar way to drawing the cycloid.

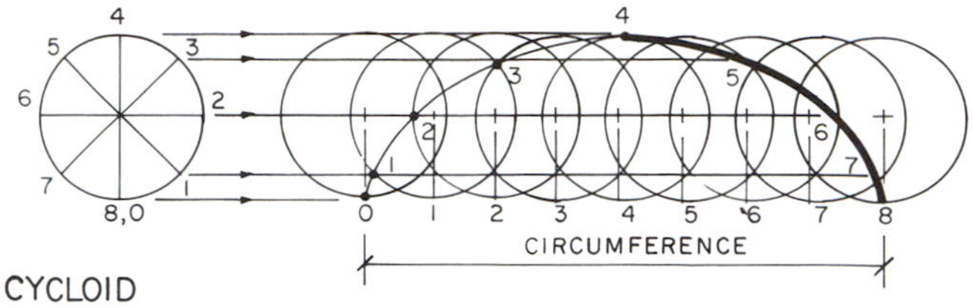

CYCLOID

FIG. 3.6

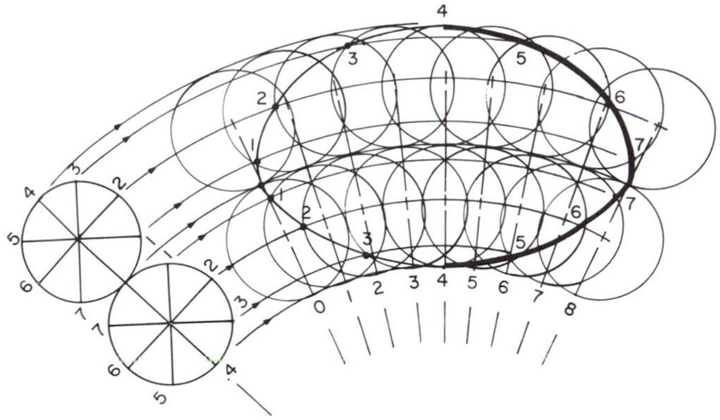

EPICYCLOID AND HYPOCYCLOID

FIG. 3.7

Involutes are a series of connected arcs swung from the corners of a square, polygon, triangle, or diameters of a circle. Each arc is made from successive corners of the original figure, and each radius used is a multiple of the previous radius. The greater the number of sides of the generating figure, the greater the number of arcs and the smoother the involute. The involute derived from a circle is dependent upon the number of diameters originally chosen.

The Spiral of Archimedes is a two-dimensional curve made by a moving point unwinding away from a fixed point with constantly changing curvature. To construct the Spiral of Archimedes, divide a circle into equal radial subdivisions (eight in the example); draw an equal number of concentric circles; and connect the intersections of the radials with their appropriate circles.

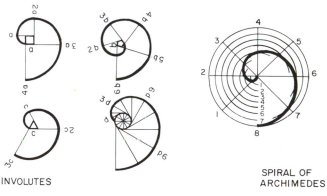

INVOLUTES

SPIRALS

FIG. 3.8

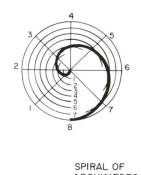

SPIRAL OF ARCHIMEDES

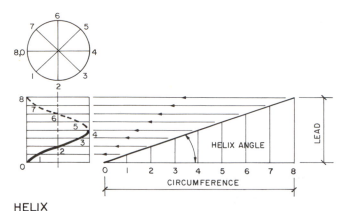

CURVED LINES (THREE-DIMENSIONAL)

A helix is a three-dimensional curve generated by a point moving on the surface of a cone or cylinder with a uniform rate of upward rise. To draw a helix, given the radius of the cylinder and the height of one complete revolution of the helix (the lead), lay the circumference out as a straight line (either calculate the circumference or graphically lay it out as described on pages 88-89); subdivide both the plan of the cylinder and the straight line into an equal number of subdivisions; draw the lead at right angles to the straight line; construct a diagonal from the end of the straight line to the lead; use this diagonal line to transfer heights to the elevation; and make projections from the plan to locate points along the helix.

SPATIAL OBSERVATION: *The helix in elevation reverses the curvature at the center line. Also, the partial curve on page 65 is a partial helix.*

HELIX ANGLE
LEAD
CIRCUMFERENCE

HELIX

FIG. 3.9

FLAT PLANES

DIAGONALS

Diagonals are used to draw a square given the length of one side; to find the center of a quadrilateral (see page 50); and to reduce or enlarge the size of a given plane. Enlargement or reduction must be done realizing that the lines of an enlarged or reduced plane are parallel to their original counterparts.

GIVEN LINE
GIVEN PLANE
GIVEN PLANE

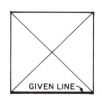

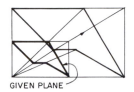

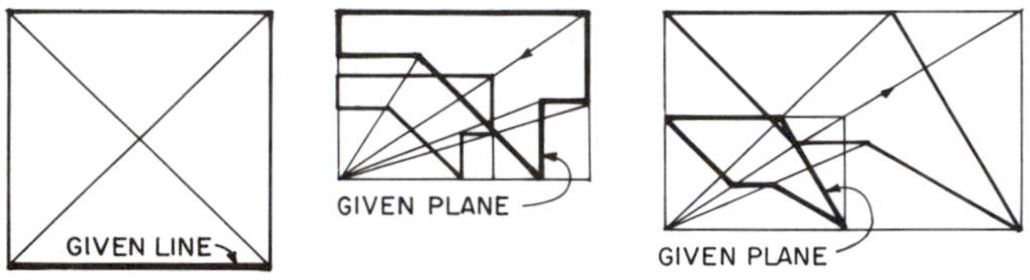

USE OF DIAGONALS

FIG. 3.10

TRIANGLES

The sides and three internal angles of an equilateral triangle are all equal. An isosceles triangle has two angles and two sides equal. A right triangle has one 90° angle plus two 45° angles. A scalene triangle has no equal sides or angles.

VERTEX
ALTITUDE
EQUILATERIAL
ISOSCELES
RIGHT
SCALENE
C
HYPOTENUSE
X
A
OPPOSITE
B
ADAJACENT
SUM OF INTERIOR ANGLES = 180°
AREA = 1/2 ANY BASE x ALTITUDE
SINE X = A/C
COSINE = B/C
TANGENT = A/B
COTANGENT = B/A
SECANT = C/B
COSECANT = C/A
A²+B² = C²

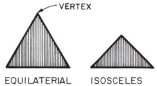

TRIANGLES FORMULAS

FIG. 3.11

Quadrilaterals are four-sided planes. Parallelograms have opposite sides parallel and, within this group, squares and rectangles have four 90° internal angles. Squares and rhombuses are equal-sided figures, while rectangles and rhomboids only have opposite sides equal in length. (When drawn in axonometric drawing (see Chapter 5), a square always appears as a rhombus or rhomboid. Further, a square, when drawn in isometric, appears as a rhombus that has two 120° internal angles and two 60° angles.)

The trapezoid is a quadrilateral that has only two sides parallel. A trapezium is a quadrilateral that has no sides equal in length or parallel.

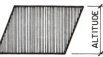

SQUARE   RECTANGLE   RHOMBUS   RHOMBOID
PARALLELOGRAMS

TRAPEZOID   TRAPEZIUM

QUADRILATERALS

PARALLELOGRAM: AREA = BASE x ALT.
              SUM OF INTERIOR
              ANGLES = 360°
TRAPEZOID: AREA = 1/2 SUM OF
              PARALLEL SIDES x ALT.
TRAPEZIUM: AREA = SUM OF AREAS OF
              TRIANGLES FORMING
              THE TRAPEZIUM

FORMULAS

FIG. 3.12

POLYGONS

A polygon is an equal-sided flat plane that can be both circumscribed and inscribed by a circle. Although triangles and squares are technically polygons, the polygon is generally considered a plane of more than four sides. Names of particular polygons are determined by their number of sides.

A number of construction methods are used for drawing polygons. The hexagon is simply drawn by using a 30°/60° triangle, and the octagon by using a 45° triangle. Any polygon can be drawn by the two methods shown. For Method 1, given the length of a side (AB in the example), use AB as a radius and swing a semicircle from point A; divide the semicircle into the same number of subdivisions as the number of sides for the desired polygon; strike radial lines through the subdivisions from point A; and then swing arcs from successive corners until they intersect their appropriate radials. Be careful using this method: accuracy depends on a series of successive steps, each dependent upon the accuracy of the preceding step.

Method 2 is inherently more accurate than Method 1. Given the maximum height and the number of sides for the polygon, draw a circle using the maximum height as the diameter; divide 360° by the number of sides (360°/7=51.4° in the example); using a protractor or adjustable triangle, measure the degrees between radial lines; and, where the radials intersect the circle are the corners of the polygon.

PENTAGON   HEXAGON   HEPTAGON   OCTAGON
(5 SIDES)   (6 SIDES)   (7 SIDES)   (8 SIDES)

NONAGON (9)
DECAGON (10)
DODEGON (11)

METHOD I
(GIVEN ONE SIDE)

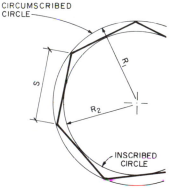

CIRCUMSCRIBED CIRCLE

INSCRIBED CIRCLE

METHOD 2
(GIVEN MAXIMUM DIMENSION)

POLYGONS

n = NUMBER OF SIDES

$$AREA = \frac{nSR_2}{2}$$

ANY SIDE $S = 2\sqrt{R_1^2 - R_2^2}$

FORMULAS

FIG. 3.13

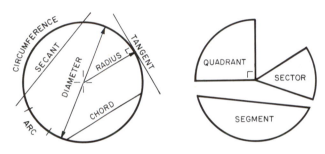

CONIC SECTIONS

FIG. 3.14

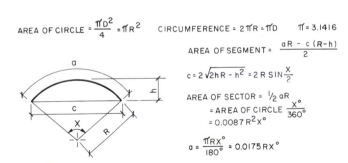

PARTS OF CIRCLE

$$\text{AREA OF CIRCLE} = \frac{\pi D^2}{4} = \pi R^2 \qquad \text{CIRCUMFERENCE} = 2\pi R = \pi D \qquad \pi = 3.1416$$

$$\text{AREA OF SEGMENT} = \frac{aR - c(R-h)}{2}$$

$$c = 2\sqrt{2hR - h^2} = 2R\sin\frac{X}{2}$$

$$\text{AREA OF SECTOR} = \frac{1}{2}aR$$

$$= \text{AREA OF CIRCLE}\frac{X°}{360°}$$

$$= 0.0087 R^2 X°$$

$$a = \frac{\pi R X°}{180°} = 0.0175 R X°$$

FORMULAS

FIG. 3.15

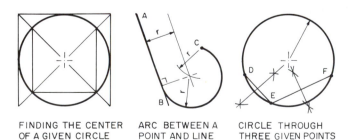

FINDING THE CENTER OF A GIVEN CIRCLE   ARC BETWEEN A POINT AND LINE   CIRCLE THROUGH THREE GIVEN POINTS

CENTERS, TANGENTS AND CHORDS

FIG. 3.16

CONIC SECTIONS

Sections that cut through a right-angled cone (the axis is perpendicular to the base) form one of the following two dimensional planes: a circle, an ellipse, a parabola, or hyperbola. The perimeters of these planes can be theoretically defined as the path of a point moving in relationship to fixed points or lines.

CIRCLES

A circle is the path (circumference) of a point moving around a fixed point (center) at a constant distance (radius). A diameter is the distance across the circle of a line running through the center, and a chord is a line running across the circle but not through the center. A secant is a line intersecting the circle at two points and, like the chord, does not pass through the center. A tangent is any exterior line that touches the circle at one point (point of tangency) and, by definition, must be at right angles to a radius at the point of tangency.

To construct a circle, use a compass or circle template.

To find the center of any given circle, either inscribe or circumscribe three sides of a square inside or outside of the circle and draw diagonals. The center of the circle will be at the intersection of the diagonals.

Chords and tangents can be used to draw combinations of circles, arcs, and lines. (The inscribed square in Fig. 3.16 forms chords and the circumscribed square forms tangents.) On page 59, for instance, a circle was drawn tangent to two given lines. The same process could be used to draw an arc of given radius between two given lines. A similar method is used in Fig. 3.16 (center) to draw an arc tangent to given line AB and passing through given point C.

A circle or arc can be drawn through any three given points. To construct this circle or arc, connect the three points by two lines (these lines become chords), and make perpendiculars at the center of these two lines. The intersection of the two perpendiculars is the center of the circle or arc.

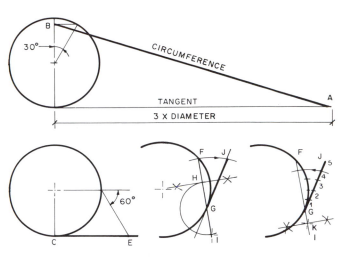

Rectifying a circle or arc is the laying out of the true length circumference or arc in a straight line by graphic means. To rectify a circle (Fig. 3.17, top), draw a tangent to a circle equal in length to three times the diameter; on a diameter perpendicular to the tangent, construct a radius at 30°; draw another line back to the diameter at right angles to the radius; and connect this last junction (point B) to the end of the tangent (point A).

To rectify a quadrant of a circle (Fig. 3.17, bottom left), draw a tangent from the end of one of the two radius forming the quadrant; from an extension of the other radii strike a 60° line back to the tangent; and from this point (E in the example) back to the point of tangency (point C) is the rectified arc of the quadrant.

To rectify any arc of a circle (FG in Fig. 3.17 center), draw a tangent at point G and another line through FG; bisect the chord FG; swing an arc equal in radius to GH from G until it intersects the extension of FG at point I; and swing a third arc using IF as a radius until it intersects the tangent at point J. GJ is the rectified arc.

To divide an arc into equal segments (Fig. 3.17, right), divide a rectified arc into the desired number of subdivisions (five in the example), and, using K as a center, swing a series of arcs back to the original arc, starting with point 4.

Although these rectifying methods are an alternative to calculating lengths, they are accurate to well over one part in a hundred. The subdivision of a given arc, however, is more approximate.

RECTIFYING CIRCUMFERENCES AND ARCS

FIG. 3.17

Ellipses are important geometric figures in architectural drawing not only because they are part of multiview drafting, but they are the representation of circles in both perspectives and axonometrics, which are forms of paraline drawing.

An ellipse can be defined four ways: two definitions are derived from sections taken through solids, and the others are two-dimensional in origin. An ellipse is a conic section created by a plane cutting through both sides of a cone at an angle less than the side slope of the cone. An ellipse is also the result of a plane cutting through both sides of a cylinder at any angle other than 90° to the central axis. (The angle of an ellipse, which is marked on templates, is the angle between the viewing angle and the edge view of the original circle. As the degree diminishes, the ellipse becomes more elongated. The longer dimension of the ellipse is the same as the diameter of the original circle.)

In the third definition of an ellipse, it is the projection of a circle onto any image plane not parallel to the edge view of the circle.

The fourth definition is related to the parts of an ellipse: the axis and foci. Every ellipse has two unequal axes at right angles to one another. The longer one is called the major, and the shorter one, the minor. Two theoretical points (foci) are located on the major axis. In the fourth definition, then, an ellipse is the path of a point moving in relationship to the foci. The distances from the foci to any point on the ellipse are constant and equal in length to the major axis.

Ellipses have tangents that can be constructed at any point along the ellipse by drawing lines from the two foci through the point and bisecting the external angle between these two lines.

If the length of both axes is known, the foci can be found by swinging an arc from the end of the minor axis, with a radius equal to half the major axis, until it intersects the major axes. These crossing points are the foci.

Although many methods can be used to draw an ellipse, only a computer, template, and ellipse machine will produce a perfect ellipse. Even then, the ellipse machine has limitations of size, and templates are restricted by only having certain ellipse angles and sizes. All of the following methods for constructing an ellipse are approximations; some approximate by connecting points with a French curve, and others by using a compass.

The fourth definition of an ellipse provides a useful method for large construction, called the Pin and String method. Three pins or stakes are inserted into the drawing surface—one at each focus and the third at the end of the minor axes. A string or cord is looped around the three uprights, and then the pin at the end of the minor axes is replaced with a drawing tool. The tool is then moved in a taut rela-

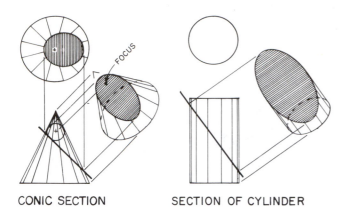

CONIC SECTION   SECTION OF CYLINDER

FIG. 3.18

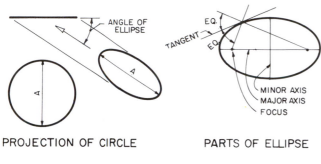

PROJECTION OF CIRCLE   PARTS OF ELLIPSE

FIG. 3.19

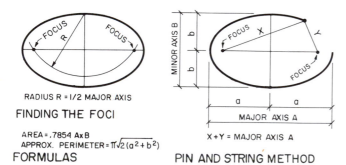

RADIUS R = 1/2 MAJOR AXIS

FINDING THE FOCI

AREA = .7854 A x B
APPROX. PERIMETER = $\pi\sqrt{2(a^2+b^2)}$

FORMULAS

X + Y = MAJOR AXIS A

PIN AND STRING METHOD

FIG. 3.20

tionship to the string, tracing the shape of the ellipse (the length of string is equal to twice the major axis). This technique is sometimes called the Gardner's Ellipse. For smaller ellipses, the drawing tool is difficult to keep exactly perpendicular to the drawing surface, affecting the uniformity of the ellipse.

The second technique for constructing an ellipse is the use of a trammel—a piece of paper or cardboard with half the major and minor axes marked on it. To use the Trammel method, move the trammel with point A always on the major axis and point B in contact with the minor axis or its extension. A series of points are established at C and, when connected freehand or by a French curve, they form the ellipse.

A third method for constructing an ellipse is the Concentric Circles method. Two concentric circles are drawn, one using the major axis as a diameter and the other, the minor axis as a diameter. A series of diameters are next drawn through the common center, intersecting both circles. From the points on the outer circle, lines are drawn parallel to the minor axis, and from points on the inner circle, lines parallel to the major axis. Where these lines intersect are points along the ellipses. The concentric circle method may be the most accurate approximate technique.

Several methods are suitable for drawing an approximate ellipse with a compass. To use the Four Centers method, the length of both axes must be known. In Fig. 3.22, the end of the major axis (point A) is connected to the end of the minor axis (point C). Next, a semicircle, with a radius of half the major axis, is swung from the intersection of the two axes until it intersects the extension of the minor axis at point E. Another arc is made from point C, with a radius of CE, until it crosses line AC at F. Last, line AF is bisected, and where this bisector cross the two axes, or their extensions, are the centers for arcs that form the quarter ellipse. (The bisecting line crosses the minor axis or its extension but never an extension of the major axis.) The other two centers can be located by a similar process or by measurement from the two already located. (The two centers on the major axis are not foci.) Although the four centers method was done classically with a compass, a scale and adjustable triangle (for the bisector) are more practical for construction.

The Conjugate method, the first inscription technique, relies on an initial parallelogram being given. With this method you must visualize a diameter and parallel chords of a circle cast onto a parallelogram, holding one diameter of the circle (lines AB at right) constant in both geometric figures. In their new location, the chords and diameters are conjugate. By definition, conjugate diameters and chords are parallel to the sides of the parallelogram, and the conjugate diameters strike each side at the midpoint of the parallelogram. In the Conjugate method, a circle is first drawn using half the longest conjugate diameter (line AB) as a radius. Next, a diameter of this circle (DIAM.) is made perpendicular to line AB. The ends of the diameter are con-

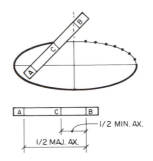

TRAMMEL METHOD

FIG. 3.21

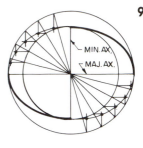

CONCENTRIC CIRCLES METHOD

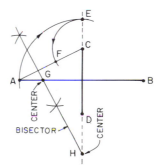

FOUR CENTERS METHOD

FIG. 3.22

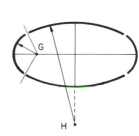

CONJUGATE METHOD

FIG. 3.23

nected to the ends of conjugate diameter CD. Chords are then drawn within the circle parallel to the diameter, and likewise transferred to the parallelogram. These conjugate chords are parallel to the conjugate diameter CD and describe points along the ellipse. (Chords used in this process can be evenly or unevenly spaced.) The ellipse formed by this technique will be as accurate as the projections.

The Parallelogram method for ellipses can be used when either the axis of the ellipse or conjugate diameters are given. This is another inscription technique. Construct a parallelogram from the given axes (or construct the conjugate diameters if the parallelogram is known). First, divide the one-half major axis or conjugate diameter into equal parts. Do the same with one half the short side of the parallelogram. Next, from the end of the minor axis or conjugate diameter, connect lines to the divisions along the short side of the parallelogram. Finally, from the opposite ends of the minor axes or conjugate diameter, extend lines through the major axis subdivisions until they intersect the first set of lines. The intersection points are points along the inscribed ellipse.

The inscription methods previously described are applicable to any parallelogram and, consequently, any axonometric drawing. The Inscription Within a Rhombus method is, as the name implies, only applicable to the rhombus. This technique is the second using compasses and is subject to distortions when drawing elongated ellipses.

A rhombus must be given or drawn first. Lines are then drawn from the ends of the conjugate diameter, at right angles to the sides of the parallelogram. These four lines intersect, and will always intersect the major axis of the ellipse (the same as the longest diagonal of the rhombus) and the minor, or extension of the minor axis (the shorter diagonal of the rhombus). These four points are used as centers for the arcs to draw an approximate ellipse. (Only two centers are shown here. The other two are found by the same process or by measurement from the two points already found.) The Inscription Within a Rhombus method is successively more accurate for ellipses with a rhombus diagonal ratio (labelled DIAG. RAT. in drawings in Fig. 3.26) of 1 to .6 (longer to minor diagonal) and larger. For lower diagonal ratios, this method is less accurate. The Conjugate method or Parallelogram method should be used for ratios of less than 1 to .4.

The Modified Inscription Within a Rhombus method is a variation on the Inscription Within a Rhombus method and produces better shaped ellipses below a 1 to .6 diagonal ratio. The first line is drawn from the end of the conjugate axes perpendicular to the longest diagonal of the rhombus. Where this line crosses the longest diagonal of the rhombus is the center for the shorter arc. A second line is then drawn through this center, perpendicular to the side of the rhombus. The center for the longer radius arc is located by extending the second line until it crosses the extension of the minor axes of the rhomboid. In effect, this method makes longer radii for swinging the longer arcs.

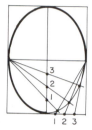
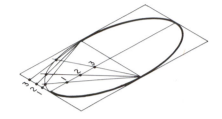

PARALLELOGRAM METHOD

FIG. 3.24

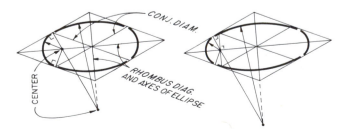

INSCRIPTION WITHIN A
RHOMBUS METHOD

MODIFIED INSCRIPTION
WITHIN A RHOMBUS METHOD

FIG. 3.25

Fig. 3.26 (above) shows a series of comparisons for the Inscription Within a Rhombus technique and the Modified Inscription Within a Rhombus method. Ellipses with a half major axis to minor axis ratio of 1 to .6 (ellipse angle approximately 35°) or larger should be drawn with the Inscription technique. Ellipses less than 1 to .6 should use the Modified method. Below a ratio of 1 to .4 (ellipse angle 25°), the Conjugate or Parallelogram methods will produce far better shaped ellipses.

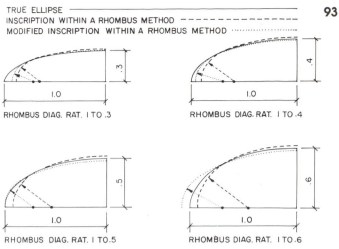

INSCRIPTION WITHIN A RHOMBUS COMPARISON

FIG. 3.26

All of the inscription techniques for approximate ellipses previously described rely solely on using conjugate diameters and not the true length axis of the ellipse. If a parallelogram is given and a perfect ellipse larger than template size is sought, a computer or an ellipse machine must be utilized. Fig. 3.27 shows the process for finding the direction and length of the axis. First, draw the conjugate diameters. Construct a circle using half the longest conjugate diameter AB as a radius. Draw a diameter at right angles to AB. Then, connect C to E and C to F, and bisect angle ECF. Last, draw a line through the crossing point of the conjugate axis point parallel to the bisector. This is the direction of the major axis. The length of both axes can be calculated form the formulas above. (With a rhombus, the major and minor axes of the ellipse will be concurrent with the longest and shortest diagonals of the rhombus.)

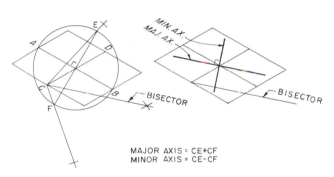

DIRECTION AND LENGTH OF ELLIPSE'S AXES

FIG. 3.27

PARABOLAS

A parabola, the third conic section, is the result of a plane cutting through a right-angled cone parallel to the slope of the cone. A parabola is also the path of a point moving in relationship to a fixed point (the focus) and a fixed line (the directrix) with the right angle distance from the directrix to the moving point always equal to the distance from the focus.

Given a parallelogram, a parabola is drawn using the Parallelogram method for parabolas. Divide one half the shorter side of the parallelogram into the same number of subdivisions as one longer side. On the shorter side and from each subdivision, draw lines parallel to the longer side. From the subdivisions on the longer side, draw lines to the midpoint of the shorter side. Where these lines intersect, the parallel lines are points on the parabola.

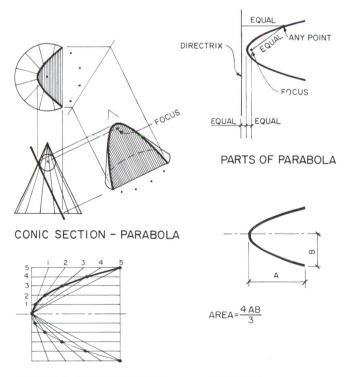

CONIC SECTION – PARABOLA

PARTS OF PARABOLA

PARALLELOGRAM METHOD

FORMULA

$$AREA = \frac{4\ AB}{3}$$

FIG. 3.28

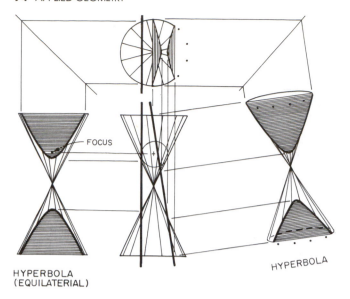

HYPERBOLA
(EQUILATERIAL)

HYPERBOLA

CONIC SECTIONS - HYPERBOLA

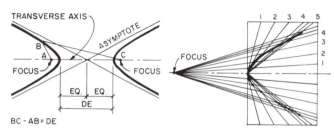

PARTS OF HYPERBOLA   PARALLELOGRAM METHOD

FIG. 3.29

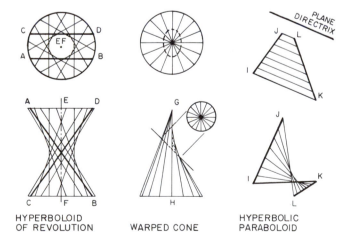

HYPERBOLOID
OF REVOLUTION   WARPED CONE   HYPERBOLIC
PARABOLOID

WARPED SURFACES

FIG. 3.30

HYPERBOLAS

The hyperbola is the last of four conic sections but, unlike the other three, the cutting plane intersects two right-angled cones. If the section is parallel to the central axes of the cones, the hyperbola is technically an equilateral hyperbola. (In general, a hyperbola is thought of as an equilateral hyperbola). A hyperbola is also the path of a point moving in a constant relationship to the two foci. The relationship is equal to the difference in lengths from the two foci to any point on the hyperbola. This difference must also be equal to the distance between the two curves measured along the transverse axis (Line DE in Fig. 3.29). The hyperbola can be extended to infinity where it will meet the asymptotes.

Using the Parallelogram Method for Hyperbolas, subdivide rhe sides of the parallelogram in a similar manner to the construction of a parabola. From the subdivisions on the half of the shorter side, draw lines to the opposite foci of the hyperbola. From the subdivisions on the shorter side, draw lines to the midpoint of the opposite shorter side of the parallelogram.

WARPED PLANES

A warped surface is a curved plane that cannot be unrolled into a flat plane. This surface is generated by a moving straight line (the generatrix) in relationship to fixed controlling lines, curves, or planes (the directrices). Warped surface must have three directrices. Generatrices for warped surfaces have the following characteristics:

1. Generatrices are always straight lines.
2. No two locations of a generatrix will be on the same two-dimensional plane; they are always skewed to one another.
3. Generatrices can never intersect one another.

Both the hyperoboloid of revolution and the warped cone have three lines as directrices. The hyperboloid of revolution has skewed lines AB and CD as generatrices rotating around a central axis (directrix EF) connecting two circles (directrices). The skewed lines are always in contact with the circles.

The elevation of the hyperboloid of revolution is a hyperbola and the directrices trace circle at the top and bottom of the warped surface. With slightly different directrices, an ellipse can be formed at the top and bottom; the surface is then called elliptical hyperboloid. For practical drawing, the circle or ellipse can be the starting point for construction. There are numerous variations for the elliptical hyperboloid or the hyperboloid of revolution. For instance, different-sized circles or ellipses can be used as the starting points, and the central axis can be oblique.

A warped cone (Fig. 3.30, center) has the central axis as one directrix and two circles as the other directrices. One circle is at an angle to the other. Generatrices connect the two circles at equal subdivisions and meet the central axis.

The hyperbolic paraboloid has two line directrices (skewed lines IJ and LK in Fig. 3.30, right) and one plane directrix (only edge view shown). The generatrix is always in contact with the two directrices and parallel to the plane directrix.

The conoid has one straight line (AB), one curved line (a semicircle in the illustration), and one plane as the directrices. Generatrices must be parallel to the plane directrix.

Like the warped cone, the cylindroid has one line as a directrix (line AB) and a plane and two curves as directrices. Generatrices are parallel to plane directrix and touch the two curved directrices. Usually the curves are of similar type.

The oblique helicoid has one curved plane (the surface of a cylinder) as a directrix. A sloping line is also a generatrix and other generatrices move upward or downward at a constant angle (angle X in the illustration) to the axis of thecylinder, while always remaining in contact with the surface of the cylinder.

Sections can be taken through warped planes. A section through a conoid or a cylindroid can be used as transitions between different-shaped openings in a building.

Since all generatrices are non-intersecting straight lines, each generatrix can be the location of a beam in architectural construction.

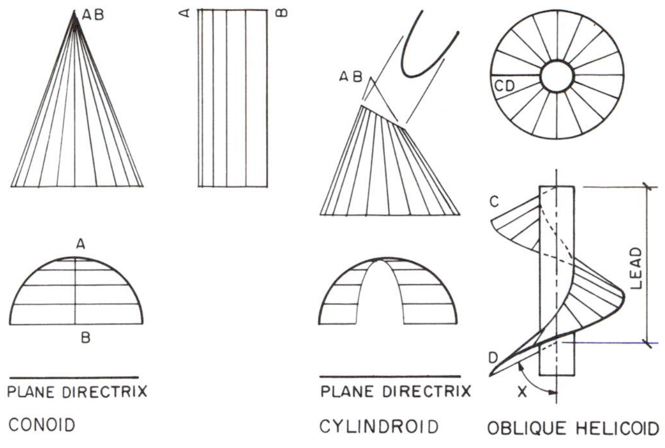

PLANE DIRECTRIX
CONOID

PLANE DIRECTRIX
CYLINDROID

OBLIQUE HELICOID

WARPED SURFACES

FIG. 3.31

SOLIDS

Solids bounded by flat surfaces are polyhedrons. In the illustrations that follow, the five basic solids, prisms, and pyramids are regular polyhedrons. The other solids shown are defined by generatrices and directrices.

Any solid that has one end sliced off by a plane that cuts through the central axis not parallel to the base is a truncated solid. The adjective "right," when applied to solids, means the central axis is at right angles to the base. Oblique solids have their central axis at an angle other than 90° to the base.

The five regular solids, known as the "Five Platonic Solids," are regular polyhedrons whose flat surfaces are polygons with each surface having equal-length sides and angles. Like polygons, the prefix to "hedron" describes the number of sides: tetrahedron = four triangles; hexahedron (cube) = six squares; octahedrons = eight triangles; dodecahedron = twelve pentagons; and icosahedron = twenty triangles.

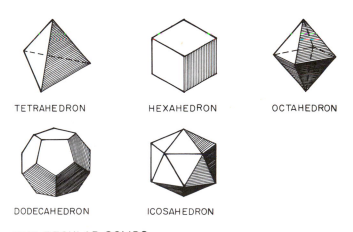

TETRAHEDRON   HEXAHEDRON   OCTAHEDRON

DODECAHEDRON   ICOSAHEDRON

FIVE REGULAR SOLIDS

FIG. 3.32

SQUARE   CUBE   OBLIQUE RECTANGULAR

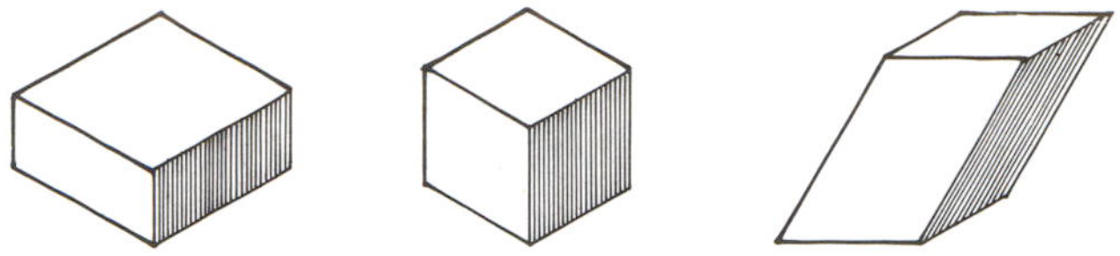

PRISMS – PARALLELPIPEDS

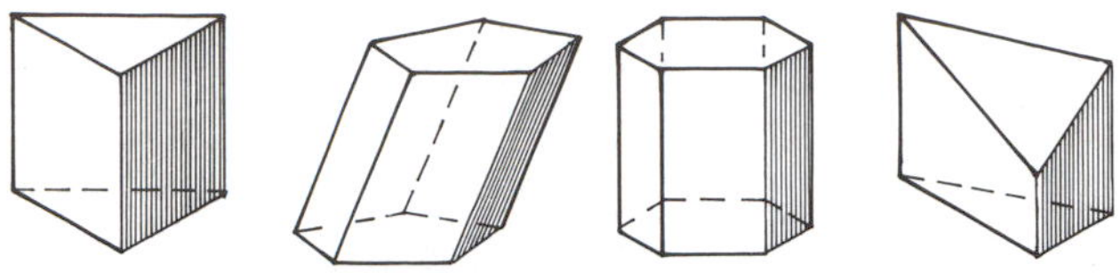

Prisms have equal, parallel polygons for bases and three or more parallelograms for sides. If the bases are parallelograms, the prism is a parallelepiped.

RIGHT TRIANGULAR   OBLIQUE PENTAGONAL   RIGHT HEXAGONAL   TRUNCATED TRIANGULAR

PRISMS

FIG. 3.33

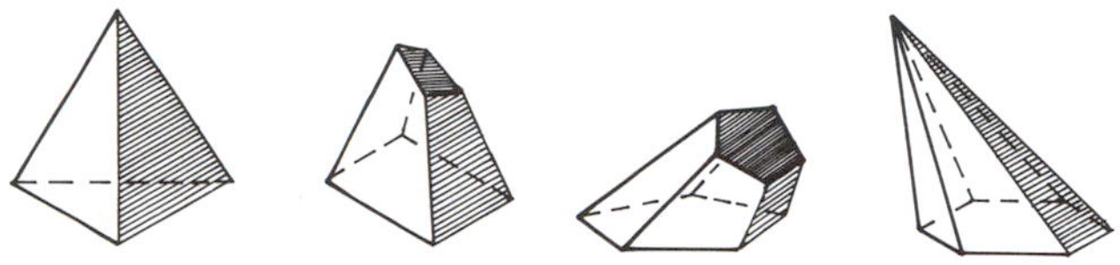

RIGHT TRIANGULAR   RIGHT TRUNCATED RECTANGULAR   OBLIQUE TRUNCATED PENTAGONAL   OBLIQUE HEXAGONAL

PYRAMIDS

FIG. 3.34

Pyramids have any polygon as a base, triangles for sides, and the sides meet at a common point (the vertex of the pyramid).

SOLIDS WITH SINGLE-CURVED SURFACES

Solids with single-curved surfaces are caused by a straight line always in being in contact with some curved plane directrix.

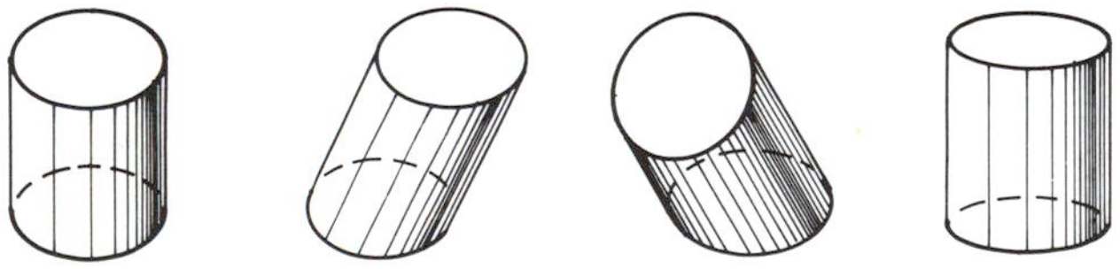

RIGHT   OBLIQUE   OBLIQUE TRUNCATED   ELLIPTICAL

CYLINDERS

FIG. 3.35

Cylinders are defined by surfaces generated with a moving straight line (the generatrix), so the line is always in contact with two identical curved planes (the directrices). Cylinders are generally considered to have conic sections as the directrices, but any regular or irregular curves can serve as the directrices.

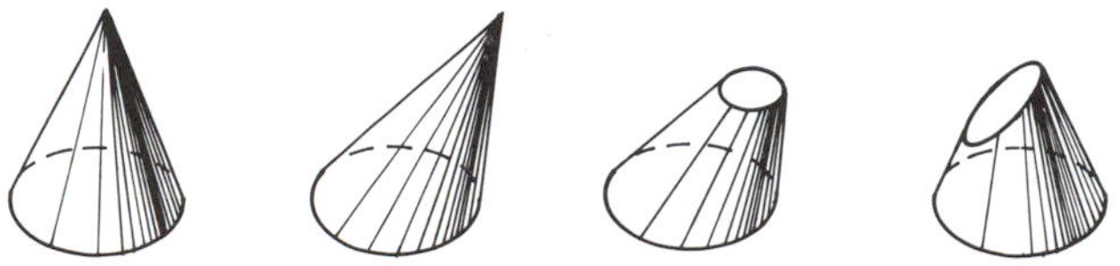

RIGHT   OBLIQUE   FRUSTUM   TRUNCATED

CONES

FIG. 3.36

Cones are defined by surfaces generated with a moving straight line generatrix always in contact with one curved plane directrix. All generatrices in cones meet at a common vertex. A frustrum is a cone or pyramid that has had the top sliced off by a plane parallel to the base.

Solids with double-curved surfaces are generated by moving curved lines. They have no straight line elements. A surface of revolution, the most common type of double-ruled surface, is created by revolving a curved line about an axis as directrix.

Spheres are obtained by revolving a circle about one of its diameters.

Tori are generated by revolving any conic section about any axis not on the plane of the section. The path of revolution for a torus can be circular or any conic section. Although they are not technically tori, other sections such as squares, rectangles, and triangles can be rotated about an axis following the same paths as the torus.

Paraboloids and hyperboloids have their respective curves as plane directrices. The second directrix is their central axis at right angles to plane directrices. The generatrix is a paraboloid or hyperboloid that changes shape as it rotates.

Both prolate ellipsoids and oblate ellipsoids have ellipses as directrices and generatrices. The rotation for a prolate is around the minor axis of one ellipse, and the oblate around the major axis.

FORMULAS FOR SOLIDS

SPHERE   TORUS   PARABOLOID   HYPERBOLOID

PROLATE ELLIPSOID   OBLATE ELLIPSOID

SOLIDS WITH DOUBLE CURVED SURFACES

FIG. 3.37

VOLUME = AREA OF BASE x H

PRISMS AND CYLINDERS

VOLUME = AREA OF BASE x 1/3 H

PYRAMIDS AND CONES

VOLUME = VOLUME OF WHOLE
MINUS VOLUME OF MISSING

FRUSTRUMS OR TRUNCATED

 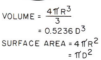

VOLUME = $\dfrac{4\pi R^3}{3}$
= 0.5236 D^3
SURFACE AREA = $4\pi R^2$
= πD^2

SPHERE

VOLUME = AREA OF SECTION x A
SURFACE AREA = PERIMETER OF
SECTION x A

TORUS OR ANY CIRCULAR RING

VOLUME = AREA OF BASE x 1/2 H

PARABOLOID

VOLUME = $\dfrac{\pi ABC}{6}$

ELLIPSOID

FORMULAS - SOLIDS

FIG. 3.38

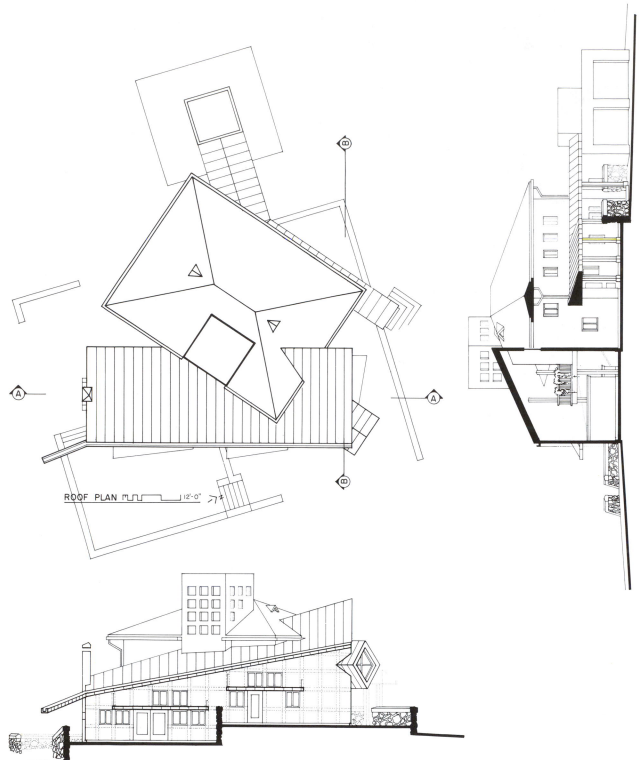

ROOF PLAN ⌐⌐⌐⌐__ 12'-0"

EAST ELEVATION ⌐⌐⌐__ 12'-0"

SECTION BB ⌐⌐⌐__ 12'-0"

CHAPTER 4

ARCHITECTURAL PLANS, SECTIONS, AND ELEVATIONS

The technical basis for coordinating plans, sections, and elevations, standardized by Gaspard Mongue in the late eighteenth century, came at a time when the first formal schools of architecture were established. One school, the École des Beaux-Arts in Paris, became the dominant architectural force in the western world during the nineteenth century. As intra-school design competitions were the backbone of the curriculum at the Ecole, drawing was heavily emphasized. The instructors, students, and graduates of the École introduced a new concept in architecture: Drawings could concretely represent a design idea and at once be a work of art.

In practical terms, drawings made at the beginning of the architectural process are conceptual, often done freehand. These sometimes beautiful "thumbnails" serve as explorations of relationships between ideas, organization, space, and form. As designs begin to solidify, the sketches are turned into "hard line" drawings (ones done with straight edges and a scale). The drawings are continually refined until a final set is given to a contractor for construction.

During this process, an architect makes two basic types of drawings: design or presentation drawings and working or construction drawings. Although design drawings include paralines and perspectives, architects spend well over ninety percent of their time during design and working drawing phases creating multiviews.This chapter therefore concentrates on the types, conventions, symbols, and uses of multiview drawing. All are standard and form a universal language understood by anyone anywhere associated with the building industry.

The chapter begins with three buildings. The first demonstrates all of the multiview types and their permutations with both imperial (feet and inches) and metric (meters) scales. The second building has more complicated forms, and the third shows projections from a building with more than one plan geometry.

ARCHITECTURAL MULTIVIEWS

There are only three kinds of architectural multiviews: plans, sections, and elevations. Each of these types have subtypes. Plans, for instance, include site plans, which depict the relationship of a project to the environment or man-made context; roof plans, often combined with site plans; floor plans showing building layout; and, in working drawings, large-scaled detailed plans of building components. Sections and elevations also have subtypes based on what kinds of information must be conveyed.

Floor plans are the result of horizontal image planes slicing through a building with the portion of the building above the cutting plane removed. Sections and elevations are the product of vertical planes slicing through the building with either a part of the building taken away for a section or the ground in an elevation removed. A floor plan is traditionally "taken" four feet above the floor, while the location of the cut for a section and elevation is based on what will produce the most informative view. If there is a change in ceiling heights, an outside space contained within the building (a court), or a special relationship to the ground on either side of the building there are reasons to take a section at a particular location. These are even reasons to draw more than one. The cut of the exterior surface for an elevation is usually made just outside the building, but the ground or other outside features may suggest moving the cutting plane away from the building.

Differential lineweight should be used in all architectural multiviews to indicate spacial depth. All solids cut by an image plane are drawn with the thickest and darkest of lineweight; some examples include ground, walls, floors, doors, cabinets, and window glass. Thickening of lines is done on the inside of measured dimensions. The next weight of line should be considerably lighter and applied to all objects distant from the cut of the image plane. The lightest are imaginary lines, such as dimension lines, center lines, and lines from written notes.

All multiviews should incorporate the scale of the drawings and titles, including names of rooms or spaces, since the person who made the drawings is often not present when someone else examines them. Names can either be put directly on the drawings or numbered and cross referenced to a chart. Some form of arrow, with an identification by letter or number, appears on plans to show where a section was taken and in what direction the viewer is looking.

Drawings are visually more important than titles. To ensure this dominance, a good rule of thumb is that main titles for a drawing at 1/4" = 1'0" scale should be no larger than 1/4". For smaller scale, they should be smaller, and for larger scale, they should be larger. Less important written information should appear even smaller. If mechanical lettering, press-on letters, or templates are used, the line weight should be lighter than the darkest line on the drawing.

DRAWING PROCEDURE

The strategy for laying out a hard line set of drawings depends on the plans, sections, and elevations being related. Projection from one drawing to another should be used at every possible occasion to avoid mistakes associated with measuring and remeasuring dimensions. As the architectural process advances toward working drawings, the plan becomes the governing drawing for horizontal dimensions and the section controls vertical dimensions. Both plans and sections are laid out starting with the longest dimensions to once again avoid mistakes—in this instance, mistakes of small dimensions not adding up to the total. For this reason, plans are started at the perimeter of a building.

Although some architectural designers start drawing on the computer, many wait until the subjective nature of the design process approaches the need for speed, and then enlist the more rational capabilities of the computer.

When drawing floor plans, the larger the project, the smaller the scale and, if possible, all drawings in a presentation set (with the exception of site plans) should be at the same scale. One quarter inch equals one foot (1:50 metric) is typically used in small construction, like a house. Scales of 3/16" = 1'0" and 3/8" = 1"0" are unconventional and almost never used.

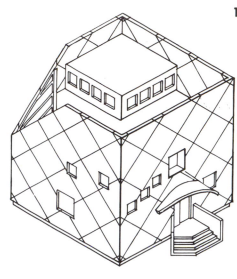

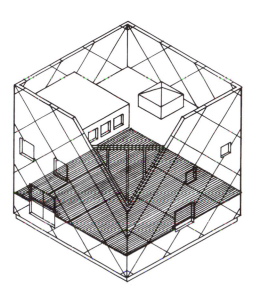

HORIZONTAL IMAGE PLANE — PLAN

BUILDING A: GENERAL DESCRIPTION

This small house (Fig. 4.1), a formal design exercise of cubes and squares, has two floors with the first raised two feet off the ground. A large triangular skyline dissects the external form, allowing light to penetrate into the living/dining area two floors below. In addition, light enters from two other sources: square windows scattered on the facade and a pyramidal skylight above the second floor landing.

The entry is also a cube achieved by lowering the standard 8'-0" (2.44M.) ceiling height to 7'-6" (2.29M). A portion of the second floor bedroom expands upward to create, like the entry, yet another cube.

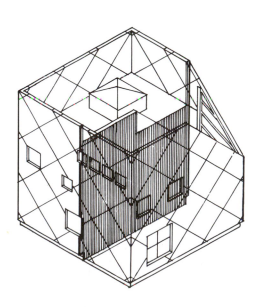

VERTICAL IMAGE PLANE — SECTION

FIG. 4.1

Figs. 4.2 through 4.6 show how one arrives at plans and sections by simply "slicing" and isolating different parts of the building.

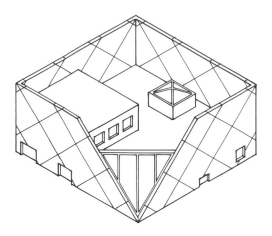

FIG. 4.2

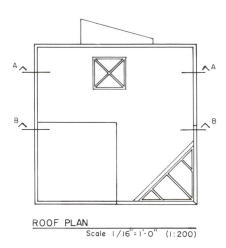

ROOF PLAN
Scale 1/16"=1'-0" (1:200)

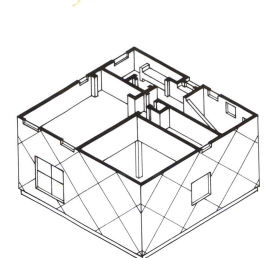

FIG. 4.3

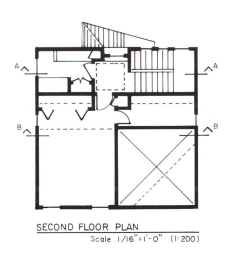

SECOND FLOOR PLAN
Scale 1/16"=1'-0" (1:200)

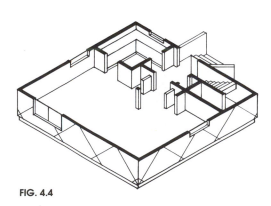

FIG. 4.4

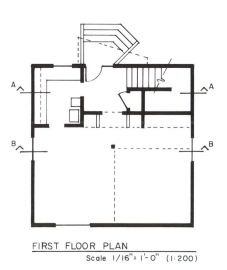

FIRST FLOOR PLAN
Scale 1/16"=1'-0" (1:200)

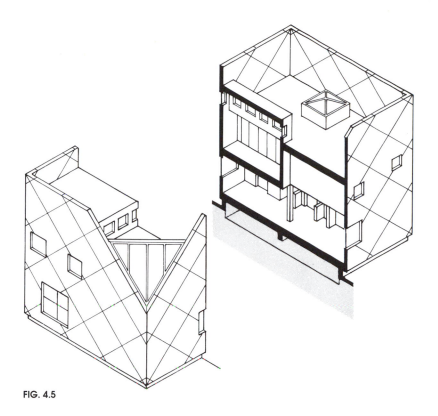

FIG. 4.5

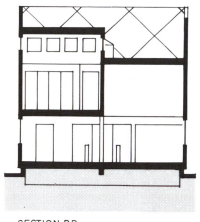

SECTION BB
Scale 1/16"=1'-0" (1:200)

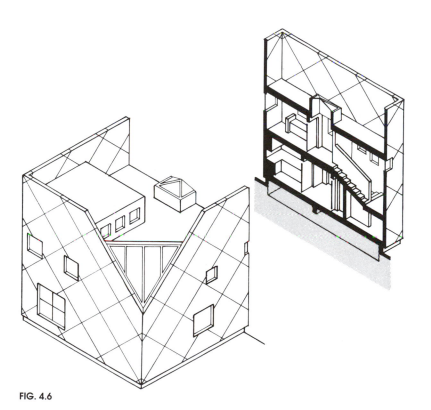

FIG. 4.6

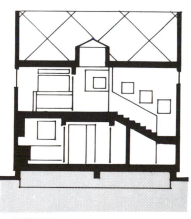

SECTION AA
Scale 1/16"=1'-0" (1:200)

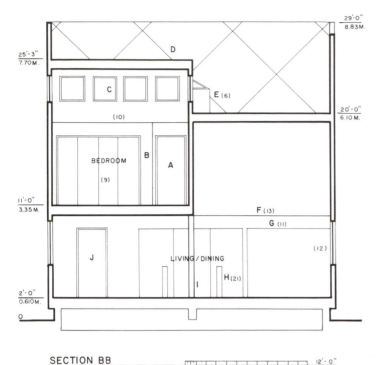

SECTION BB

FIG. 4.7

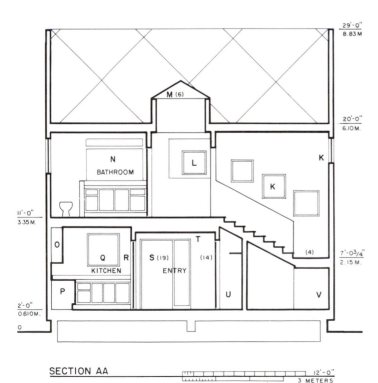

SECTION AA

FIG. 4.8

BUILDING A: SECTIONS

Building A is planned for wood frame construction in the United States: vertical framing members, studs, supporting horizontal beams called joists. When finished materials are added, wall thickness is very close to 6", floors above the ground 12", flat roofs 12", and pitched roofs 8" to 12". These dimensions can be assumed for the majority of residential wood construction during the early stages of architectural design.

As a project proceeds toward working drawings, dimensions are added to plans and sections. In addition, heights, or elevations above ground, are put on both drawing types. Although the drawings on these two pages are design sections and plans (excluding horizontal dimensions and notes), they do indicate elevations above ground (elevation 0'-0") to demonstrate the concept.

Plans and sections are cross referenced on drawings by letters or numbers in parentheses. Both plans and sections must be studied at the same time to gain a clear understanding of the project.

SECTION BB

A. Entry door to bedroom (Doors vary in width according to need; 6'-8" is the conventional height.)
B. Intersection of walls at right angles
C. Clerestory windows above roof (See page 106 for plans.)
D. Parapet wall beyond cut of section (Parapet: an extension of an exterior wall above the roof line.)
E. Part of pyramidal skylight beyond
F. Line of 8'-0"-high ceiling intersecting vertical wall above (8'-0" is the conventional height for residential rooms.)
G. Line of 7'-0"-high ceiling with short wall above
H. 3'-6" high wall below plan cut
I. 6" square freestanding column
J. Pocket door (one that slides into a wall) leading to kitchen

SECTION AA

K. Windows in stairway (High window, cut in section, is above the second floor image plan cut. This image plane only cuts through two of the three windows seen in Elevation, but for clarity, all three are shown in Second Floor Plan.)
L. Recession with window (Recession is on center line of house and the offset window shares a rotational, corner relationship with other openings on the second floor landing. See Plan.)
M. Pyramidal skylight
N. 32"-high bathroom cabinet, mirror, and light
O. 14"-deep upper kitchen cabinets
P. 36"-high x 24"-deep lower kitchen cabinets
Q. 3'-4"-square kitchen window
R. Kitchen pocket door leading to entry
S. 3'-0"-wide by 6'-8"-high entry door with glass sidelight (Doors vary in width but must be at least 3'-0" for entry to any building.)
T. 7'-6"-high entry ceiling to match entry plan dimensions (Forms a cube.)
U. 2'-0"-deep entry coat closet with shelf
V. Inaccessible space under stair

SECOND FLOOR PLAN

1. Edge of triangular skylight above plan cut (Dashed lines in plan, unless otherwise noted on drawing, indicate something above.)
2. "X" is a symbol for no floor present (In this example, the space is open from the second floor ceiling down to the first floor. A large "X" is also used to indicate elevator and mechanical ductwork shafts.)
3. Shelf above, in storage closet
4. Intermediate stair landing (Stair goes down from second floor (Elevation +11'-0") to Landing (+7'-03/4"), and then descends in the opposite direction to the First Floor (+2'-0"). At the beginning of the stairs descent is an arrow marking the down direction (DN) and the total number of vertical risers (17R). See pages 109 and 144-145 for more detailed presentation of stairs.)
5. Curved/straight entrance canopy below Second Floor with supporting diagonal rod (For Elevation, see page 112.)
6. Pyramidal skylight above
7. Medicine cabinet with shelves above and below plan cut
8. Linen closet; doors and shelving above and below (Doors are shown open in Plan and closed in Section with the "swing," or path of door travel, drawn with the lightest of lines in Plan. Minor doors, such as closets, are indicated partially open. When there would be an overlapping of two door swings, both doors are drawn partially open, even though one door may be a major door. For example, door to bathroom conflicts with bathroom closet doors. Cabinet doors are never shown open in Plan.)
9. Bifold closet doors in bedroom (See page 144.)
10. Line of 8'-0"-high ceiling with vertical clerestory wall above

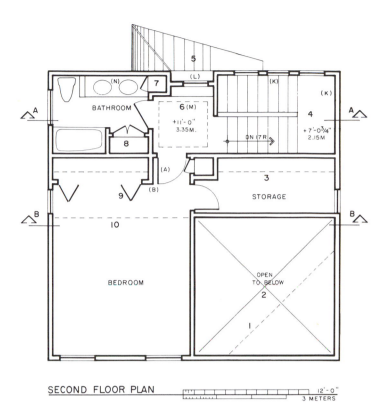

SECOND FLOOR PLAN

12'-0"
3 METERS

FIG. 4.9

FIRST FLOOR PLAN

11. Line of 8'-0"-high ceiling with vertical wall above
12. 4'-4" square window with sill 3'-0" above the floor (The image plane of Plan slices through the building 4'-0" above the floor. This plane cuts through the glass—darker line—with the wall thickness shown below—lighter lines. Similarly, any window cut by a section shows only the glass in dark lineweight.)
13. Line of 7'-0"-high ceiling and short wall above
14. Coat closet, door, and shelf above
15. Light diagonal line with an "S" or "Z" = "break line" (This symbol indicates an incomplete drawing. Incomplete in this case because the rest of the stair is above the plan cut.)
16. Line of entrance canopy above
17. Outside stair to bring a person entering from ground (Elevation 0'-0") up to the first floor (Elevation +2'-0")
18. Outside wall below plan cut
19. 3'-0" x 6'-8"-entry door with glass side panel
20. Refrigerator (Not attached to wall and, like moveable furniture, drawn as an independent object.)
21. 3'-6"-high wall below plan cut (light lineweight)

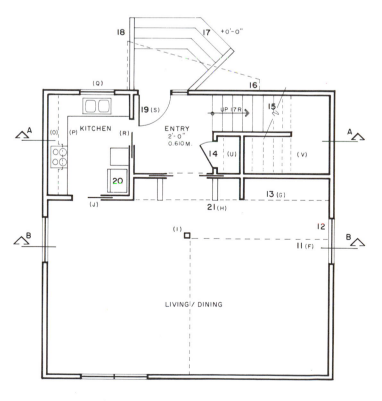

FIRST FLOOR PLAN

12'-0"
3 METERS

FIG. 4.10

Floor plans are generally taken 4'-0" above the floor, but some circumstances arise where additional plans must be drawn at non-conventional heights to fully describe a building. In fact, plans can be drawn at any horizontal level. Building A, for instance, needs a plan at +22'-0" (11'-0" above Second Floor Plan) to show the location of clerestory windows (for Elevation, see pages 112 and 113). Section CC in Fig. 4.15 must be examined first to understand this Plan. It points out the Plan at +22'-0", slices through the parapet walls and the glass of the triangle skylight, and leaves part of the skylight above +22'-0", expressed as dashed lines in Plan at that level.

BUILDING A: SPECIAL SECTION

None of the previous drawings adequately describe the large triangular skylight. To accomplish this, Section CC must be taken at right angles to the slope of the skylight. It shows the true slope (slopes are expressed either in degrees—this example 54°—or more usually as a ratio of vertical to horizontal, holding 12 constant for horizontal—this example, 18 in 12), the height of the short parapet walls supporting the skylight, and the relationship to perimeter walls. This section also indicates the true length of the altitude of the triangle. A true-sized view of the skylight is drawn by projecting at right angles from the edge view (Section CC) and using 13'-9" from the Roof Plan.

Although Section CC theoretically cuts through the 6" free-standing column on the first floor, columns are never shown as a cut object in Section. This is because they would be confused with walls. Section CC depicts 6" walls cut at an angle, making the drawn thickness greater than 6" (+/-8.5"); all windows are seen at an angle, hiding the frames on one side in Section CC.

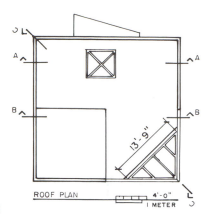

FIG. 4.11

ROOF PLAN

13'-9"

4'-0"
1 METER

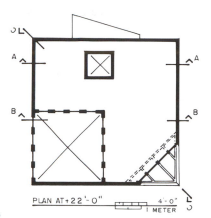

FIG. 4.12

PLAN AT +22'-0"

4'-0"
1 METER

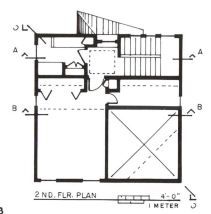

FIG. 4.13

2 ND. FLR. PLAN

4'-0"
1 METER

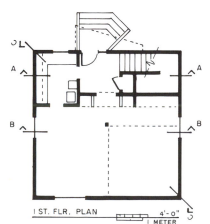

FIG. 4.14

I ST. FLR. PLAN

4'-0"
1 METER

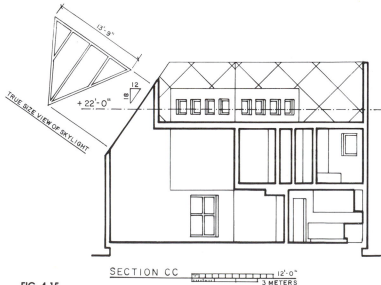

FIG. 4.15

SECTION CC

TRUE SIZE VIEW OF SKYLIGHT

13'-9"

+22'-0"

18
12

12'-0"
3 METERS

A reflected ceiling plan is the reverse of a floor plan: the viewer is looking up rather than down. Also different, the image plane is cut just below the ceiling. Drawing this type of multiview is a simple matter of tracing the floor plan and making the necessary corrections. For example, a reflected ceiling plan with a 6'-8"-door in a space with a conventional 8"-0" ceiling indicates the solid wall above the door. Windows that do not go all the way to the ceiling would also show a solid wall.

Reflected ceiling plans typically locate lighting fixtures and air conditioning grills in working drawings. In other instances, an architect might elect to draw a reflected ceiling plan of exposed structural beams and mechanical ductwork, a highly decorative or patterned ceiling, or complicated changes in ceiling heights.

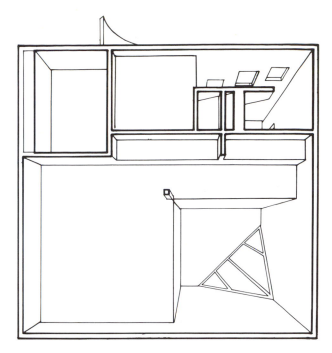

PERSPECTIVE LOOKING UP

FIG. 4.16

Fig. 4.17 shows Building A's reflected ceiling plan with its varying ceiling heights. Ceiling elevations are noted for the various levels related to the First Floor (Elevation 2'-0"). The upper kitchen cabinets touch the ceiling; the cut of the image plane is above the intermediate stair landing (cut at +/-7'-6", landing at 7'-0-3/4"). Consequently, the viewer sees the second floor ceiling at +19'-0".

Reflected ceiling plans are seldom used with residential buildings because lighting fixtures are usually drawn on floor plans (see page 135).

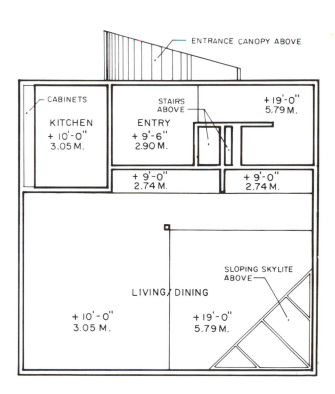

SECOND FLOOR PLAN

FIG. 4.17

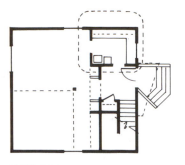

FIRST FLOOR PLAN

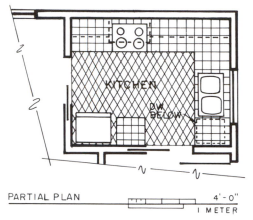

PARTIAL PLAN   4'-0"
           I METER

FIG. 4.18

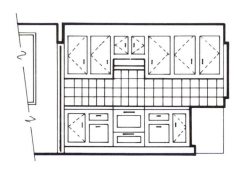

KITCHEN ELEVATION   4'-0"
           I METER

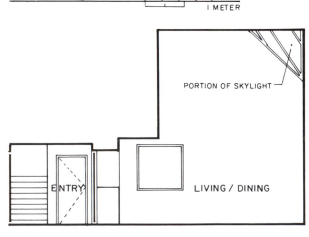

PORTION OF SKYLIGHT

ENTRY   LIVING / DINING

INTERIOR ELEVATION   8'-0"
           2 METERS

FIG. 4.19

BUILDING A: PARTIAL PLANS

Partial plans are enlargements of a segment of a floor plan that show more detail or provide more room for dimensions, symbols, or notes on working drawings. The limits of a partial plan are marked by snap lines to indicate that the plan is incomplete. In addition, the smaller-scaled plan must show what portion of the full plan is enlarged. This is usually done with a dashed line rectangle with rounded corners.

The kitchen plan in Fig. 4.18 indicates tile on the floor and counter tops, the location of appliances, and what is above and below the plan cut. Kitchen counters are 36" high and below the plan cut. Upper cabinets are normally 18" above counter height, making them above the plan cut. The dishwasher is under the counter, noted as such (D.W. below), and drawn with a light dashed line. The refrigerator, although theoretically cut by the plan cut, is never shown with a heavy line.

BUILDING A: INTERIOR ELEVATIONS

Interior elevations, similar to partial plans, usually appear only in working drawings. This type of drawing produces much the same information that a section does, but without floor and wall thickness. At scales of 1/4" = 1'-0" or less, cabinets are presented in profile only without depicting shelving inside. The image plane cuts through the exterior wall and window on the right of this drawing. The inside half thickness of the wall is seen beyond in elevation.

Dashed lines that form an arrow in elevations are the standard working drawing symbol telling the viewer which way the door swings: The arrow points to the hinge side. This indication is used for both cabinet and full-height doors.

The second interior elevation looks in the opposite direction and shows the entire First Floor from the approximate centerline of the house. Left to right, the drawing portrays: the entry with the stair leading to the Second Floor; the coat closet door; the pocket door in Section between entry and living/dining; ceilings at 7'-6", 7'-0" and 8'-0"; the short 3'-6"-high wall; and the double-height living/dining ceiling (17'-0" high or +19'-0").

Risers, treads, and nosings are the major visible components of a stair. When they are put together without a landing, these elements constitute a stair "run" (in any run of stairs, there is always one more riser than treads). The most common kinds of stairs are the straight run from floor to floor and a "switchback" where the run goes to a landing and continues in the opposite direction. (The latter are used in Building A. See page 145 for other stair types.)

Code requirements set minimum standards for stair construction. For nonresidential buildings, treads must usually be no less than 11", risers a maximum of 7", no more than 13'-0" vertical rise without a landing, and landings must be the same width as the stair width—minimum 36". Handrails can be no less than 34" and no more than 38" above nosing. Guardrails or walls at landings should be no less than 42" in height.

For the early stages of design, assume 6" risers and 12" treads. For example, if a building has 10'-0" from floor to floor, a straight run of stairs would require 20 risers at 6" and 19 treads at 1'-0". An even simpler method to determine the ample length of a run is to subtract one foot from two times the floor to floor height.

The interior stair for Building A (a 28' cube) is diagrammatically shown in Fig. 4.21. It is the technical basis and rationale for the stair design.

After subtracting 8'-6" for the kitchen width plus walls and 7'-6" for the entry, 11'-0" was left for the first stair run and a 3'-6" intermediate landing. Calculations were made to obtain the number and sizes of risers/treads, length of run, and the vertical height to intermediate landing. Overall dimensions were then laid out and subdivided using the Subdivision of a Given Line method. (See Chapter 3, page 83).

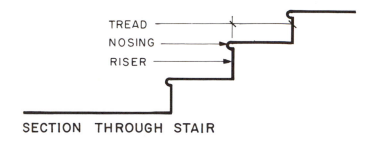

SECTION THROUGH STAIR

FIG. 4.20

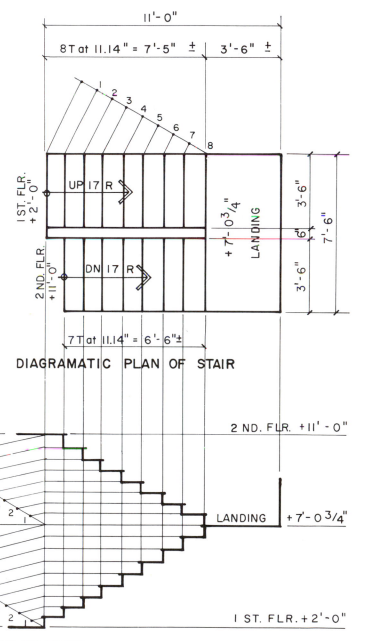

DIAGRAMATIC PLAN OF STAIR

DIAGRAMATIC SECTION OF STAIR

FIG. 4.21

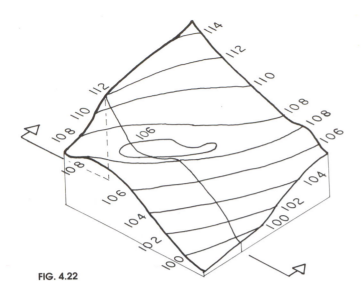

FIG. 4.22

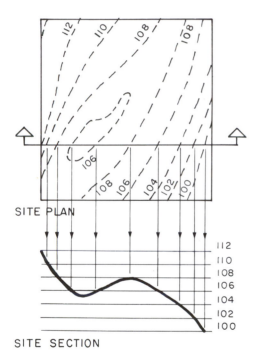

SITE PLAN

SITE SECTION

FIG. 4.23

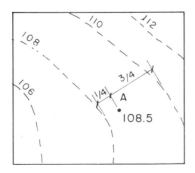

FIG. 4.24

BUILDING A: CONTOURS

Topography is the surface configuration of a land area, and the vertical difference in ground height is represented in drawings by contours. Contours are imaginary lines of constant horizontal level drawn with dashed lines in plan. Each contour is given a number identifying its height in relationship to other contours; the numbers are labelled on the uphill side of dashed lines. Some characteristics of contours are:

1. Contours can never cross one another.
2. The closer the contours are in plan, the steeper the ground slope, and conversely, the further apart, the flatter the slope.
3. Equally-spaced contours indicate a constant slope.
4. When a contour closes upon itself, either a convex or concave ground form is present.

Contours are obtained by either aerial photography or, more normally, by surveyors on the ground. In both cases they are drawn at engineering scales—1″ = 20′, 1″ = 40′, etc. Unless the ground is exceptionally steep or aerial photography is used for whole regions, contours are usually "taken" (mapped) for two-foot differences in ground elevation. Elevation numbers are referenced to one of two datum planes: 100 is arbitrarily assigned to the lowest point on a given site or to elevation 0, the mean high tide of the ocean. The United States Coast and Geodetic Survey Department (U.S.G.S.) has mapped the whole country for five contours and established thousands of permanent "bench marks" throughout the country. From these concrete bench marks, surveyors can establish an elevation at any site referenced to 0 elevation and number local contours.

Sections through vertical contours are drawn by first selecting a location for the vertical image plane in plan and then projecting the points where contours cross this plane into section.

The projection lines and horizontal lines in Section in Fig. 4.23 serve only as guide lines and are never drawn in a finished section.

If the elevation of a point not on a contour line is needed, it is found by extrapolation: An imaginary line is drawn through the point connecting adjacent contour lines, and the desired elevation is proportional to the relative distance between the two contours. From the example in Fig. 4.24, point A is one quarter the distance between elevation 108 and 110. Therefore, the elevation of point A is approximately 108.5′.

Ground elevations are given in decimal percentages of a foot to match the engineer's scale used in drawing. Architectural elevations (heights), on the other hand, are usually expressed in feet and inches.

During the architectural process, contours have multiple uses. The topography and the consequent contours of a site can strongly influence floor plan configuration, building location, and orientation to the sun.

Contours are shown on site plans along with built objects on the ground. Roof plans are the usual representation of the building on a site plan, at least for design presentations, but some building codes require a foundation wall plan on construction drawings. In either case, contours are not shown within the perimeter of the building.

The cube house, Building A, has been adapted to a sloping site and a simplified site plan illustrated in Fig. 4.25. On pages 104 and 105, the building was referenced to 0'-0" as ground but, with adaption, this elevation height becomes approximately 117'-0" for the architectural portions of the drawing and 117. 0 for ground; the heights of other horizontal planes have changed accordingly. For instance, to top of the parapet wall (T.O.W.) becomes 146'-0" (117'-0" + 29'-0" = 146'-0"). (See Section BB on page 104.)

Site section DD in Fig. 4.26 explains the relationship of the building to the topography. Section DD, on the left side, cuts through a sloping section of the parapet wall, making it less than 146'-0". Although contour lines are not shown within the building Plan, a dashed line representing the original slope is often drawn in Section.

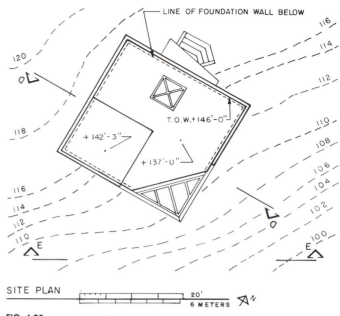

SITE PLAN

FIG. 4.25

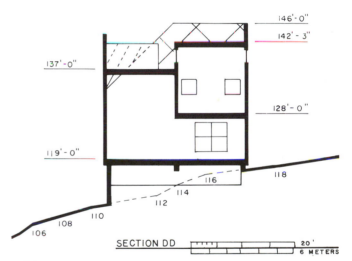

SECTION DD

FIG. 4.26

BUILDING A: EXTERIOR ELEVATIONS

The auxiliary Elevation in Fig. 4.27 is drafted using Section EE from the Site Plan in Fig. 4.25. Pulling the image plane away from the building gives a better three-dimensional representation of the house on the uphill ground slope than an image plane just outside the building. The intersection of the foundation wall with the building is drawn by projecting the intersection point of the contours and foundation wall from the Site Plan.

A note here on line weight: The section cut on this page receives the heaviest line weight, with lighter lines for elements further back in space (even a dotted line for the far parapet wall). On a more sophisticated level, wedge-shaped lines are used for those lines receding into space. This technique is hard to master and, to be effective, it should be almost unnoticed.

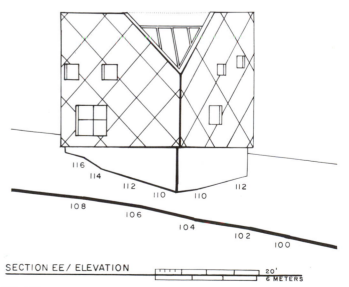

SECTION EE / ELEVATION

FIG. 4.27

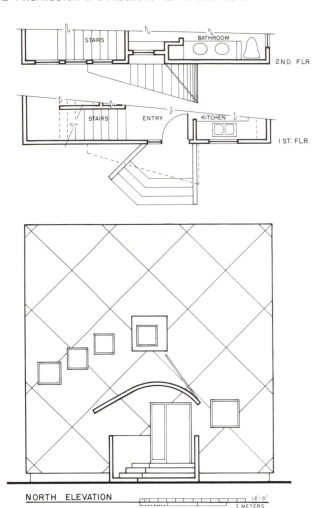

NORTH ELEVATION

FIG. 4.28

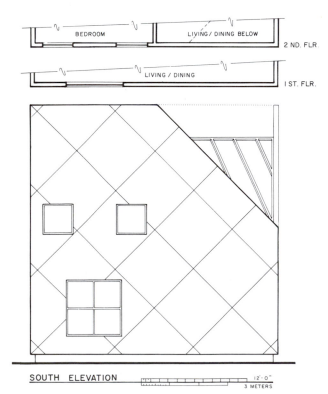

SOUTH ELEVATION

FIG. 4.29

The auxiliary elevation in Fig. 4.27 is a useful drawing type for presentation. (Some may refer to an auxiliary elevation as a transmetric, but the term "auxiliary elevation," though it assigns an unjustified subordinate role, is an older, more commonly used title.) The elevations in Figs. 4.28 and 4.29, however, are more typical orthographic projections onto image planes parallel to each side of the building. Exterior elevations are usually drawn on separate sheets laid over plans. This is done with a triangle for alignment, rather than actually drawing projection lines.

Titles for elevations are given according to the points of the compass: An elevation that faces south is titled South Elevation, northwest is called Northwest Elevation, etc.

The entrance canopy for Building A was designed by selecting the tangent/arc relationships in North Elevation and deciding to slice the form in Plan. To draft the East and West Elevations of the canopy (shown in Fig. 4.30), the arc was subdivided in North Elevation, projections were made into Plan, where the subdivision points became lines, and then both points and lines were taken into the two new elevations.

The view of a cylinder perpendicular to its central axis will show equal subdivisions of a circle as lines get progressively closer together toward the edge (see page 67). These lines give a three-dimensional effect of curvature (a type of shading). In the Plan of the entrance canopy in Fig. 4.30, less than a half circle is present. Lines here do get closer together toward the edges but only slightly, thereby negating the feeling of curvature. The partial second floor plan in Fig. 4.28 subjectively exaggerates the closeness of lines, creating a believable curvature.

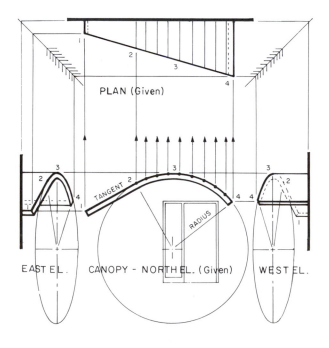

FIG. 4.30

Of all the possible graphic treatments for exterior elevations, the use of differential lineweights and thickness is the easiest and quickest. This technique can be applied to any stage of design or working drawings and produces a subtle, understated quality that does not interfere with the designer's intentions.

Some architects believe that drawings relying solely on lineweight have a mechanical appearance, unsuitable for less composed, freer designs. Nonetheless, the nature of Building A is one of a carefully considered, controlled composition and consequently, the technique is appropriate. Other techniques will be discussed later in this chapter.

To fully employ lineweight, one must understand the major difference between making a drawing and viewing it. Drafting is done 10" to 15" from a drawing, while presentations are often seen from 10' to 15' away. A drawn line may be legible at 10", but at 10' it all but disappears. Consequently, the drafter must adapt by using heavier lineweight without eliminating the light/dark line relationships.

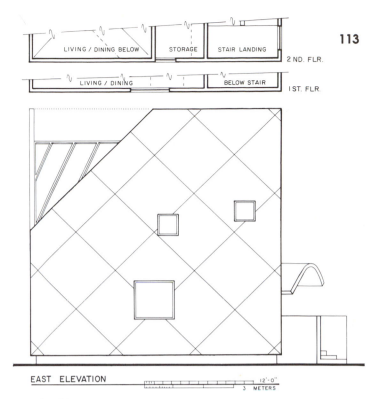

EAST ELEVATION

FIG. 4.31

The elevations in Figs. 4.28 through 4.32 were drawn with ink on plastic drafting film at 1/4" = 1'-0" and were then reduced. The cut ground lineweight is drawn at quadruple #2 (.60mm. pen); the entrance canopy and front edge of the exterior walls in North Elevations at #21/2 (.70mm.); the outline of the cube at #2; wall openings for doors and windows at #0 (.35mm.); frames inside wall openings and diagonal grid at #4x0 (.18mm.); and the entrance canopy and exterior walls in East and West Elevations at #0 for closest and #4 x 0 for the furthest.

This combination of lineweights for this particular design at 1/4" = 1'0" makes the originals read well for presentation viewing distances. If the drawings were done at a larger or smaller scale, the lineweight would be proportionally heavier or lighter.

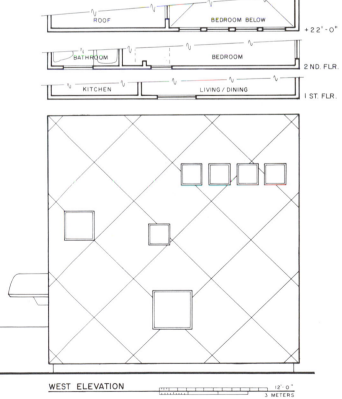

WEST ELEVATION

FIG. 4.32

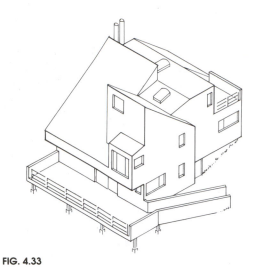

FIG. 4.33

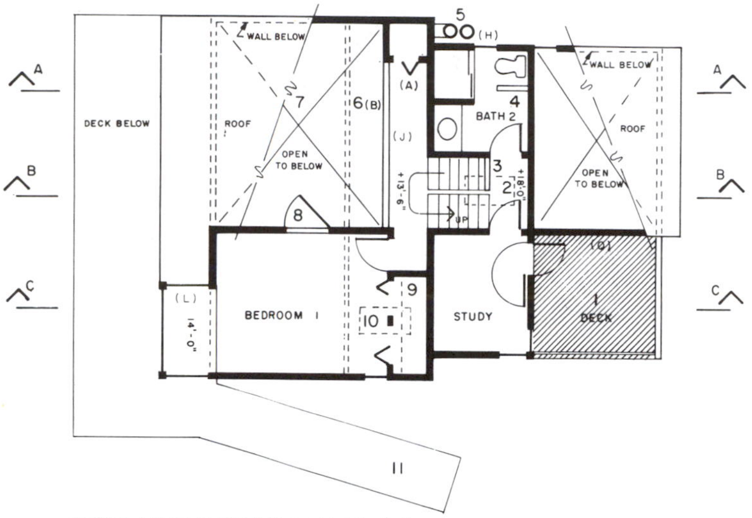

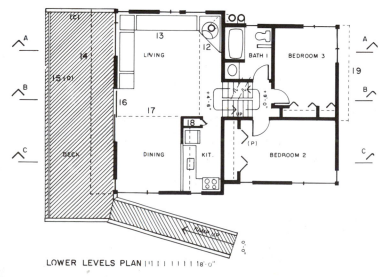

UPPER LEVELS PLAN |' | | | | | | | |8'-0"

FIG. 4.34

LOWER LEVELS PLAN |' | | | | | | | |8'-0"

FIG. 4.35

BUILDING B: FLOOR PLANS

The design of Building B, a small vacation house, responds to a narrow, sloping site by using split level plans and developing the necessary spaces upward into a tall house. On the uphill side, a basement digs into the ground and the floors above are one half level (4'-6") higher than the downhill levels. (The basement Plan is not shown.) The locations of broken image planes in the Plans are shown with dashed/dotted lines in Section AA, Fig. 4.36. This house, similar to Building A, turns inward, depending on large interior volumes, rather than strongly integrating the interior and exterior. The plans and sections for Building B are also similar to the drawings for Building A in that they are a composite of presentation and working drawings.

The graphic treatment of cut elements by solid black rather than by dark lines is a matter of personal choice and also of the scale of the drawing. At scales of 1/8" = 1'-0" or less, solid black is the only alternative, but at 1/4" = 1'-0" or greater, cut elements such as walls and floors can be represented with lines only (the Plans and Sections of Building A, for instance). Solid black ensures legibility at a greater viewing distance than line, but lacks the finesse of light versus dark lineweight.

UPPER LEVELS PLAN

1. Exterior wood deck
2. Skylight above stair
3. 3'-6" wall below plan cut
4. Low privacy wall below plan cut
5. Prefabricated metal flues (one from fireplace in living area and one from furnace in basement)
6. Large beam above supporting roof joists
7. Break line with living area below (Break lines are always drawn at an angle so they won't be confused with construction lines.)
8. Interior window connecting Bedroom 1 with living area below
9. Bedroom closet with top of closet as a desk top in study one-half level above bedroom (Study and bedroom are open to one another over the desk top; see Section CC. Upper Levels Plan had to be drawn for either the closet or desk top. Closet was the condition selected for drafting even though it indicates a separate, closed room.)
10. Skylight above Study/Bedroom 1
11. Ramp below

LOWER LEVELS PLAN

12. Prefabricated metal fireplace
13. Built-in "L"-shaped couch with continuous back touching walls
14. Line of roof overhang above
15. 3'-6"-high guardrail
16. Sliding glass doors
17. Line of vertical bedroom wall above
18. Narrow broom closet
19. Roof overhang above

SECTION AA

A. Storage closet beyond section cut
B. Large wood beam supporting transverse roof rafters in both upper living space and Bedroom 1
C. 3'-6"-high deck end wall beyond
D. Pipe railing
E. 6" wood column sitting on 8" concrete pier with 12" square "footing" (Footings are portion of foundation that transmit loads directly to soil. The bottom of a footing must be below possible frost line for a particular building location. This varies widely from one geographic area to another.)
F. 12" continuous concrete foundation wall with 18" concrete footing (Footings usually not shown in design drawings. Foundation walls are normally 6" wide for wood frame construction. In this building, rear and side walls for basement must be 12" thick to retain earth pressure. Using a consistent 12" for all walls proved more economical than changing to 6" for other foundation walls. Image plane for Section cuts through this wall and footing, but not pier represented by E.)
G. Original ground line

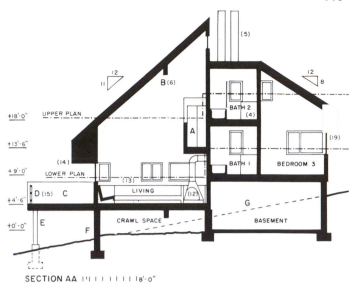

SECTION AA

FIG. 4.36

SECTION BB

H. High window in Bedroom 3
I. Clerestory window
J. 3'-6"-high wall below plan cut
K. Large beam in "crawl space" supporting floor joists

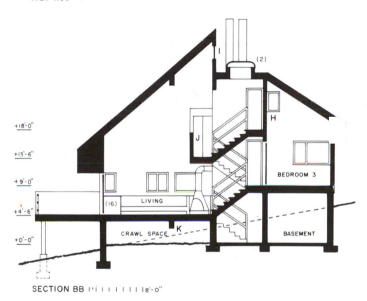

SECTION BB

FIG. 4.37

SECTION CC

L. Window above plan cut; shown in Plan for clarity
M. Built-in furniture (Shown in less detail than other two sections because these objects are further away from section cut than Section AA or BB. Same principle was used when displaying the deck below in Upper Levels Plan.)
N. Lower kitchen cabinets
O. Door in basement leading to stairs (Basement plan not shown.)
P. Bifold closet door (Doors shown on swing side of all walls; see detail on page 134.)
Q. Vertical wood siding in Elevation beyond

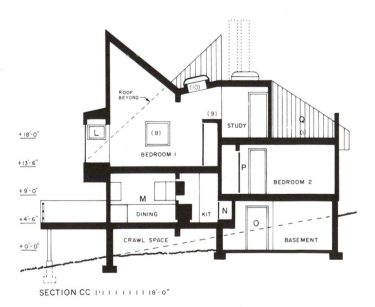

SECTION CC

FIG. 4.38

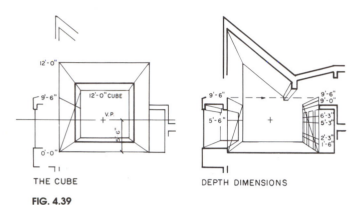

TWO POINT PERSPECTIVE   HALVING   UNEQUAL SUBDIVISION

ONE POINT PERSPECTIVE   EQUAL SUBDIVISION   EQUAL MULTIPLICATION

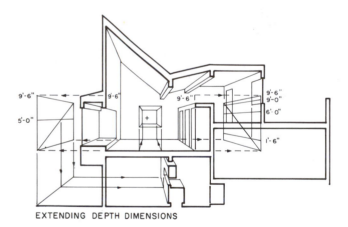

THE CUBE   DEPTH DIMENSIONS

FIG. 4.39

EXTENDING DEPTH DIMENSIONS

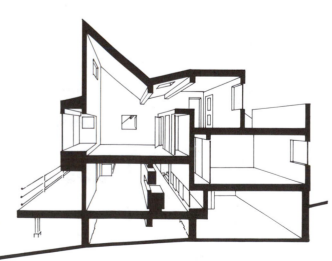

SECTIONAL PERSPECTIVE

FIG. 4.40

BUILDING B: SECTIONAL PERSPECTIVES

Once drawn, sections can be readily changed into sectional perspectives for design presentations. This type of drawing discloses interior volumes more clearly than a section, particularly if the design is intricate or the viewers are laypersons.

There are two basic kinds of perspectives: one point and two point. In the latter type, all parallel horizontal lines converge to one of two vanishing points (V.P.) on the horizon at the viewer's eye height (usually at 5'-4" or 5'-6"). With both one and two point perspectives, equal length lines subject to perspective convergence get progressively closer together as they approach the vanishing point.

A one point perspective has one set of horizontal lines parallel to the horizon. Although one point perspective is less convincing than a two point for exterior views, one point appears believable when applied to a sectional perspective.

Many methods can be used for constructing perspectives, but the easiest and fastest method (other than employing a computer program) is the Estimate a Cube method. With this method, a cube is estimated at the beginning of the process and depth dimensions are obtained by multiplying or subdividing the original assumption. The following mechanical techniques are used in this process:

1. To halve the perspective distance between two given lines (AB and CD in Fig. 4.39), draw diagonals from the ends of the two lines. The mid-distance between the two lines is at the intersection of the two diagonals (EF). (This process can be repeated indefinitely. For example, GH is midway between AB and EF.)
2. To subdivide the distance between two lines, scale the depth dimensions on the leading line. Extend the dimension points as lines to the vanishing points. Draw a diagonal between the two given lines. The desired depth dimensions occur at the intersection of the diagonal and the corresponding perspective line.
3. To multiply a given depth dimension, divide the leading line in half. Extend the midpoint as a perspective line to the vanishing point. Draw a diagonal from the end of the leading line through the midpoint of the second line. Where this diagonal intersects the perspective line from the leading line is an equal multiplication of the given depth dimensions.

BUILDING B: ELEVATIONS

As discussed earlier, there are two basic graphic methods for communicating spacial depth in orthographic drawing. The use of dark lines in the foreground and lighter ones further back essentially establishes the foreground and pulls the drawing away from the image plane (or vice versa). This technique is related to natural seeing: Distant objects become less distinct, have less contrast, and show less detail than closer objects. Although no examples of this visual phenomenon using tone have been presented thus far in this book, everyone is familiar with distant hills being lighter than nearer ones.

The second graphic method for depicting spacial depth is to establish the background with a darker tone. This pushes the drawing forward by foiling lighter planes against darker ones. (See pages 60, 62, 68, 70, and 79). This abstract method will be applied to architectural drawings later in this chapter.

North and South Elevations for Building B use a combination of both push and pull methods. Darker lines come forward while lighter lines recede, pulling elements back into space. The closely spaced dashed lines, representing shingles on the roof, create a graded tone from dark at the near edge of the roof to light at the furthest edge. The vertical surface adjacent to the dark edge of the roof is pushed forward and the gradation pulls the plane back into space.

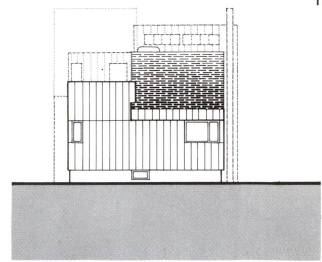

NORTH ELEVATION   1'| | | | | | | | | 8'-0"

FIG. 4.41

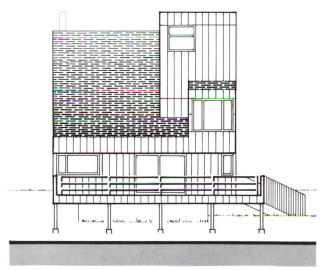

SOUTH ELEVATION   1'| | | | | | | | | 8'-0"

FIG. 4.42

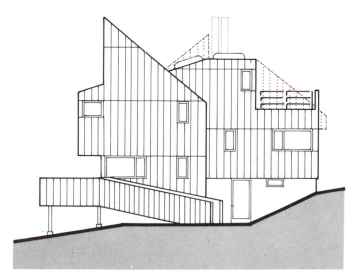

EAST ELEVATION   1'| | | | | | | | | 8'-0"

FIG. 4.43

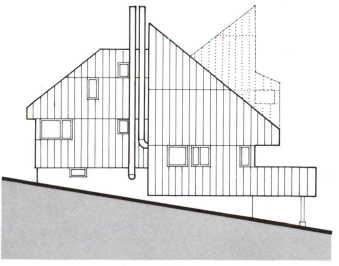

WEST ELEVATION   1'| | | | | | | | | 8'-0"

FIG. 4.44

BUILDING C: GENERAL DESCRIPTION

All of the previous multiview drawings in this chapter were orthographic projections from building surfaces parallel to one side of the conventional six-sided theoretical box. There were only two exceptions: Section EE Elevation for Building A and the roofs of Building B. Building C, the last of the three major example buildings, has two sets of orthogonal (right-angled) geometry, one for the first floor and another for the upper two floors. Consequently, all sections and elevations have surfaces that are and are not parallel to image planes.

The upper two floors of this building have a roof made up of two sloping surfaces. The first floor has an upper section composed of a quarter-round portion combined with a flat portion and a lower flat roof section.

The drawings for Building C demonstrate complicated projections from one drawing to another. Therefore, projection lines were kept on the drawings. Further, the drawings are architectural demonstrations of principles explained in Chapter Two. The following descriptive geometry techniques apply on the following five pages:

1. Dimension transfer lines; see page 45
2. Visibility; see page 47
3. Circles appear as ellipses; see page 54
4. Lines penetrating planes; see pages 58 and 69
5. A cutting plane to establish a solid on an oblique plane; see pages 69 and 75
6. Drawing an elevation of an object with compound geometries; see page 76

SITE PLAN   24'-0"   N

FIG. 4.45

FIG. 4.46

The three drawings in Fig. 4.47 assume Plan and Section were developed first. The problem was to draw the Rear Garden Elevation. All three plans were overlaid in order to draw projections, but for clarity only the third floor is shown.

The elliptical profile of the quarter-circular roof and the intersection of this roof in Elevation were resolved by dividing the circle into six parts in Section AA, projecting these divisions into Plan where the points became lines, and then projecting the points from both Section AA and Plan into Elevation.

Only the second and third floor portions of the Garden Elevation are "true to scale" (true size). No single elevation of this building will produce a true-sized elevation for the entire building.

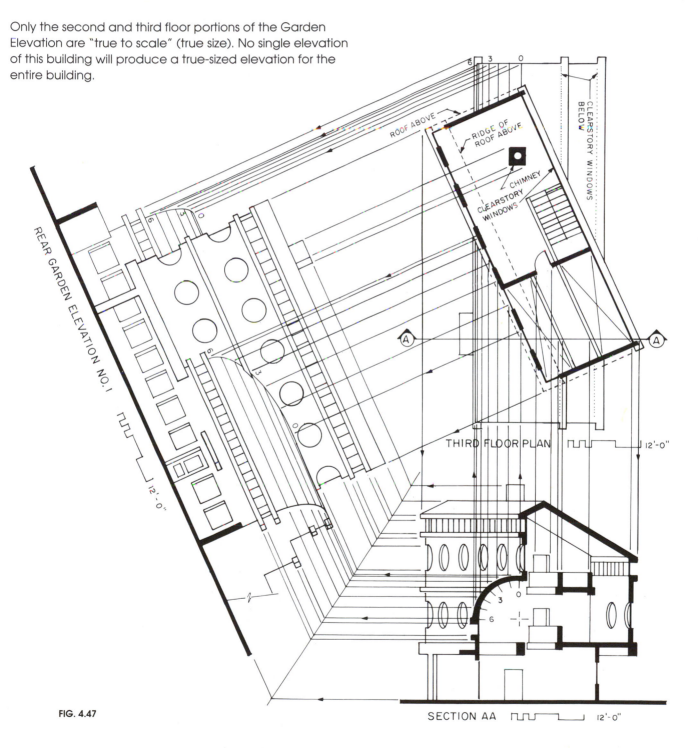

FIG. 4.47

SECTION AA   12'-0"

Rear Garden Elevation 2 (Fig. 4.48), in contrast to the one in Fig. 4.47, depicts the first floor true-to-scale but not the second and third.

The circular windows are seen at an angle, making them ellipses. The half wall thickness for these windows is shown on one side of the ellipse. Also note that Section BB cuts the quarter-circular roof at a location that is less than a quarter-circle.

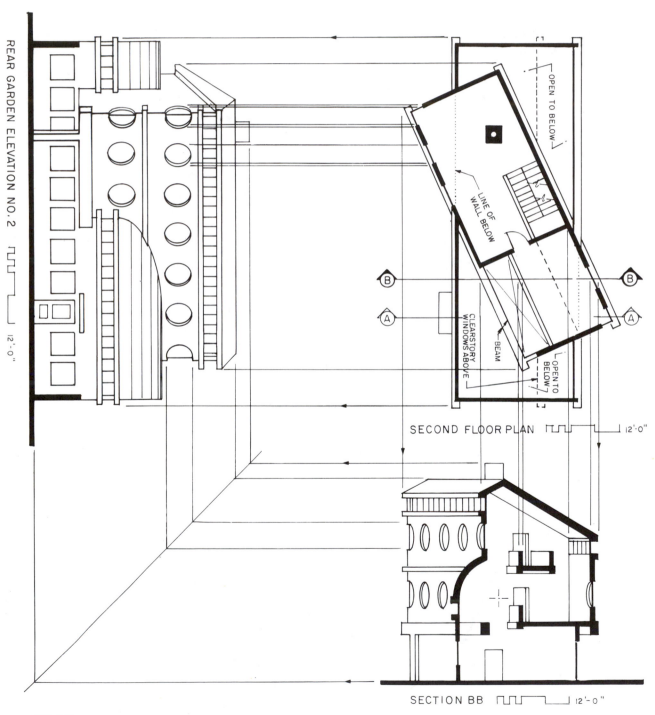

FIG. 4.48

Section CC in Fig. 4.49 is taken at right angles to the second and third floors. The dimensions for these two floors are true to scale. Section AA, however, shows elongated horizontal dimensions for the upper floors.

A second method for drawing the ellipse—the representation of the quarter-circular roof in Section CC—involves finding the half major and minor axis and using a template ellipse machine or computer. This method could have been used for the major ellipse in Rear Garden Elevation 1 and 2 instead of projecting lines and points.

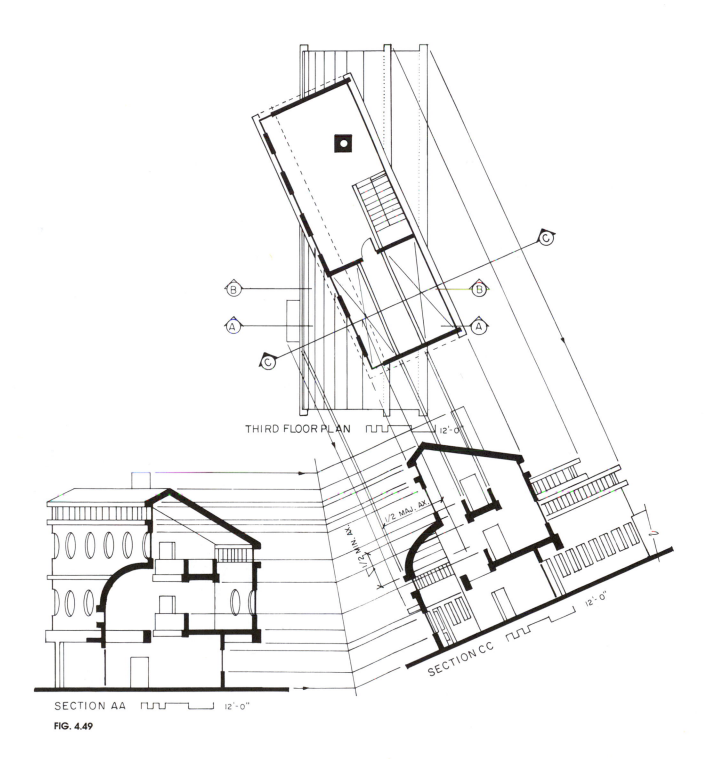

THIRD FLOOR PLAN   12'-0"

SECTION CC

SECTION AA   12'-0"

FIG. 4.49

Additional sections were needed to fully describe the spacial qualities of this building. Section EE amplifies the description and Section DD shows the two-part roof covering the first floor. (Section EE cuts the lower floor walls at an angle. They are slightly wider than the walls for the upper two floors.)

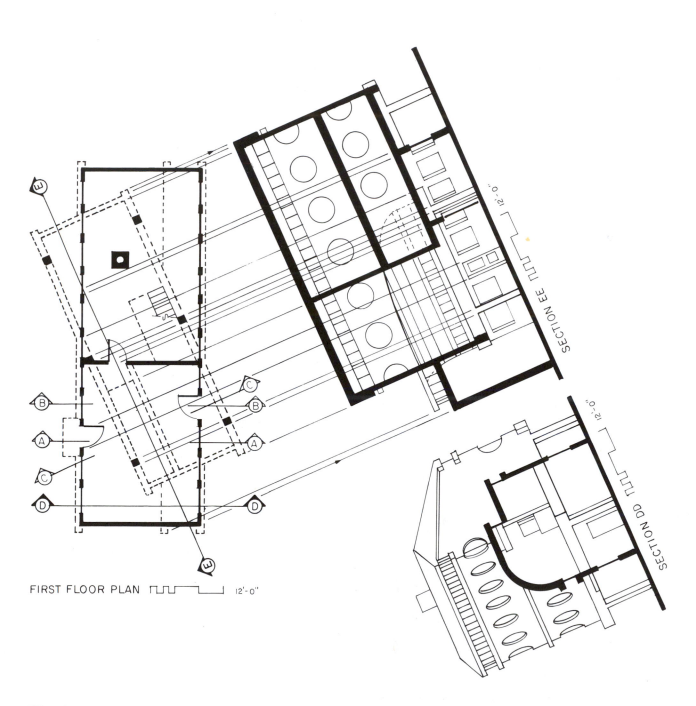

FIRST FLOOR PLAN

SECTION EE

SECTION DD

FIG. 4.50

The sculptural structure signifying the entry has not been drawn yet. The cylindrical pole and the thin triangular prism are abstracted as a line and triangle in Elevation 1 and Plan 1 in Fig. 4.51; the point of intersection between these two elements is found in these two drawings. The desired thickness of the thin prism is established in Elevation 2 and Plan 2. Visibility is checked in Plan 3 and Elevation 3: The prism does not touch the building. Finally, the chimney is drawn in Front Elevation by assuming a vertical cutting plane in the Roof Plan.

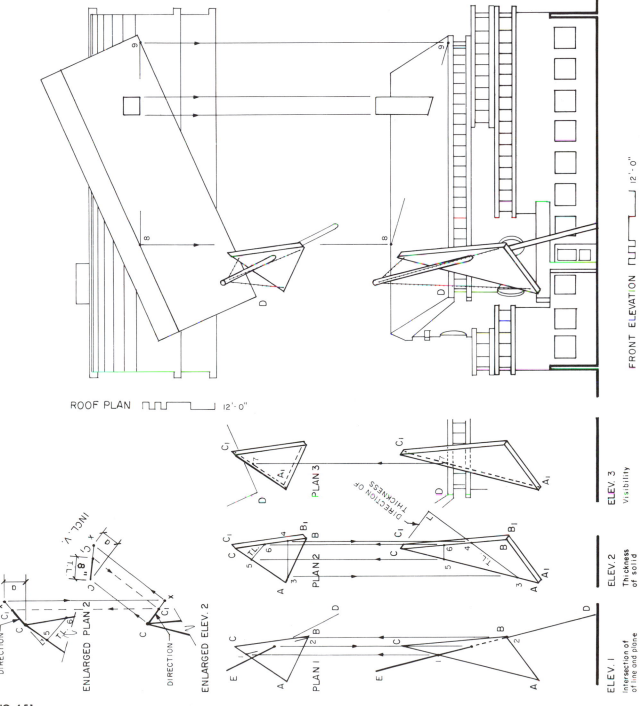

FIG. 4.51

SECTIONS: SOME EXAMPLES TO NOTE

The plans for Building B used a broken image plane in order to incorporate the split level configuration. Sections can also be broken in numerous ways (Section 1 on page 74 is one example). The section in Fig. 4.53 is another example. It had to be adjusted for the overlapping areas, indicated by the cross hatched area in Plan. Orthographic projection rules have been violated, but the end result better conveys the nature of the design. (For more drawings of house in Figs. 4.52 and 4.53, see pages 98, 167, 197, and 214.)

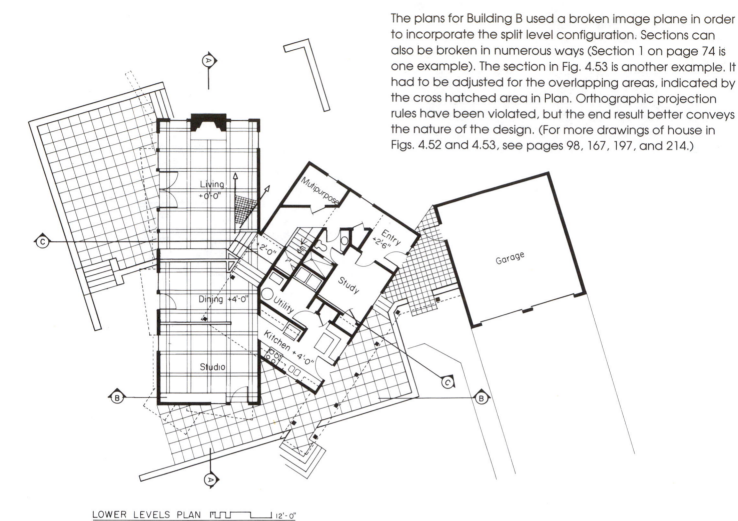

LOWER LEVELS PLAN 12'-0"

FIG. 4.52

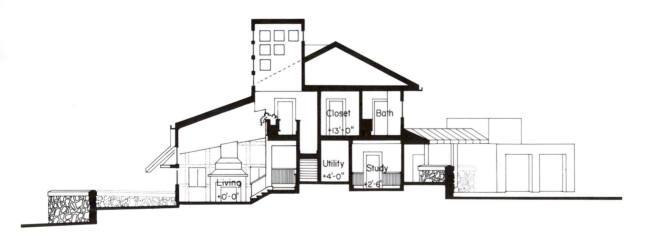

SECTION CC 12'-0"

FIG. 4.53

Figs. 4.54, 4.55, and 4.56 are drawn with different presentation methods. In Fig. 4.54, the use of solid black for all cut elements makes a strong visual impact even though the black/white spacial movement has been reversed. This type of drawing would read well at a distance and poses little problem for reproduction. Large areas of black are best outlined with pen and then filled in with a brush on a non-buckling drawing surface.

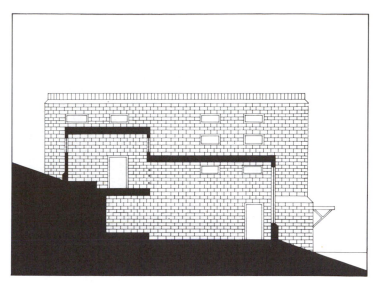

FIG. 4.54

Fig. 4.55 utilizes shades and shadows for a very spacial and realistic illustration. The original drawing was executed on vellum paper with ink, 6B lead pencil for shadows, and 2B for the background concrete block wall in sunlight. When rendering shadows, the tone should be slightly darker nearest the casting edge. Note how the white walls, roofs, and floors in section come forward.

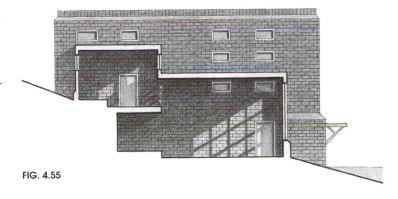

FIG. 4.55

The presentation technique in Fig. 4.56 has been photographically reversed. Some architects do not favor this drawing type because of its abstract, "slick" quality. If the cut ground had been solid white, it would have overpowered the building part of the section. The ground was therefore rendered by applying 30% gray sticky-backed transfer tone.

The location of all three longitudinal sections is indicated in Site Plan on the following page. Paralines of this project can be seen in Chapter 5.

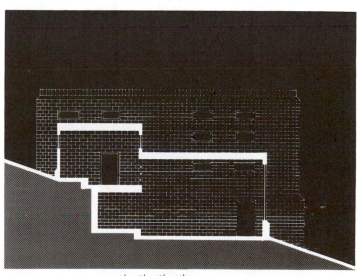

SECTION AA   0 4' 8' 12' 16'

FIG. 4.56

Most architectural presentations are done in a clear, rational, and literally descriptive manner. Many such drawings are both communicative and, sometimes, even fine art. In some designs, the architect's sensibilities may be poetic, expressing the complex interrelationships between ideas, moods, and images.

Fig. 4.57's tonal range is compressed to the dark side and by association, the mood is on the dark, brooding side. This drawing was done on 8 1/2" x 11" vellum paper with a #4x0 pen and then shaded using 6 B to B wooden pencils.

Section BB

0 4' 8' 12' 16'

FIG. 4.57

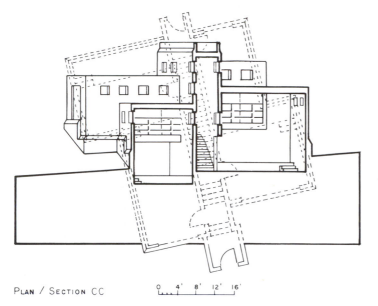

Plan / Section CC

0 4' 8' 12' 16'

FIG. 4.58

The Section in Fig. 4.58 is overlaid with a plan to form a composite drawing. The heavier lineweight Section comes forward and the dashed Plan recedes. (The overlapping of different views of the same object originates in the Cubist paintings of the early-twentieth century. The architectural application of combining different multiviews, even at different scales, can produce graphically stunning results.)

SITE PLANS: SOME EXAMPLES TO NOTE

The site plan in Fig. 4.59 contains some basic conventions and information found on working drawings: contours, property line indications with bearings, and distances from property lines to the building (minimums set by local codes). Note how the contours appear in relationship to the street. The center of the street is higher than the gutter to allow for water runoff, and the sidewalk is higher than the gutter.

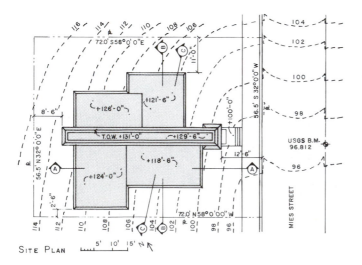

Site Plan   5' 10' 15' N

FIG. 4.59

Site plans for design presentations differ significantly from working drawing site plans. In the latter, information is conveyed to a contractor concerning the what and where of construction, without emphasis on design intent. Design site plans, on the other hand, focus on the architect's design strategies by using appropriate graphic techniques. These techniques can vary from the more expressive treatments similar to those applied to Figs. 4.57 and 4.58 to the more straightforward approaches on this page.

If a building, or a series of buildings, have pitched roofs, parallel roof surfaces can be given tones to imply shade caused by the sun (Fig. 4.60). A three-dimensional quality is consequently added to the site plan. This should never be used on working drawing site plans.

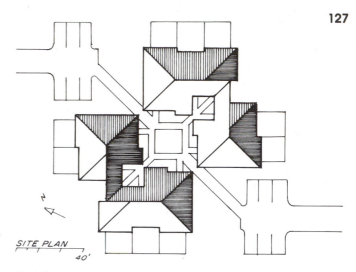

SITE PLAN 40'

FIG. 4.60

The building in Fig. 4.61 has a strong contextual relationship to the existing built environment. What is new construction should be immediately apparent. Vicinity maps often accompany site plans to orient the viewer.

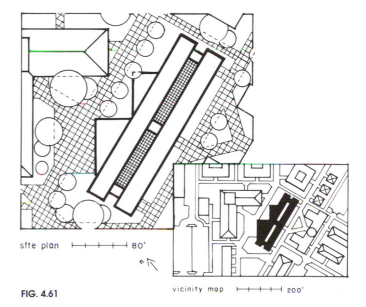

site plan 80'

vicinity map 200'

FIG. 4.61

Rendering shades and shadows in a site plan gives a full three-dimensional feeling to the drawing. In Fig. 4.62, the gray establishes the abstract middle ground, the black recedes, and the white pops forward.

If black is used for shadows instead of gray, a 30% gray tone (sticky-backed transfer tone in Fig. 4.62) works well for a middle ground. When applying tone to any drawing, if time allows it's best to reduce the line drawing to a small size and test different tones before finishing the original.

SITE PLAN 25' 6 METERS

FIG. 4.62

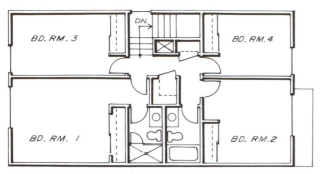

SECOND FLOOR PLAN 12'-0"

FIG. 4.63

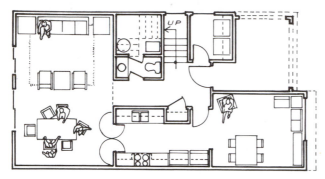

FIRST FLOOR PLAN 12'-0"

FIG. 4.64

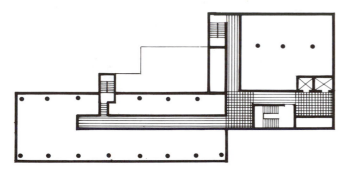

Second Floor Plan 48'-0"

FIG. 4.65

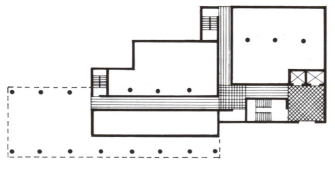

First Floor Plan 48'-0"

FIG. 4.66

FLOOR PLANS: SOME EXAMPLES TO NOTE

Floor plans, like sections and site plans, can be drawn in numerous ways—from literal to very abstract. The examples in Figs. 4.63 through 4.67 are literal. Darkening one side of walls creates a shadow and a three-dimensional sense, as exemplified in Fig. 4.63. This technique only works when the plan has a scale of 1/4" = 1'0" or larger.

Note that in the Second Floor Plan, one of the two bathrooms has a shower. The conventional way of indicating a shower is to draw a very small circle—which represents the drain—and an X—the floor slope.

Adding furniture and people to a floor plan gives a visual scale to the drawing, which helps laypersons who, more often than not, have trouble reading architectural drawings. This technique (Fig. 4.64) implies that the designer's intentions are in the direction of livability rather than the abstract nature of architecture. (Neither direction is right or wrong, better or worse than the other.)

Horizontal circulation or corridors in any building can be made prominent in plan by applying tones or patterns. The emphasis on circulation in architectural drawings goes back at least to the École des Beaux-Arts, the dominant 19th-century architecture school founded by Napoleon.

Furniture, people, and floor patterns have been drawn in Fig. 4.67, a plan of a renovated 1870s Victorian house. The gray surrounding the Plan is the abstract middle ground, the walls come forward, and the Plan between the walls recedes deeper into space than the middle ground.

To create the tones, 9" x 12" sticky-backed transfer tone sheets were used. This limits the drawing's size, as any drawing larger than 9" x 12" would require using more than one sheet of transfer tone, producing a noticeable (and unavoidable) seam.

A 9" x 2" drawing is small when seen at normal presentation viewing distances. This problem, as well as the one involving the use of more than one sticky-backed transfer tone sheet, can be overcome by drawing at the maximum 9" x 12" size and enlarging by either photographic or instant copy process. The original 7 1/2" x 9 1/2" drawing in Fig.4.67 was inked on plastic drafting film and seven instant copies were made at 50% reduction. In trials one and two, 20% and 30% gray was applied respectively to the areas surrounding the Plan. In both cases, the gray was approximately the same value as the Plan itself. In trial three, 40% was used for the surrounding area. As a result, the whole Plan came forward. In the fourth trial, 40% plus 10% over the Plan between walls produced much the same results as the previous try. In the fifth trial, 20% plus 10% made the whole drawing flat. When 20% was used for both in the sixth trial, the walls came forward and the area between the walls receded. The Plan area, however, receded more than the walls came forward. In the final trial, 30% was used for the area surrounding the Plan and 20% over the Plan between walls. Not quite enough spacial movement or "punch" was achieved. To increase "punch," add 40% to the surrounding area and 30% in between. The eighth and final try, illustrated in Fig. 4.67, uses the last combination with 20% added to the people and furniture.

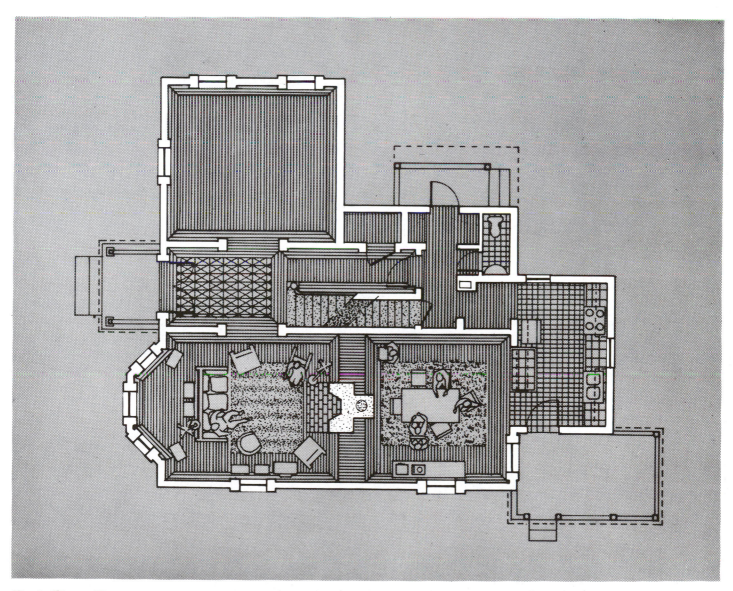

First Floor Plan ————————————————————————————————————•–•–•–•––• 12'- 0"

FIG. 4.67

EXTERIOR ELEVATIONS: SOME EXAMPLES TO NOTE

Architects and students become so accustomed to drawing with straight edges that they neglect freehand drawing. Even though lines do not always connect or are may not even be straight, human perception makes allowances for these "errors" in freehand drawing. Line drawing is the fastest method for doing architectural presentations, yet freehand tracing of hardline sketch drawings is even faster.

Street Elevation — • • • • • • • 16'-0"

FIG. 4.68

Another elevational treatment is to draft a symmetrical building half in section and half in elevation (Fig. 4.69). This assumes a broken image plane cutting through the ground in front of the building, along the center line, and then across the building.

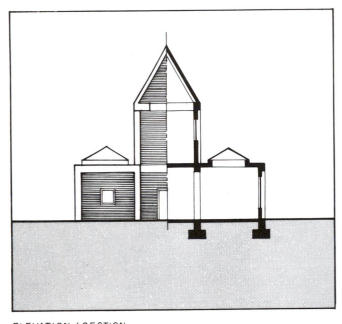

ELEVATION / SECTION

20'-0"

FIG. 4.69

Fig. 4.70 shows how each elevation of an essentially flat building can be unfolded into what is technically called a "developed elevation". It shows all elevations in one drawing. (This type of drawing is sometimes referred to as transmetric, but the word "developed" is more descriptive.)

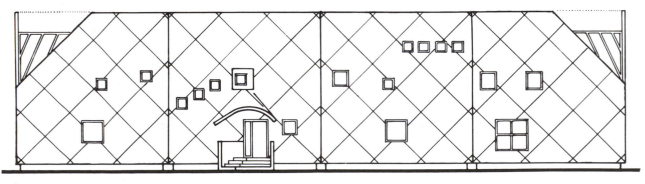

DEVELOPED ELEVATION 16'-0"
4 METERS

FIG. 4.70

Tone, applied to elevations, usually produces drawings that are more readable at normal presentation viewing distances of 10' to 15'.

A line drawing can be enlivened by adding tone to the cut ground in front of the building (Fig. 4.71). If the tone is limited to 10% to 40% gray, the ground will not visually overpower the line drawing.

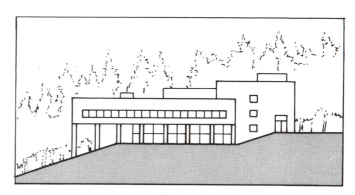

Elevation   72'-0"
FIG. 4.71

In Fig. 4.72, tone has been applied to everything but the nearest faces of the building. Consequently, these surfaces become very prominent. This example has a full range of values—from near black to pure white—but the balance of toned areas is on the dark side, insinuating a gathering storm or that the sun is setting behind the viewer.

Elevation   72'-0"
FIG. 4.72

The majority of toned drawings (excluding the more expressive), however, look best with a balance of middle grays, white, and a limited area of black or near black (Fig. 4.73).

To execute toned drawings, sticky-backed transfer tone sheets are available in a variety of tones, textures, and patterns. For example, the sky in Fig. 4.72 was made with a graded tone and the trees in Fig. 4.73 with a textured tone.

Elevation   48'-0"

FIG. 4.73

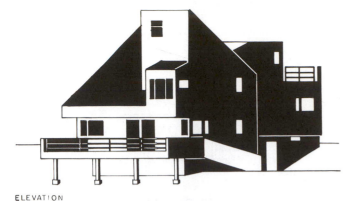

ELEVATION

FIG. 4.74

The auxiliary elevation in Fig. 4.74, rendered in stark black, communicates a strong, uncompromising design attitude. Such a radical drawing approach should only be used when the building design is in the same sensibility, otherwise the technique will look out of place. (Frank Lloyd Wright switched some of his presentation techniques to pure black and white drawing in the 1910-1911 Wasmuth Volumes, which, in turn, were highly influential in the early years of European Modernism.)

SOUTH ELEVATION ||||| | | | 16'-0"

FIG. 4.75

The appeal of the elevation in Fig. 4.75 is not so much in the delineation of the trees, bushes, and rocks, but in the layering of these elements over each other and the building. The illustration of page 80 also uses overlapping coupled with exaggerated lineweight, and the illustration on page 36 does the same with more subtle use of differential lineweight. The overlapping of abstract layers generates three dimensionality.

While the middle example is literal and puts the building in a natural setting, Fig. 4.76 stresses the abstract form of the building by using parallel lines, gradation of tone, and black shadows. It was popularized in the early 1960s for architectural drawing. (This technique has its origins in etchings of the eighteenth and nineteenth centuries.)

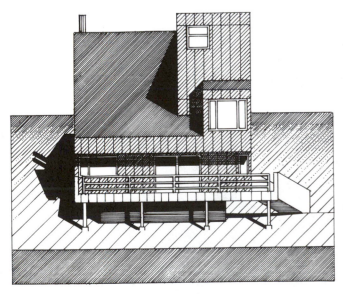

SOUTH ELEVATION ||||| | | | 16'-0"

FIG. 4.76

The plan and two elevations in Fig. 4.77 are rendered in an abstract/literal technique partially inherited from the École des Beaux-Arts. The cloudy sky's Romantic quality blends with the surreal landscape, floating multiviews, and mechanical projection lines. In this drawing, the cotton ball method was applied to an ink line drawing done on vellum. The borders of the drawing were "masked off" with drafting tape, grindings from a hand-held pencil sharpener sprinkled over the drawing (pencil or pastel rubbed over a sand paper paddle would have also worked), and rubbed in with a cotton ball. The clouds and front elevation were then erased with a kneaded eraser (avoid either erasing the ink drawing or fingerprints on the surfaces, as both will cause noticeable unevenness when the lead is applied).

PLAN / ELEVATIONS

|___|_|_|___|___|___| 20'-0"

FIG. 4.77

DRAWINGS AND SCALE

When drawings are done at a larger or smaller scale, line weight changes, titles become larger or smaller, and more or less detail is shown. In the elevations in Fig. 4.78, for example, both fixed and operable window frames are drawn in the larger scale South Elevation. The Plan at Door Jamb and Plan at Window Jamb are drawn at an even larger scale than any of the elevations and consequently show the components that make up the assemblage as the scale gets larger.

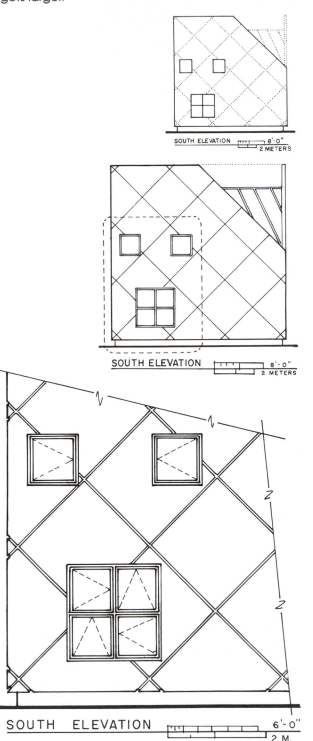

SOUTH ELEVATION   8'-0" 2 METERS

SOUTH ELEVATION   8'-0" 2 METERS

SOUTH   ELEVATION   6'-0" 2 M.

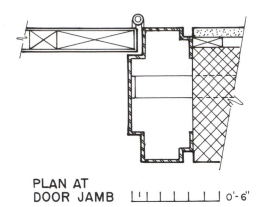

PLAN AT
DOOR JAMB   0'-6"

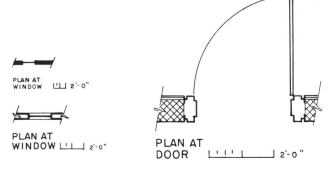

PLAN AT
WINDOW   2'-0"

PLAN AT
WINDOW   2'-0"

PLAN AT
DOOR   2'-0"

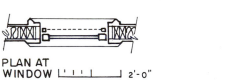

PLAN AT
WINDOW   2'-0"

PLAN AT
DOOR   2'-0"

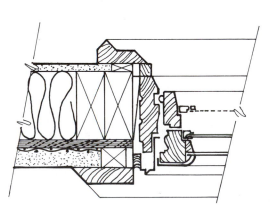

PLAN AT
WINDOW JAMB   0'-6"

FIG. 4.78

A set of working drawings for an architect-designed house usually has ten to thirty sheets of drawings, and for a large building, there are literally hundreds. Each sheet may contain up to twenty individual drawings, all of them interrelated. Many of the symbols found on working drawings are cross referenced to more detailed drawings found elsewhere, and still other symbols make reference to schedules for doors, windows, and light fixtures. Once you are able to "read" and understand the standard symbols and abbreviations, much of what initially appears overwhelming becomes clearer.

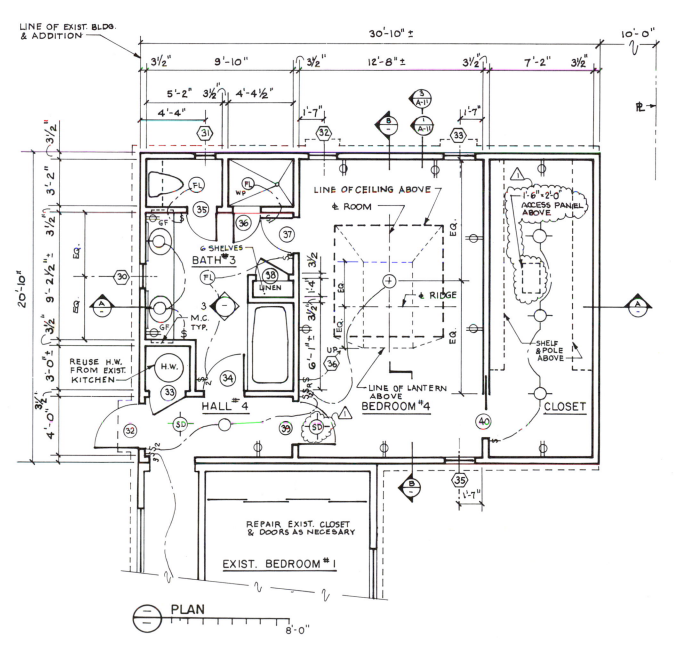

FIG. 4.79

Figs. 4.79 through 4.90 contain reduced drawings for a bedroom addition to a conventional, inexpensive suburban one-story house. The major design element is the lantern (a windowed superstructure crowning a roof or dome). To understand the space below the lantern, both Plan and Sections must be examined at the same time.

Structural drawings are the first drawing type that a contractor consults during construction. These drawings should contain little architectural information, and, conversely, architectural plans, sections, and elevations should not show or note structural information, unless structural members are exposed.

Most structural sizes and details for conventional wood frame construction are governed by local building codes.

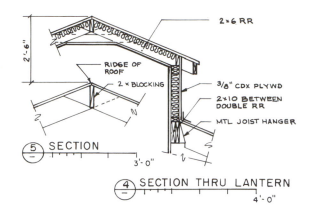

FIG. 4.80

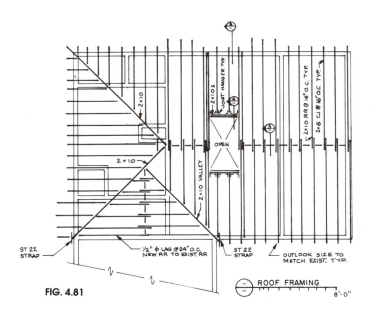

FIG. 4.81

FIG. 4.82

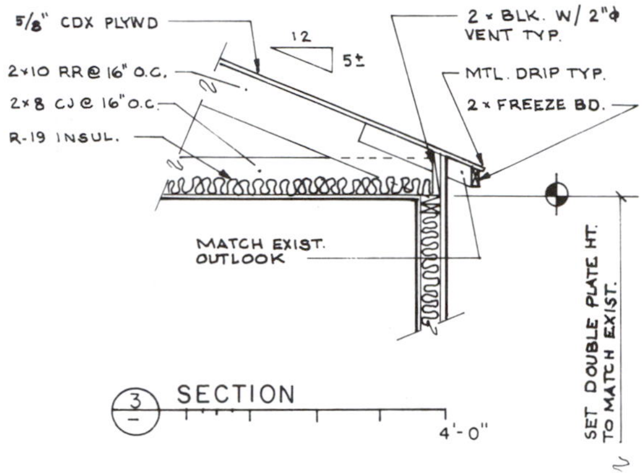

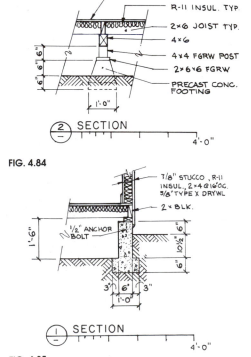

FIG. 4.83

FIG. 4.84

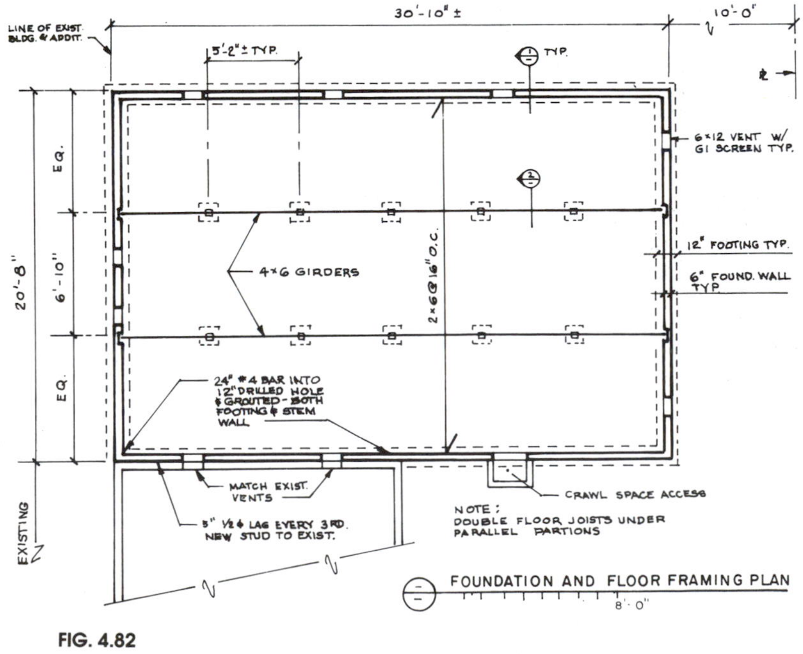

FIG. 4.85

With few exceptions, horizontal dimensions appear in plans and vertical dimensions are shown on elevations or sections. The lantern, shown in the sections in Figs. 4.87 and 4.88, is one of those exceptions because the sections explain the form better than the plan.

All interior and exterior elevations should be drawn for a building. Interior materials are charted in a room finish schedule.

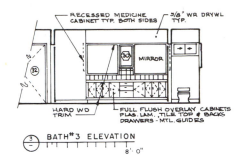

BATH #3 ELEVATION

FIG. 4.86

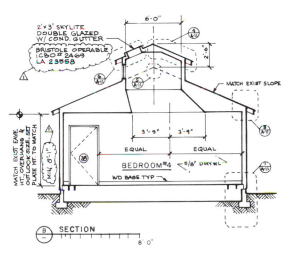

SECTION

FIG. 4.87

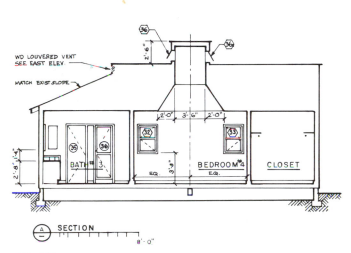

SECTION

FIG. 4.89

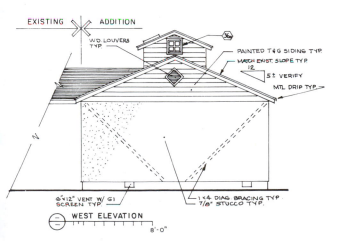

WEST ELEVATION

FIG. 4.88

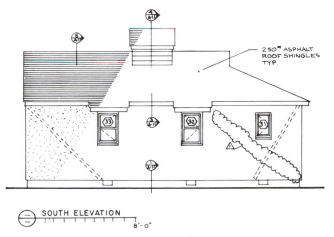

SOUTH ELEVATION

FIG. 4.90

The working drawing symbols and abbreviations listed in this book are those typically used in the United States. The symbols used in other countries vary slightly and the abbreviations are different in other languages.

Hidden; existing to be removed; something overhead; furniture not in contract for construction.

SYMBOLS

Existing contour; elevation numbers indicated on high side; on site plans.

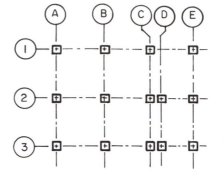

Column grids

New contour caused by site grading; on site plans.

Left: New or required point elevation. Right: Existing point elevation; on site plans.

Section; point of arrow shows in which direction the section is looking; information inside circle tells that section is drawing #2 found on sheet A-5.

Solids cut by image plane; heaviest line weight.

Wall section; larger scaled drawing #6 can be found on the same sheet.

Physical objects distant from image plane cut; medium line weight.

Interior elevations. Left: Four elevations are drawn and are on sheet A-11. Right: Only elevation 2 has been drawn and is on the same sheet.

Dimension lines; lightest line weight.

Reference symbol; detail drawing #15 can be seen on page A-32.

Center line

Revision #3 after working drawings have been issued to contractors for bidding.

Property line

Left: Information (size, kind, etc.) about door #44 can be found in door schedule. Right: Window #38 information can be found in schedule.

`501` `72`	Left: Room number; normally found in nonresidential projects. Right: Equipment number; see schedule; medium and large sized projects.
⊕ 12'-3"	Elevation height; only in sections and elevations.
PN N	Project north; elevations referenced to PN.
$ $² $³ $⁴ $ᴿ ᵂᴾ$	Electrical switches; number of poles, rheostated and waterproof.
⌀ ⌀ ⌀ ⌀ ⌀ᵂᴾ ⌀ᴳᶠ	Electrical convenience outlets: single, duplex, triplex, quadraplex, water proof and ground fall (grounded).
○ ⊕ ○	Incandescent lighting fixtures: ceiling-surface mounted, recessed, wall mounted.
▭ ▭ ▭ᴱ	Fluorescent fixtures: recessed, wall mounted, on emergency power.
○○○ ○○○ ○ ○○	Incandescent lighting track
SD	Smoke detector

MATERIAL INDICATIONS

	Earth
	Gravel on earth
	Concrete
	Concrete block
	Brick
	Glass block
	Plaster on lath
	Drywall or stucco
	Finished wood
	Rough lumber
	Plywood
	Blanket or loose insulation
	Insulation, rigid
	Acoustical tile
⊏	Metal stud
	Aluminum
	Brass or bronze
	Steel or other metal

ABBREVIATIONS

AP	Access panel		HVAC	Heating/ventilating & air conditioning
AC	Acoustical		HT	Height
ADJ	Adjustable		HC	Hollow core
A/C	Air conditioning		HM	Hollow metal
ALT	Alternate		ID	Inside diameter
AL	Aluminum		JT	Joint
AB	Anchor bolt		KO	Knockout
AD	Area drain		LAB	Laboratory
ASB	Asbestos		LB	Lag bolt
BRG	Bearing		LAM	Laminated
BVL	Beveled		LAV	Lavatory
BIT	Bituminous		LVR	Louver
BLK	Block		MAS	Masonry
BD	Board		MO	Masonry opening
BN	Boundary nail		MTL	Metal
BOT	Bottom		MFD	Metal floor decking
CAB	Cabinet		MOV	Movable
CI	Cast iron		NIC	Not in contract
CIP C	Cast-in-place concrete		NTS	Not to scale
CB	Catch basin		OPG	Opening
CLG	Ceiling		OPP	Opposite
CJ	Ceiling joist		PNT	Painting
CER	Ceramic		PNL	Panel
CT	Ceramic tile		PLAS	Plaster
COL	Column		PLAM	Plastic laminate
CMU	Concrete masonry unit		PLWD	Plywood
CPR	Copper		QT	Quarry tile
CORR	Corrugated		RAD	Radius
DP	Damproofing		RCP	Reinforced concrete pipe
DEMO	Demolish		RES	Resilient
DIAG	Diagonal		RO	Rough opening
DIAM	Diameter		ROW	Right of way
DIM	Dimension		RR	Roof rafter
DS	Downspout		SC	Solid core
DT	Drain tile		SPC	Spacer
DF	Drinking fountain		SST	Stainless steel
EF	Each face		STD	Standard
EMER	Emergency		ST	Steel
EQ	Equal		TC	Terracotta
EXH	Exhaust		TZ	Terrazzo
EB	Expansion bolt		THK	Thick
EXP	Exposed		T&G	Tongue & groove
FB	Face brick		TYP	Typical
FOS	Face of stucco		UNF	Unfinished
FGRW	Field grade redwood		VERT	Vertical
FIN	Finished		VAT	Vinyl asbestos tile
FA	Fire alarm		WC	Water closet
FLR	Floor-flooring		WP	Waterproofing
FD	Floor drain		WR	Water resistant
FTG	Footing		W/	With
FND	Foundation		WO	Without
GA	Gauge		WD	Wood
GI	Galvanized iron		WB	Wood base
GC	General contractor		WPT	Working point
GD	Grade		WI	Wrought iron
HDW	Hardware			

All buildings have roofs, windows, and doors. Most have stairs and many have elevators. How to draw these basic elements, their variations, nomenclature, and a few general notes are presented in the following pages.

Roofs

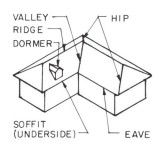

VALLEY — | — HIP
RIDGE —
DORMER—

SOFFIT
(UNDERSIDE) —   — EAVE

The eave of a sloping roof is the lowest horizontal edge and the ridge is the highest horizontal edge. A sloping line of intersection between two roof planes is a hip if the external angle between the two surfaces is more than 90° and a valley if the angle is less than 90°. A dormer is a windowed structure on the sloping surface of a roof.

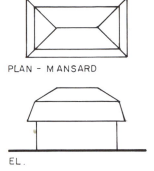

PLAN - MANSARD

Both a mansard and gambrel roof have a steeper slope breaking from the eave than the slope to the ridge.

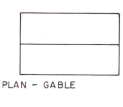 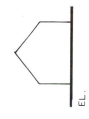

PLAN - GABLE

EL.

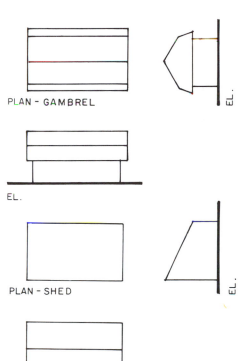

PLAN - GAMBREL

EL.

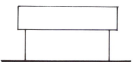

PLAN - HIPPED

45°

Roofs always have a slope to allow rainwater to run off. Even a flat roof has a 1/4" per foot minimum slope. With pitched roofs, the slope is determined by the roofing material and visual appearance. If two intersecting surfaces of a roof have the same slope, a 45° angle is formed in plan.

PLAN - SHED

EL.

Shed roofs have a single pitched surface.

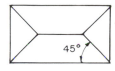

PLAN - DUTCH-HIPPED

EL.

PLAN - SAWTOOTH

EL.

A sawtooth roof is industrial in origin, but is sometimes used in architecture. More often than not the steeper section has windows in it.

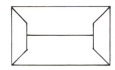

EL.

A Dutch-hipped roof has a vertical surface, with or without windows interrupting the slope of the roof.

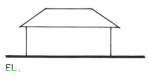 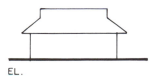

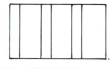 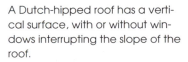 

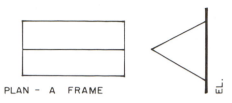

PLAN - BUTTERFLY

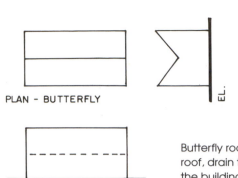

EL.

Butterfly roofs, like a sawtooth roof, drain toward the inside of the building rather than the outside.

PLAN - A FRAME

EL.

A building with an "A" frame roof has no side walls and provides a complete structural system.

Windows

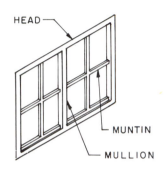

HEAD

MUNTIN

MULLION

Within a window area, muntins are small, secondary members subdividing the glass area. Mullions are larger vertical members. The head of a window is the top.

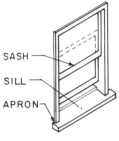

SASH

SILL

APRON

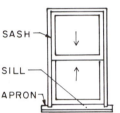

SASH

SILL

APRON

EL. - DOUBLE HUNG

One of the oldest and most commonly used windows is the double hung. The operable frames, or sashes, slide up or down. A system of counterweights within the side wall hold the sash in a fixed position once opened or closed.

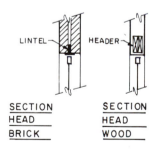

LINTEL

HEADER

SECTION HEAD BRICK

SECTION HEAD WOOD

The wall above a window or door must be supported. In non-wood construction, this function is accomplished by a horizontal structural steel shape or a concrete beam called a lintel. In wood construction, a couple of wood headers achieve the same result.

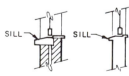

SILL

SILL

SECTION SILL BRICK

SECTION SILL WOOD

The bottom of a window usually has a sill to shed rainwater that runs down the window. Windows are either fixed or operable. There are three basic types: sliding, hinged, and pivoted.

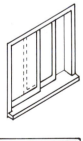

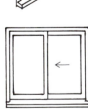

EL. - SLIDING

A slider or sliding window operates by one frame moving horizontally behind the other, which is normally fixed.

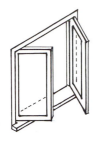

Casement, awning, hopper, and jalousie windows are hinged. The casement is side-hinged and opens outward by a crank on the inside.

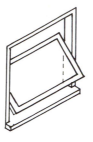

Pivoted windows can have their rotational points at either the sides or top and bottom.

EL. – CASEMENT

EL. – PIVOTED

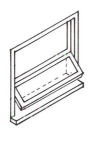

An awning window is hinged along its upper edge and opens outward.

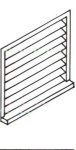

Jalousies have a series of narrow, frameless, horizontal pieces of glass ganged together and operated by an inside crank.

FIXED

EL. – AWNING

EL. – JALOUISE

A hopper window is hinged along its lower edge and opens inward.

STRIP

Windows can be combined in various ways. A number strung together, with or without fixed frames, form a strip window.

EL. – HOPPER

PICTURE

A picture window has one large, fixed pane of glass in the center, flanked by two smaller sashes.

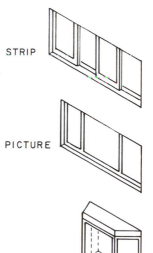

BOW

A bow window protrudes from the face of a building and can be any form in plan.

Doors

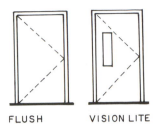

FLUSH   VISION LITE

Doors are manufactured in many widths but the standard height is 6'-8" with 7'-0" readily available. Vision lights of glass can be inserted into doors to provide privacy at a distance and a view close up. Knobs and hinges are almost never shown in architectural drawings.

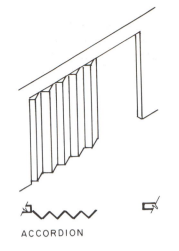

ACCORDION

With large interior openings, doors can be broken into sections, hinged along each side, and slid along a track. The bi-fold door illustrated earlier in Building A was an example of this type of door.

An accordion door has many hinged sections and can be used as a movable partition. With extremely large openings, multiple unhinged sections are linked together and rolled sideways or upward.

Vertical Circulation

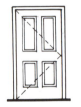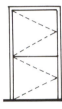

PANELED   DUTCH

Paneled doors are made up of various raised trim pieces, panels, and sub-panels to give a decorative appearance.

Dutch doors have two operable sections.

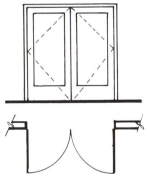

FRENCH

French doors are two individual doors in one opening.

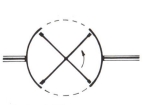

REVOLVING

Revolving doors have three or four individual "wings," pivots at top and bottom, and a circular enclosure.

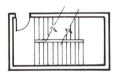

SWITCH BACK

Stairs are provided for convenience and escape during a fire. In case of a fire emergency, the stair must be in a fire resistant shaft, provide a path down from any floor, and exit directly to the outside. Besides the code information provided earlier with Building A, a distance of 100' to 120' is required from any building location to a fire stair. Two fire stairs are generally needed in nonresidential buildings.

The switch back, or U-shaped stair gives only one path of escape from each floor.

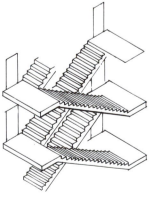

SCISSORS

Scissor stairs are made up of two straight runs from floor to floor. They have the advantage of providing two means of egress from each floor, but corridors are normally limited to 20' "dead end" corridors.

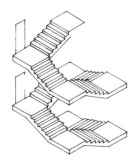

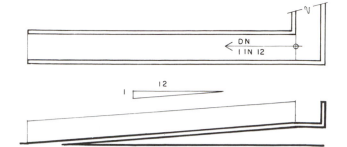

The Kahn stair, named after American architect Louis Kahn, has a spacious interior volume. This stair is also known as the "donut stair".

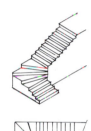

KAHN

Handicapped codes require that a public building be accessible by persons in wheelchairs. An elevator is one means of accomplishing this, and a ramp is another. Ramps are limited to a 1 in 12 slope, and usually a level landing is required for every 5'-0" of rise. Handrails are needed and must, like stairs, not be less than 34" or more than 38" in height.

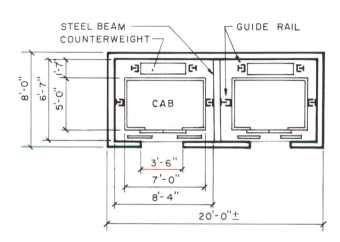

Winders are stairs, treads, and risers arranged at corners to save plan space for residential building. Like the spiral stair, they are not legal for use as fire stairs.

WINDERS

Elevators (also known as lifts) have a cab that moves inside a fire-resistant shaft. There are two basic types of elevators: hydraulic and electric gearless. The design of both is complicated and depends on a number of determinates, including the number of people occupying the building, the structure's height, and the desired time of vertical travel. Taller buildings require an increase in the number of elevators and cab size. Only in rare situations are there less than two elevators in a building. If only one is provided, a breakdown cripples convenient vertical circulation.

A hydraulic elevator moves up and down by a telescopic piston, and though less costly than the electrical gearless, it has a limit of about 50' in height. The electrical gearless is faster than the hydraulic and is used in all buildings over four floors in height.

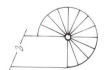

SPIRAL

A spiral staircase becomes a dramatic sculptural element in a room and saves plan space. Nevertheless, spiral staircases are somewhat inconvenient to use.

Both types move on guide rails. The electrical gearless is lifted by cables and has a slightly deeper shaft than the hydraulic. The drawing shown above shows a small gearless elevator in more detail than you would normally find in architectural drawings. The more usual presentation below calls for only drafting the shaft walls with an X inside, which indicates there is no floor.

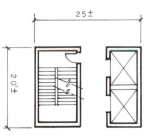

This is a typical vertical circulation core with two elevators and a fire stair. As a rough guide, the overall dimensions would be satisfactory for a five-story building (most codes would require one more fire stair).

CHAPTER 5

PARALINES

Paralines are a much older drawing type than perspectives. After perspectives were first used in Italy during the fifteenth century, paralines all but disappeared from Western art until the second half of the nineteenth century, when a number of French painters and architects abandoned perspective as a method for representing three dimensionality. Both groups were searching for a new visual language that would fit the artistic, political, social, and industrial realities of the times. The architects were also trying to rationalize structure as the basis for architecture, and in so doing found the abstract, mechanical paraline an ideal drawing type. This preference for paralines spread during the first quarter of the twentieth century, the time when European Modernism was born. Even today many architects use the paraline because of its continuity with modernist sensibilities.

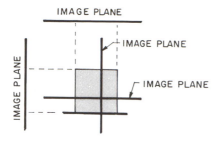

MULTIVIEWS

FIG. 5.1

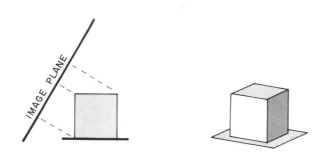

AXONOMETRICS

FIG. 5.2

Paralines differ from multiviews in that they show three dimensionality in a single drawing. Although engineers often use paralines for building, architects limit their use to design presentations.

Paralines have the following characteristics:

1. Parallel lines of an object or building that normally converge in a perspective drawing remain parallel.
2. Paralines always show either the top or bottom of an object and at least one side.

There are two basic types of paralines: axonometrics and obliques. Both are easier to construct than a perspective, and this is another major reason for their usage.

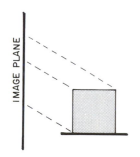

OBLIQUES

FIG. 5.3

Axonometrics are theoretically constructed by orthographic projection into inclined views. Oblique drawings also assume projections onto an image plane, but the projections are at an angle to the image plane.

Because of the pictorial quality of paralines, they are usually drawn using practical shortcuts, rather than rigorously following their theoretical methods of construction.

This chapter explains the theory of axonometrics and the practical methods of construction for both axonometrics and obliques.

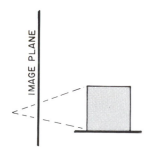
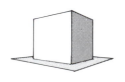

PERSPECTIVES

FIG. 5.4

THEORY

Axonometrics are a group of paralines made up of isometrics, dimetrics, and trimetrics. All three are theoretically inclined views. Each derives its name from the natural foreshortening of lines in the final inclined view: If lines are equally foreshortened along the X, Y, Z axes, the view is an isometric; if two out of three have the same foreshortening, the view is a dimetric; if all three are different, the view is a trimetric.

The amount of foreshortening produced is based on the particular viewing angles. Angle A, the horizontal direction, and angle B, the true vertical angle (the altitude angle), determine the proportions of the top and sides seen in the inclined view, the amount of foreshortening of lines along the X, Y, Z axes, and angles C and D. For angle B to be the true vertical viewing angle, it must be in an elevation whose image plane is parallel to the direction of angle A.

Only one set of angles can produce a true isometric: angle A must be 45° and angle B must be 35°16'. Effectively, the first angle looks along the diagonal of a cube and the second produces this line as a point in the inclined view. With this geometric configuration, all lines are equally foreshortened and angles C and D are both 30° to horizontal.

Although other combinations of viewing angles will, for approximate purposes, produce equal foreshortening, 30° for angles C and D matches a 30°/60° triangle and therefore make this combination both the practical and theoretical standard. (Fig. 5.6, top, also shows an isometric—Inclined View 2—looking at the bottom of the figure.)

More than one combination of angle A and B will produce a dimetric. Two are shown in Fig. 5.7.

Angle B in both Elevations 2 and 3 for the dimetric in Fig. 5.7 is approximately equal. Although the foreshortening is different for both Inclined Views 1 and 2, the amount of top surface seen is much the same. Also, angle B in Fig. 5.6 is greater than angle B in Fig. 5.7. Consequently, the former shows more of the top surface. In Fig. 5.7, note how the proportions of the sides change as angle A changes.

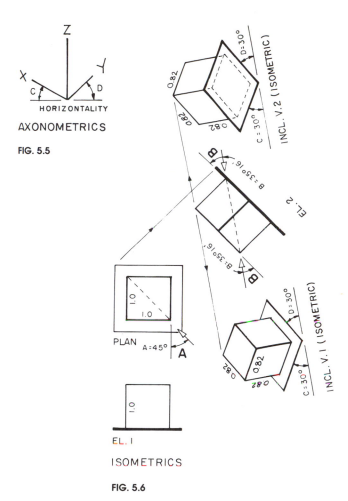

AXONOMETRICS

FIG. 5.5

ISOMETRICS

FIG. 5.6

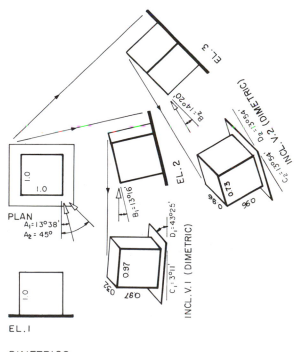

DIMETRICS

FIG. 5.7

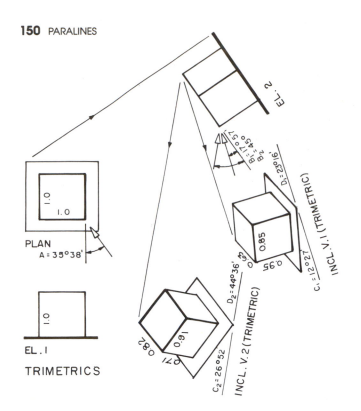

TRIMETRICS

The trimetric, like the dimetric, can be formed by different combinations of horizontal viewing angle A and the true vertical viewing angle B. Lines along all three axes for the trimetric foreshorten differently.

In the dimetric in Fig. 5.7, the horizontal viewing angle was changed in order to demonstrate how the proportions of the sides of the object changed. In the trimetric in Fig. 5.8, angle A has been held constant and the vertical viewing angle changed. This demonstrates how the amount of top surface changes, as does foreshortening in Fig. 5.8.

Given the two viewing angles, the exact amount of foreshortening along each of the three axes of an inclined view and the precise angles from horizontal can be found by following the simple trigonometry below.

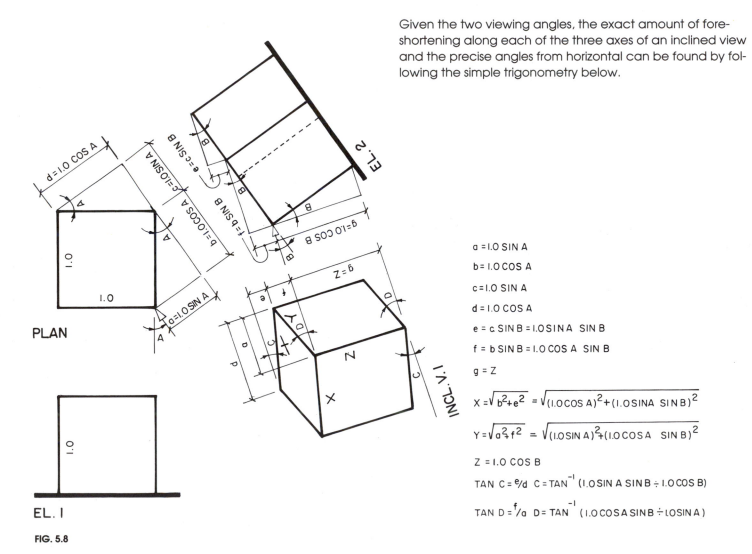

$a = 1.0 \sin A$

$b = 1.0 \cos A$

$c = 1.0 \sin A$

$d = 1.0 \cos A$

$e = c \sin B = 1.0 \sin A \ \sin B$

$f = b \sin B = 1.0 \cos A \ \sin B$

$g = Z$

$X = \sqrt{b^2 + e^2} = \sqrt{(1.0 \cos A)^2 + (1.0 \sin A \ \sin B)^2}$

$Y = \sqrt{a^2 + f^2} = \sqrt{(1.0 \sin A)^2 + (1.0 \cos A \ \sin B)^2}$

$Z = 1.0 \cos B$

$\tan C = e/d \quad C = \tan^{-1}(1.0 \sin A \sin B \div 1.0 \cos B)$

$\tan D = f/a \quad D = \tan^{-1}(1.0 \cos A \sin B \div 1.0 \sin A)$

FIG. 5.8

The twelve theoretical examples in Fig. 5.9 demonstrate what happens when viewing angles are systemically increased. Certain combinations produce a trimetric, while a relatively small increase of 15° may give a dimetric.

The difference between theoretical foreshortening and practical foreshortening in the chart below will produce axonometrics that look slightly different. However, the advantage of using practical foreshortening ratios far outweigh the differences when drawing.

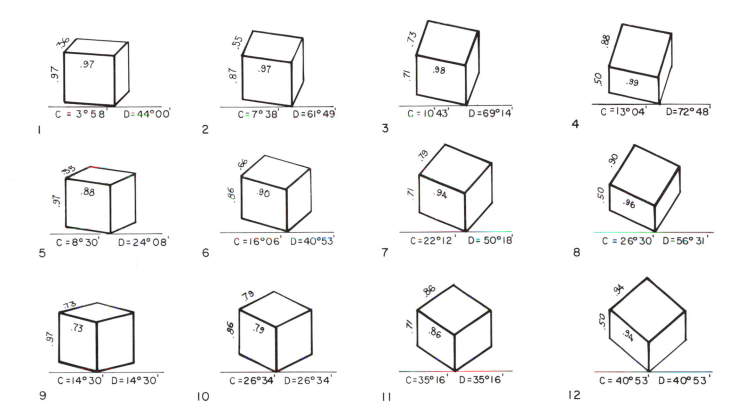

	THEORETICAL								PRACTICAL			
	ANGLES				FORESHORTENING FROM 1.0x1.0x1.0 CUBE				FORESHORTENING ASSUMES LARGEST THEORETICAL VALUE AS 1.0			
	A	B	C	D	X	Y	Z	TYPE	X	Y	Z	TYPE	
1	15°	15°	3°58'	44°00'	.9683	.3598	.9659	TRIMETRIC	1.0	.50	1.0	DIMETRIC	1
2	15°	30°	7°38'	61°49'	.9746	.5480	.8660	TRIMETRIC	1.0	.50	.80	TRIMETRIC	2
3	15°	45°	10°43'	69°14'	.9831	.7304	.7071	TRIMETRIC	1.0	.75	.75	DIMETRIC	3
4	15°	60°	13°04'	72°48'	.9916	.8756	.5000	TRIMETRIC	1.0	.80	.50	TRIMETRIC	4
5	30°	15°	8°30'	24°08'	.8757	.5479	.9659	TRIMETRIC	.80	.50	1.0	TRIMETRIC	5
6	30°	30°	16°06'	40°53'	.9014	.6614	.8660	TRIMETRIC	1.0	.75	1.0	DIMETRIC	6
7	30°	45°	22°12'	50°18'	.9354	.7906	.7071	TRIMETRIC	1.0	.75	.75	DIMETRIC	7
8	30°	60°	26°34'	56°31'	.9683	.9014	.5000	TRIMETRIC	1.0	1.0	.50	DIMETRIC	8
9	45°	15°	14°30'	14°30'	.7304	.7304	.9659	DIMETRIC	.75	.75	1.0	DIMETRIC	9
10	45°	30°	26°30'	26°30'	.7906	.7906	.8660	DIMETRIC	1.0	1.0	1.0	ISOMETRIC	10
11	45°	45°	35°16'	3.5°16'	.8660	.8660	.7017	DIMETRIC	1.0	1.0	.75	DIMETRIC	11
12	45°	60°	40°53'	40°53'	.9354	.9354	.5000	DIMETRIC	1.0	1.0	.50	DIMETRIC	12

FIG. 5.9

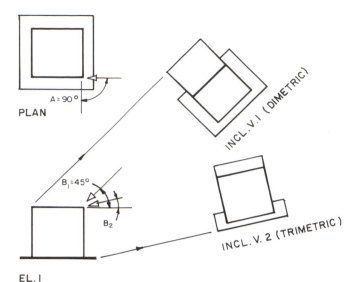

PLAN

A = 90°

B₁ = 45°

B₂

EL. I

INCL. V.I (DIMETRIC)

INCL. V. 2 (TRIMETRIC)

FIG. 5.10

Inclined views are time-consuming projections from plans to auxiliary elevations to inclined views, while axonometrics are constructed without projecting from another view, using instead predetermined angles and foreshortening. However, one type of easy-to-construct inclined view is illustrated in Fig. 5.10. Depending on the particular angle B chosen, the drawing can be a diametric (if B is 45°) or any one of a number of trimetrics (see page 46 for two examples).

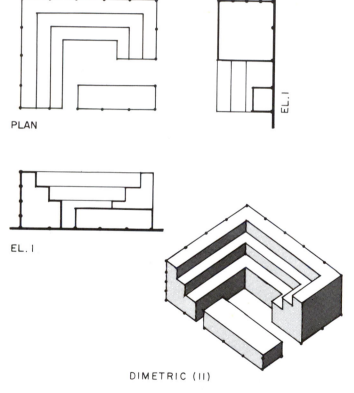

PLAN

EL. I

EL. I

DIMETRIC (II)

FIG. 5.11

CHOOSING WHICH AXONOMETRIC

Selecting which axonometric to draw for a particular project is based on the answers to several questions. Is one elevation more significant or interesting than another? How much top surface (or surfaces) should be represented (especially when drawing a group of buildings)? If all surfaces are equally important, the isometric, with its equal angles and foreshortening, is the fastest and easiest to draw.

Another determinant in selecting which axonometric to use is the choice of foreshortening ratios. Certain ratios are easier to use than others. As an example, cube #3 from the previous page has a practical foreshortening ratio of 1.0 to .75 to .75. This means that the X axis can be drawn at, say, 1/2" = 1'-0" and the other two at 3/8" = 1'-0" (1/2 x 3/4 = 3/8).

When using CAD to construct an axonometric, the choice of a convenient scale ratio is of no consequence; theoretical foreshortening ratios can be easily used.

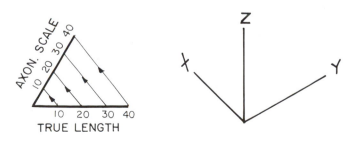

AXON. SCALE

10 20 30 40

10 20 30 40

TRUE LENGTH

Z

X

Y

FIG. 5.12

CONSTRUCTING AXONOMETRICS

If an axonometric type is chosen which does not have a convenient foreshortening ratio, an axonometric scale can be made. To make one, multiply any true length by the foreshortening ratio, draw the foreshortening length on a separate piece of paper or cardboard, and then subdivide that line. (See "Subdivision of a Given Line" on page 83). This paper serves as a scale.

Axonometric dimensions can only be measured along the three axes or on lines parallel to them. Lines not parallel to one of the axes are not directly measurable and must be found from an axonometric line to locate the ends of the nonaxonometric line. The ends are then connected. Any line parallel to such a line will be parallel in the axonometric.

In Fig. 5.13, an imaginary cube is first drawn using the 1.0, .5, .8 foreshortening ratio from trimetric cube #2 in Fig. 5.9. There are then two ways to find points B, C, and D. In the first method, the distances from the corners of the cube are measured, converted to an axonometric distance, and then applied to the paraline. The second, more simple method is less subject to mistakes. It relies on knowing that B, C, and D are at the halfway points of the edges of the cube. Also, the center of quadrilaterals can be obtained by drawing two diagonals. From these centers, the axonometric lines are then projected to the edges of the cube, finding points B, C, and D.

Although the non-axonometric line CD is not directly measurable, it can be subdivided into four equal parts. Point B is then connected to b. The two other lines on the sloping surface are drawn parallel to Bb, using the subdivisions of CD as starting points.

Once the type of axonometric is selected, there are still different approaches to drawing, and each depends on the three-dimensional configuration of the particular design. If the construction of an imaginary transparent box fits a particular project, measurements can be directly applied to the three axonometric surfaces and projected from these locations (box shown dashed in lower portion of Fig. 5.14).

Differential line weight in the Plan and both Elevations in Fig. 5.14 is used to imply spacial depth and even wedge-shaped lines (see page 111). Multiview drawings usually present planes in orthogonal relationships parallel to an image plane. Each plane can logically be treated with one particular line weight.

Line weights for axonometrics, however, differ from multiviews: the axonometric image plane is tilted in relationship to the object. Two facts become apparent. First, and on theoretical grounds, every line disappears away from the image plane, causing many wedge-shaped lines. One practical, time-saving approach is to eliminate wedge-shaped lines. Second, a judicious use of different line weight can be as effective as treating each wedge-shaped line separately (see drawings on pages 118 and 146).

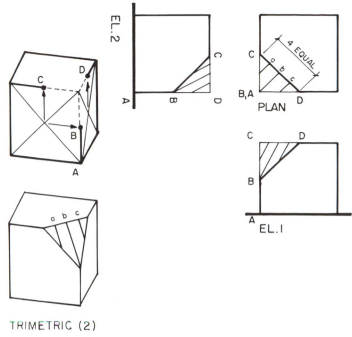

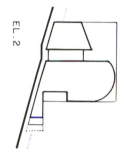

TRIMETRIC (2)

FIG. 5.13

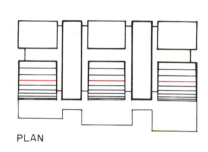

PLAN

EL.I

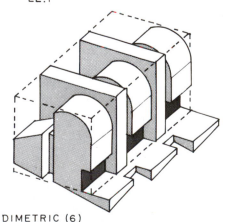

DIMETRIC (6)

FIG. 5.14

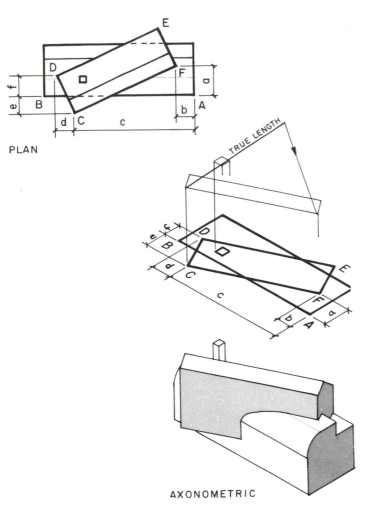

PLAN

TRUE LENGTH

AXONOMETRIC

FIG. 5.15

Should a particular design have two orthogonal geometries not at right angles to one another, offsets from one can be used from one geometry to establish the direction and lengths of a second geometry.

Fig. 5.15 (from page 118), starting with line AB, was laid out using an isometric; points C, D, and F were found by taking offsets from line AB. The direction and lengths of CD and CF have been established and all lines parallel to them in the multiview are parallel in the axonometric. Subdivisions of CF or other parallel lines can be made by the Subdivisions of a Given Line Method or by constructing a new scale. All vertical heights were kept the same for both geometries.

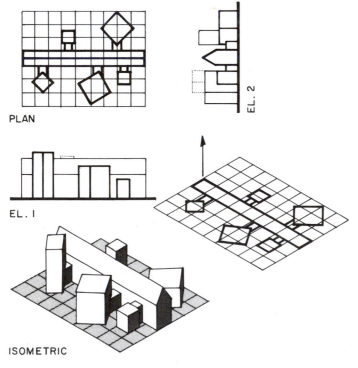

PLAN

EL. 2

EL. 1

ISOMETRIC

FIG. 5.16

Another method for constructing an axonometric involves laying out the plan in axonometric grid and then elevating the height dimensions. This strategy is appropriate when the form or forms of the building are unbroken. A grid can be useful if there are odd plan shapes or different geometries.

Imaginary boxes, offsets, and grids are not the only ways to approach axonometric drawings. Each project to be drawn may suggest one of these three methods, or even a combination. A methodical approach to any drawing always saves time.

Any curve, including circles, can also be drawn in an axonometric by superimposing a grid over a multiview and then drawing both the grid and curve on the axonometric plane. When transferring points from multiview to axonometric, locating points by eye rather than by measurement is usually accurate enough.

In the two axonometric examples in Fig. 5.17, note how the shape of the curve changes when the horizontal angle and foreshortening change.

The second curve in Fig. 5.17, represented in both Plan and Elevation, is a combination of a two-dimensional and a three-dimensional curve. The former is drawn by using a grid and the latter by offsets. These offsets can be described as coordinates (see page 82).

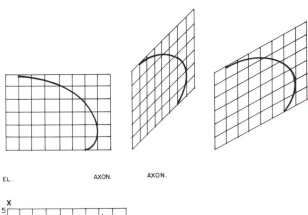

EL. AXON. AXON.

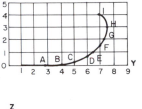

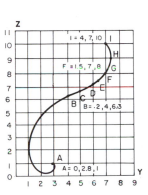

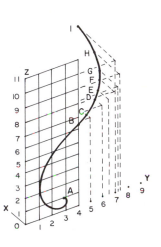

EL. AXON.

FIG. 5.17

CIRCLES IN AXONOMETRICS

A circle is only in its true shape when projected onto a parallel image plane; all other views, including axonometrics, will show the circle as an ellipse.

Ellipses have four characteristics in axonometrics:

1. Every circle can and must be circumscribed by a square and the square, when in axonometric form, is one of two types of parallelograms: a rhombus or a rhomboid. The rhombus has four equal sides and the rhomboid has unequal sides with opposite sides equal. To state this another way, the rhombus has equal foreshortening and the rhomboid does not.
2. Any inscribed ellipse must touch the two ends of both conjugate diameters (see page 91). These points are labelled A,B,C and D in the first illustration in Fig. 5.18.

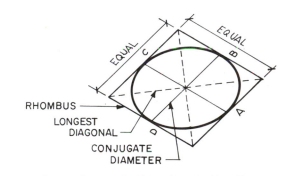

RHOMBUS — EQUAL FORESHORTENING

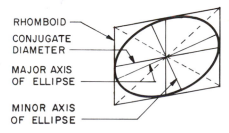

RHOMBOID — UNEQUAL FORESHORTENING

FIG. 5.18

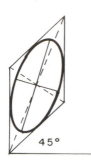

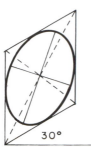

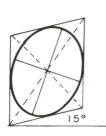

RHOMBOIDS – AXIS OF
ELLIPSE VERSUS DIAGONAL
OF RHOMBOID

FIG. 5.19

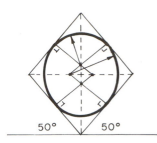

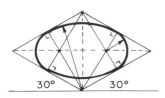

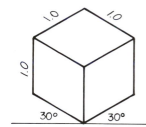

RHOMBUSES
THE INSCRIPTION WITHIN A
RHOMBUS METHOD

FIG. 5.20

3. With both the rhombus and the rhomboid, one diagonal is usually longer than the other. The major axis of an inscribed ellipse will be in the same general direction as the longest diagonal of a rhomboid. (This is useful to know when using templates.) This relationship between these two lines changes according to the amount of foreshortening and the angle to horizontal. Note how the ellipses' axes get closer to the rhomboid's diagonals as the horizontal angle gets greater in the three examples on the extreme left.

4. When an ellipse is put into a rhombus, the axes of the ellipse will correspond to the diagonals of the rhombus.

Beginning on page 91, a number of methods for fitting an ellipse within a rhomboid are given. If a precise ellipse is required, the computer or ellipse machine should be used. This, in turn, requires finding the length and direction of both axes (see page 93).

For an ellipse within a rhombus, the "Inscription Within a Rhombus Method," within the limits set in Chapter 3, is, other than using the computer or templates, the easiest method for construction.

In closing, it's important to remember a few basic facts. The geometric configuration of the isometric—equal foreshortening and 30° angles to the horizon—gives a 35° 16' ellipse (template available). Second, when using the Inscription Within a Rhombus method, two centers for the arcs are at the corners of the rhombus. The "Inscription Within a Rhombus" method does not work for the rhomboid. And last, with any particular dimetric or trimetric, one surface may be a rhomboid and another may be a rhombus.

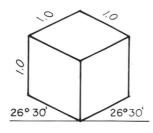

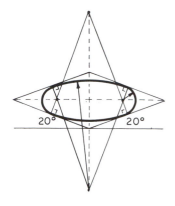

PRACTICAL

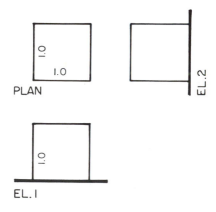

FIG. 5.21

ISOMETRICS

Of the most widely used paralines—the isometric and the plan oblique—the isometric looks the most like a perspective and, consequently, is more literal.

Many combinations of horizontal angles will, for practical purposes, produce an isometric (cube #10 from Fig. 5.9 is an example), but the conventional standard is 30°/30° with a foreshortening ratio of 1.0 to 1.0 to 1.0. This practical combination makes the isometric convenient to construct because the scale is the same as the multiviews and a 30°/60° triangle is used. In addition, the practical foreshortening ratio means the isometric will appear slightly larger than its comparable multiviews. This could be used to good effect in a set of presentation drawings.

It is helpful to know that a horizontal square plane drawn in isometric has one diagonal of the rhombus horizontal and the other vertical. This is an aid when drawing a cube or scaling a dimension in one direction, knowing the same dimension in the other direction is horizontally related. For a vertical square plane in isometric, one diagonal of the rhombus will be at 60° to the horizontal and the other at 30°. Again, the two diagonals are perpendicular to one another. These observations will allow you to equally multiply or subdivide a cube using only one dimension.

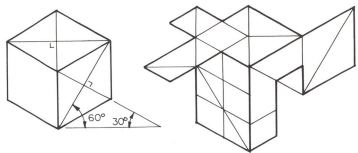

FIG. 5.22

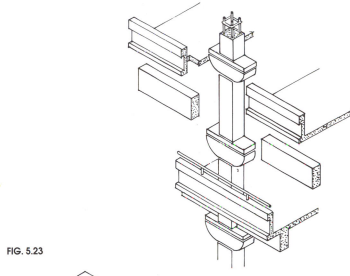

FIG. 5.23

ISOMETRICS: SOME EXAMPLES TO NOTE

Isometrics are used for purposes other than showing exteriors. They can convey the process of construction, spacial relationships, or the diagrammatic thrust of a design. Although these "take apart" drawings are usually employed for presentation purposes, there are rare occasions when they are put into working drawings to describe an assemblage or condition that's difficult to visualize. In such cases, the drawing should be clearly marked "For information only."

Fig. 5.23 is an isometric for a cutaway portion of a parking garage. The lower portion shows the final appearance, while the upper section identifies the continuous precast concrete column (poured at an off-site location and transported to the construction site) and beams plus the remainder as poured in place.

Isometrics can illustrate both the interior and exterior of a building. Parts can be imploded, exploded, hinged, and even duplicated. Graphically, tones can be added, walls cut, or floors poched (darkened between lines), and, of course, different line weights used. All of these choices occur within a drafting framework and, other than being to scale and using given angles to the horizontal, conventions are less stringent than in multiviews.

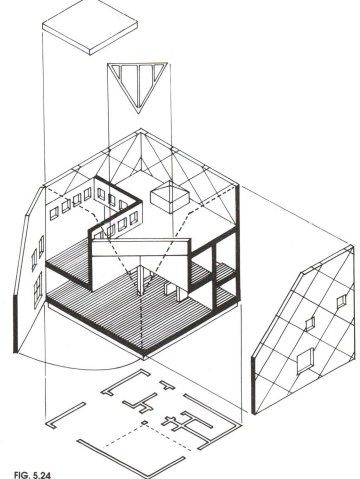

FIG. 5.24

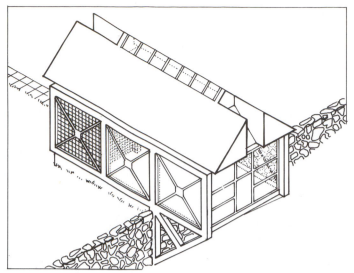

FIG. 5.25

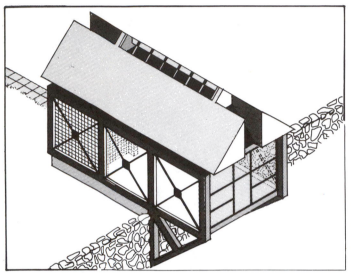

FIG. 5.26

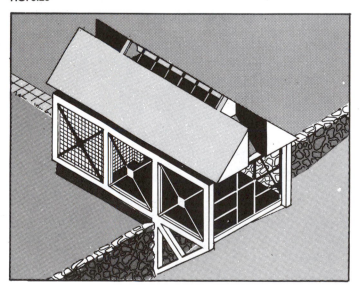

FIG. 5.27

The isometric, as well as other paralines, has traditionally been drawn in linework to represent the building as an isolated object without reference to context. Other options are available.

If an architectural design has a contextual relationship, the surroundings should be drawn (see page 146). Even when the surroundings are relatively unimportant, an isometric can relate to an abstract ground by having tones applied to the drawing, relying then on the spacial movement of lighter and darker tones (Figs. 5.27 and 5.28).

Overall tones can be applied to a drawing in various ways. Although not illustrated, a building can be "masked off" and tone applied with an airbrush, spray can, or Cotton Ball technique using pencil grindings (see pages 132 and 133). An alternative is to use sticky-backed transfer tones—a technique sympathetic to the mechanical, drafted nature of paralines (see page 129). The size of the area to be covered with this method is limited by the 9" x 12" sheet size. Otherwise, sheets will have to be butted, and an unavoidable seam will be present. To avoid the seam problem, the drawing can be done within the sheet size limitation and enlarged with instant copy or photographic processes.

Glass appears one of four ways on a building: as a reflective surface, semi-transparent plane, totally transparent plane, or as a combination of reflective and transparent planes. Figs. 5.25 and 5.26 represent glass as semi-transparent by using dotted lines for materials seen through glass. Fig. 5.27 provides total transparency. Commercial illustrators often utilize a combination of reflective and transparent planes when rendering perspectives. For the non-professional, the representations on this page are more appropriate and easier to draw.

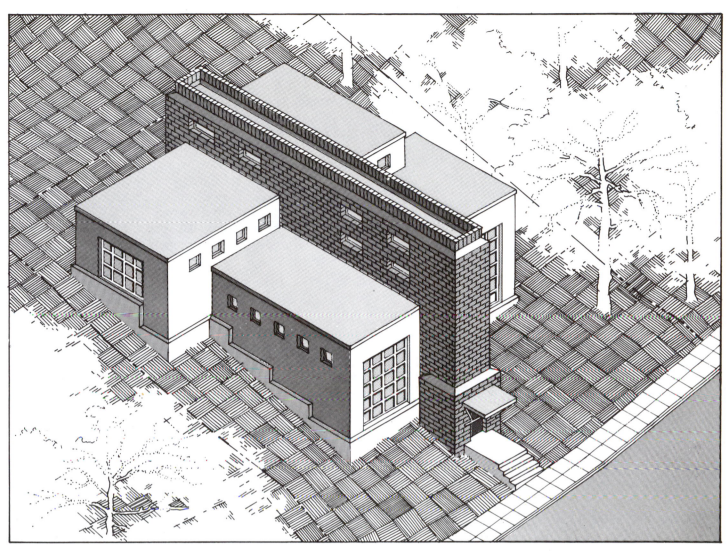

FIG. 5.28

The surroundings in a paraline can be treated in a semi-abstract fashion (as opposed to the total abstraction of the preceding Figs. 5.25, 5.26, and 5.27. In Fig. 5.28, the ground is rendered as a patchwork quilt to describe the topography and the trees are ghosted.

At a large scale, windows in any paraline will show more detail than at a smaller scale. Windows are normally near the center of a wall, and the half thickness of the wall will be seen on one side of the drawing. (It is possible to detail a window so that it is flush with the exterior of the wall.)

The drawing in Fig. 5.29 indicates a double-hung window in a brick wall; the center drawing shows a casement window in a stucco wall; and at right a flush hopper or awning window in a wall with corrugated metal siding is depicted.

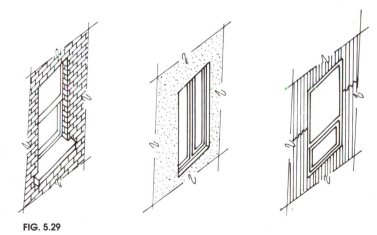

FIG. 5.29

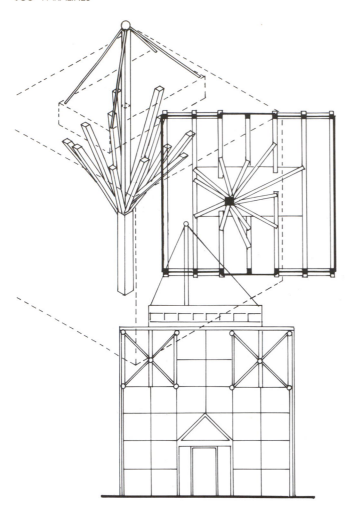

Isometrics can be included in a composite drawing to give a fuller description of a project. In the upper portion of Fig. 5.30, an elevation, reflected ceiling plan, and isometric are used in this composite of a rational/irrational design (rational on the outside versus irrational on the inside, with the central "tree" structure supporting sawed-off beams). The isometric delineates and emphasizes the tree. Without this drawing, the essence of this structural "folly" would be diminished.

Axonometrics looking up usually have two sides removed and have a tendency to look inside out, reading like an exterior view. For example, the small cube in Fig. 5.30 can be either imagined as an exterior view or as an interior looking up with two sides removed. The isometric on the lower right exhibits some of these characteristics. The isometric on the lower left has tone and differential lineweight applied to correct this inside-out phenomenon.

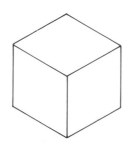

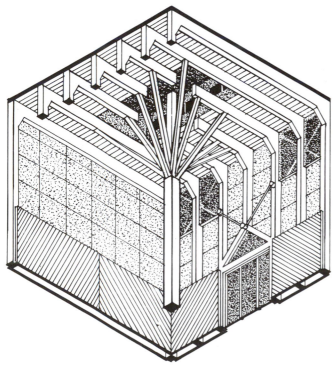

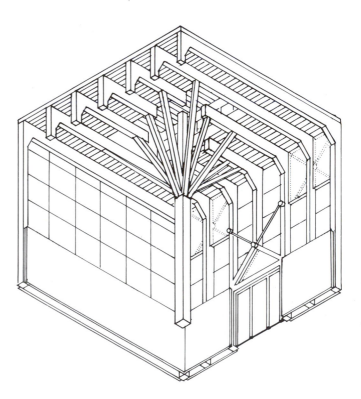

FIG. 5.30

Tilting the horizon gives a dynamic quality to Fig. 5.31; there is a tension between expecting the horizon to be horizontal and not seeing it as it would be normally. This view is similar to a photograph taken from a banking airplane. Receding lines still have a 30° angle to the horizon, an obtuse 120° between the X and Y axis, 60° between the receding lines and the vertical, and the vertical is still at right angles to the horizon.

A photograph from a banking airplane taken with a long telephoto lens will look almost exactly like the isometric in Fig. 5.31. The greater the viewer's distance from an object or building, the more the vanishing points in a perspective will move toward infinity. One definition of an axonometric—an axonometric drawing is a perspective in which the vanishing points are at infinity—is based on this phenomenon.

The isometric, besides being the easiest axonometric to draw, is constructed by a set of rules and, therefore, is inflexible. At the same time, it is the least arbitrary of all paralines.

DIMETRICS AND TRIMETRICS

Unlike the isometric, which has a fixed vertical viewing angle of 35°16', particular dimetrics or trimetrics can be used to emphasize more of the plan or elevation of a building. The dimetric in Fig. 5.32 stresses the plan while the trimetric in Fig. 5.33 shows more of the front elevation.

After foreshortened length AC in Fig. 5.33 was calculated, true-to-scale measurements were marked on a piece of paper from a predrawn elevation and remarked along line AB. Using a separate piece of paper lessens mistakes associated with scaling and rescaling dimensions.

Practical foreshortening ratios of .80, .50, and 1.0 were used for Fig. 5.33. The theoretical foreshortening ratios of .8757, .5479, and .9659 would produce a more accurate rendition of the front side of the building (see page 133 for true elevation). Note the slight difference in heights to widths.

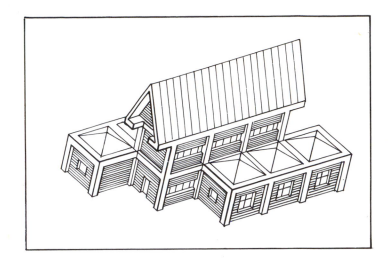

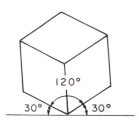

ISOMETRIC

FIG. 5.31

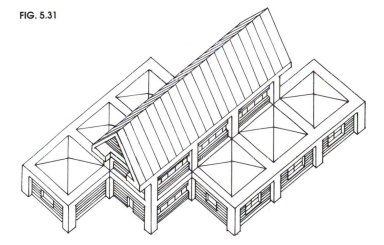

DIMETRIC (12)

FIG. 5.32

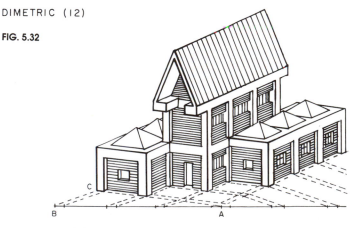

TRIMETRIC (5)

FIG. 5.33

OBLIQUES

The Plan Oblique and the Elevation Oblique are the only two types of oblique drawings. They have either the plan or an elevation of a building true to scale and, therefore, are easier to draw than any axonometric yet look more abstract. The common measure of lifelikeness in architectural drawing (the opposite of abstraction) is a perspective—a two-dimensional illusion of three dimensionality.

Many architects, designers, and students prefer the abstract nature of obliques. They feel this drawing type both better conveys the abstract quality of design and, at the same time, questions conventionality, a tenet in modern architecture.

PLAN OBLIQUE

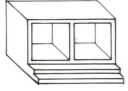

ELEVATION OBLIQUE

FIG. 5.34

PLAN OBLIQUES

Plan obliques (historically known as military projections) are the result of parallel projections from an object onto sloping image planes but the projections, unlike multiviews and axonometrics, strike the image plane at an angle. This makes graphic or mathematical derivations difficult. Consequently, drawing always starts with a predrawn plan and almost any receding line angle or foreshortening ratio (F.R. in drawings) can be used.

Plan obliques look less like perspectives than axonometrics, therefore, there is no psychological, visual standard for appearance. This is the reason why almost any receding line angle and length looks believable.

All horizontal planes (plans) in a plan oblique are true-sized and, regardless of foreshortening and angle of receding lines, these views show more of a downward view than most axonometrics. The angle of receding lines determines the relative size and visual importance of adjacent elevations: a 45° angle generates equal weight elevations, 60° stresses the ABCD elevation, and 30°, the CDEF elevation.

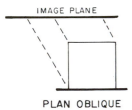

ELEVATION OBLIQUE

PLAN OBLIQUE

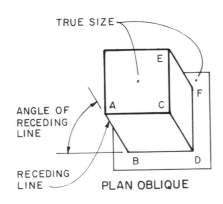

TRUE SIZE

ANGLE OF RECEDING LINE

RECEDING LINE

PLAN OBLIQUE

FIG. 5.35

When drawing a plan oblique, practicality dictates either a 45° or 30°/60° triangle. Also, foreshortening ratios below .5 or so makes for very small subordinate elevations—difficult to draw on. Foreshortening ratios approaching 1.0 look too deep, unless you want a totally abstract drawing. (The four examples in Fig. 5.36 have a .5 foreshortening ratio.)

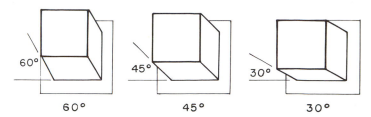

60°   45°   30°

60°   45°   30°

VARYING RECEDING LINE ANGLE, HOLDING
FORESHORTENING RATIO (F.R.) AT .5

F.R. .3   F.R. .3   F.R. .3

F.R. .45   F.R. .45   F.R. .45

F.R. .6   F.R. .6   F.R. .6
60°   45°   30°

VARYING BOTH RECEDING LINE
ANGLE AND FORESHORTENING

FIG. 5.35

The predrawn plan can be, and often is, rotated at a convenient angle. Verticals can be vertical or tilted. It is a matter of choice and the desired degree of realism.

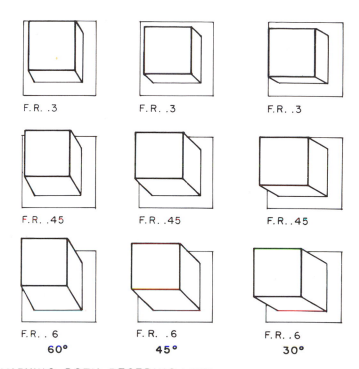

30°

60°   45°   45°

45°   60°

FIG. 5.36

30°

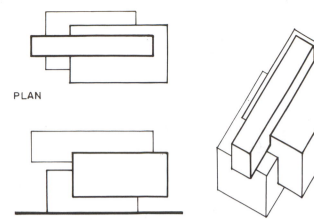

PLAN

EL.

FIG. 5.37

The most usual method for constructing plan obliques is to project up or down from a predrawn plan. This may entail drawing or overlaying plans at various levels, thereby creating a composite of plans. In the illustration in Fig. 5.37, for example, the plan oblique was drawn by projecting downward from the given plan. No foreshortening was used for heights.

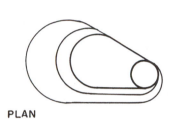

PLAN

FIG. 5.38

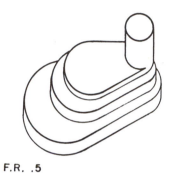

F.R. .5

Because a plan is true sized or true to scale in a plan oblique, curves and circles are also in true shape. However, any shape on a vertical surface of a plan oblique must be constructed by the same methods that apply to axonometrics.

A second way of constructing plan obliques is to tape the plans to the drafting board and move the overlay sheet of the plan oblique up or down on a common vertical line to other levels, tracing the plan for that level. In Fig. 5.38, the central axis of the tall cylinder was used as the common line.

Care must be taken when selecting the foreshortening ratio for a project that has one element considerably higher than other elements. In the upper plan oblique in Fig. 5.38, a .5 foreshortening ratio was used for convenience; the tall cylinder looks too stubby. The lower plan oblique in Fig. 5.39 employs a .75 foreshortening ratio; the cylinder height looks more believable.

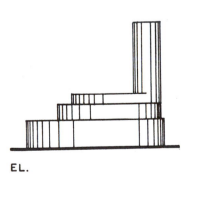

EL.

FIG. 5.39

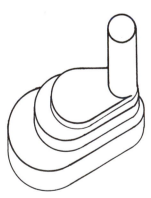

F.R. .75

The example in Fig. 5.40 is composed of a base, a lower sliced half-cylinder, columns supporting an upper half-cylinder, and small cylinders protruding from the upper element.

From examining the multiviews, Elevations 1 and 2 are equally important; consequently, 45° for the receding line angle was chosen. A .5 foreshortening ratio was used because, unlike the Fig. 5.39, there are no compositional elements that would be excessively foreshortened.

None of the rounded solids appear true sized in Plan. Therefore, all of the circles will be ellipses in the plan oblique. The lower semicylinder springs from the top of the base and height dimensions are scaled up and down from the plan at this level. Two imaginary parallelograms are drawn next, one for the 90° slice and another for the 45° sliced portion. Line AB is the shorter conjugate axis for the ellipse and CD is the longer. Both parallelograms are rhomboids. The results were reached by using the Parallelogram method (see page 92). The ellipses on the taller form are small and were drawn with a template.

In the finished plan oblique (lower right, Fig. 5.40), light lines, subjectively drawn closer together towards the edges of the curved forms, give roundness to the forms. This shading can be visually destroyed by employing heavy differential lineweight.

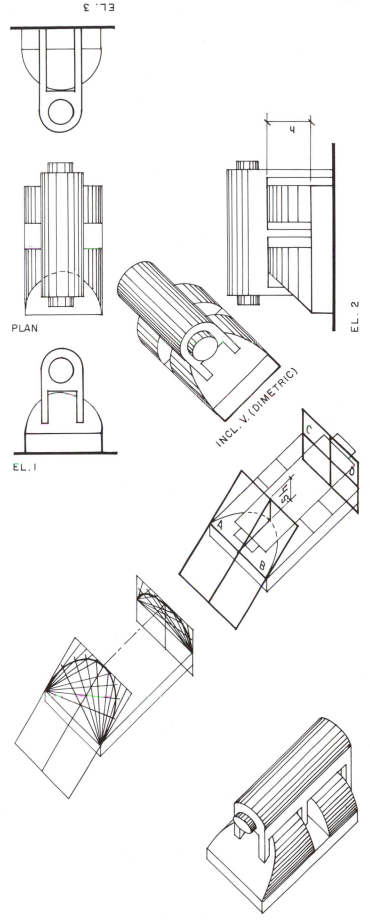

FIG. 5.40

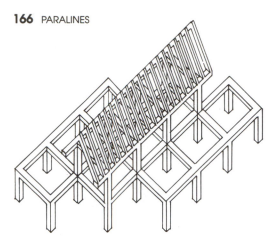

FIG. 5.41

Architects often draw separate paralines of a building to show individual aspects such structure, volumes, components, and the like. Frequently, these features are combined in a blown-apart drawing.

The structural illustration in Fig. 5.41 was drawn using a 45° receding angle and .5 foreshortening.

When squares or cubes are part of a plan configuration, a 45° angle will cause near elements to overlap far elements on the diagonal of the cube. This can create visual confusion. This is not a problem in Fig. 5.41 but, in general, careful consideration should be given to squares and cubes with 45°.

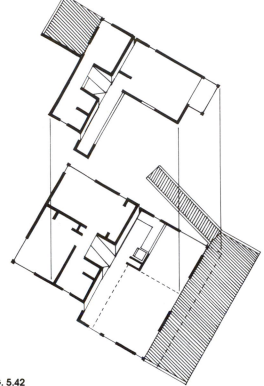

FIG. 5.42

Half-level floor plans are diagramatically shown without indicating any volumetrics or actual heights between upper and lower levels (Fig. 5.42).

Plan obliques that indicate interior volumes must have the roof, sides, or both removed. Normally walls are projected upward to a common height.

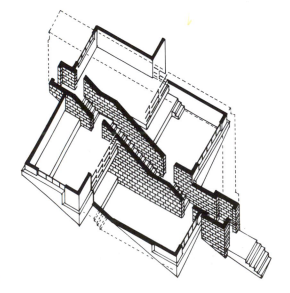

FIG. 5.43

The walls in Fig. 5.43 are not cut off at a common height. If they had been, by starting with the height element on the left, the stairs would have been hidden by the concrete block spine wall. Also, these walls would have covered up much of the far volumes. (The two spine walls are the organizational forms for this design and are therefore dashed above the plan cuts.)

Not all elements need be drawn in a plan oblique, or in any paraline for that matter, if you wish to highlight a particular feature of a design. Drawing everything puts equal emphasis on all aspects.

The intersection between the upper floor and the lower levels in Fig. 5.44 is accentuated by casting a black shadow under the upper floor, indicating a wooden floor on the second floor, applying a 20% tone to the lower levels, and leaving the drawing incomplete.

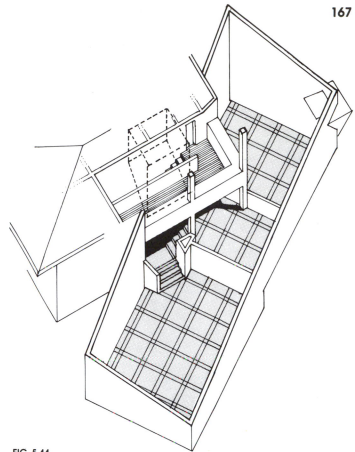

FIG. 5.44

There is a tendency to put too much detail into an illustration when drawing at a large size. Keep in mind that this will not reproduce well when reduced for portfolios, a reason for leaving some detail out of a pictorial drawing.

Windows and other details were left out of the plan oblique in Fig. 5.45 because of final drawing size. Black was arbitrarily applied to ground surfaces, adding graphic impact.

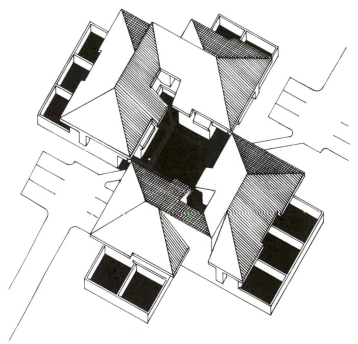

FIG. 5.45

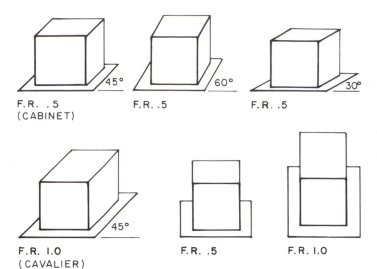

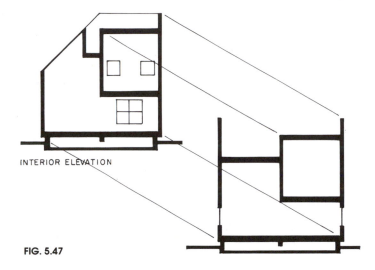

FIG. 5.46

INTERIOR ELEVATION

FIG. 5.47

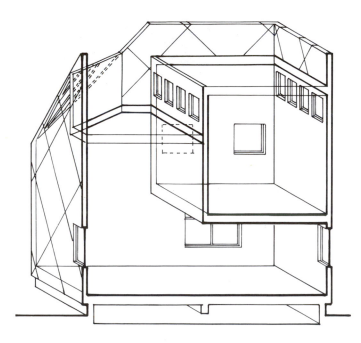

FIG. 5.48

Elevation obliques have all vertical planes (normally elevations) parallel to the image plane and are true to scale. With any given foreshortening ratio, the lower the receding angle the more of the side elevation will be shown. The exception is 90°, which will not display any side elevation.

A 45° receding line angle with a .5 foreshortening ratio has historically been known as a Cabinet Projection, and 45° with a 1.0 ratio, a Cavalier Projection. Of the six elevation obliques on the left, 45° with a .5 foreshortening ratio (F. R.), a Cabinet Projection, and 90° with a .5 ratio are the most widely used.

ELEVATION OBLIQUES: SOME EXAMPLES TO NOTE

The example in Fig. 5.47 is an exception to the normal usage of elevations for the construction of an elevation oblique. Here, two sections were used. The upper portion is a section taken just inside the exterior wall and can be thought of as either an interior elevation with floor and wall thickness drawn or as a section. The other small drawing is a section.

In the larger, finished elevation oblique in Fig. 5.48, two portions of roof have been removed but are still indicated by light lines in section. The section portion was given the heaviest lineweight to establish the visual foreground. Next and almost as heavy in lineweight, the place where the roofs were removed was articulated to define the interior volumes and the difference between inside and outside. Receding planes were treated both as solid and transparent.

Although Fig. 5.48 can be superficially related to a "wire frame" drawing done on a computer, it is entirely different because not all lines are shown. Selecting what to draw and what not to draw couples with differential lineweight to do away with any similarity.

One of the advantages of an elevation oblique with a 90°
receding angle (Fig. 5.49) is the ability to use sticky-backed
sheets of architectural materials. (The plan oblique offers
the same presentation possibilities.) Both types of drawings
can, of course, be rendered using material indicators in
computer files.

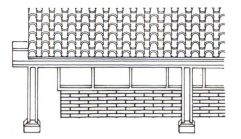

FIG. 5.49

Figs. 5.50 and 5.51 are drawn at different foreshortening
ratios—the latter at .75 and the former at half that ratio.
Neither is more correct than the other, only the bottom
example is looking down more on the building.

Figure 5.50 uses a 60% tone for the roofs and a textured pattern for the ground, both sticky-backed transfer tones. Note
how the roof recedes into the texture and the elevations
come forward.

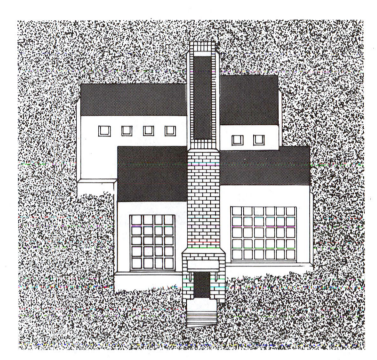

FIG. 5.50

The pure black and white of Fig. 5.51 gives maximum spacial movement and graphic impact. This technique is very
sympathetic to both the architectural design and the drawing type.

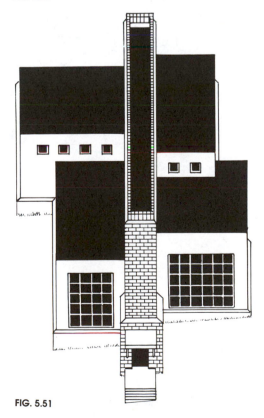

FIG. 5.51

CHAPTER 6

SHADES AND SHADOWS

Light from the sun, shade, and shadow appear in the earliest known drawings, the 20,000-year-old cave paintings of animals in Lascaux, France. Ever since—and long before—the illusions of paralines and perspectives, shades and shadows have been used to depict three dimensionality in almost all cultures. Along with the overlapping of pictorial elements, shades and shadows remain one of the best methods for representing spacial relations in drawing and painting.

Sunlight has had a profound influence on architecture in two ways: first, in the very forms and spaces of buildings; and second, in architectural drawing and the planning of actual projects. Sunlight, climate conditions, and available building technology have been major parameters defining architectural development, both for everyday indigenous building and as well as for "high" architecture. The ancient Egyptian pyramids had religious and symbolic relationships with the seasonal paths of the sun. Later, the classical Greeks developed sophisticated undercutting of their stone decorations which, in turn, cast precise, long shadows under the bright Mediterranean sun. The creation of relatively efficient columns and arches allowed for large areas of glass in soaring Gothic cathedrals, all of which were located in a mild climate with overcast skies. Much later, these same climatic conditions fostered the spectacular design of all-glass railroad stations and exhibition halls of the nineteenth century.

In response to the crowded, dark urban slums of the seventeenth and eighteenth centuries, sunlight—or the lack of it—became major health concerns. Building standards were originated and techniques for greater sun control explored during the first quarter of the twentieth century in Germany and Russia. Presently, the questions of when and how much sun enters a building can be very accurately calculated and controlled by natural and built means. This leads to greater human comfort, while it limits the natural resources expended for heating and air conditioning.

Shades and shadows were taught extensively at the École des Beaux-Arts, the citadel of nineteenth-century architectural drawing. There, the drawing approach was highly influenced by the naturalism of French contemporary landscape painters. The pictorial rendering of shades and shadows has changed since those days because of electric lights, still cameras, movies, and changes in artistic sensibilities. As American architect Louis Kahn commented in a 1960s lecture, "I was born in the wrong century—in the century of yellow light and blue shadows. This is the century of white light and black shadows."

This chapter delves into the unchanging basics of shades and shadows using both descriptive geometry methods and practical shortcuts for multiviews. Shades and shadows are infrequently used in paraline drawing, so the short section on paraline shadows has been limited to isometrics using set angles for the sun's rays. As in other chapters, only a few examples of technique, attitudes, and sensibilities are included. Due to the scope of this book, the important environmental control aspects are mostly left to other sources.

SOLAR ANGLES

The length of shadows is determined by the angle of the sun's rays striking the earth. This angle has two components: angle A, the horizontal angle, and angle B, the vertical angle. A is defined in degrees, minutes, and seconds, either as a bearing or azimuth from North or South. Altitude angle B is also defined in degrees, minutes, and seconds but from the horizon. Both component angles change according to the specific geographic location, time of day, and month of the year.

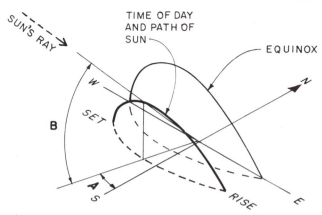

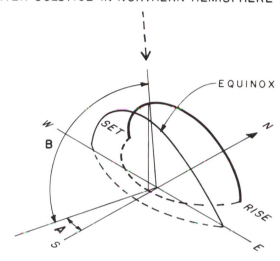

SUN AT WINTER SOLSTICE IN NORTHERN HEMISPHERE

On approximately March 21 and September 22, day and night are equal in length; these two days are called solar equinoxes and the sun rises in the true East and sets in the West. At other times of the year, sunrise and sunset do not occur in true East or West (note difference in 6.1 top and bottom). The summer and winter solstices occur when the axis of the earth is tilted the most in relationship to the sun. This condition causes summer or winter in the northern hemisphere and vice versa in the southern. During the winter in the northern hemisphere, the rays of the sun are lower in the sky than in the summer. To state this another way: For any given angle A, angle B will be greater in summer than winter.

SUN AT SUMMER SOLSTICE IN NORTHERN HEMISPHERE

FIG. 6.1

Precise angles can be found from model measurements in sun chambers, calculations, or charts. To use these angles for drawing, horizontal direction A must first be plotted in Plan. Altitude angle B is then drawn in an elevation whose image plane is parallel to the direction of A (Elevation 1 in Fig. 6.2), and then angle C can be found in any other elevation by projection and by transferring height h.

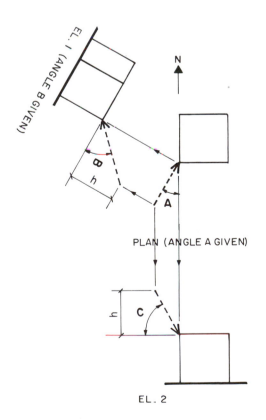

FIG. 6.2

SUN'S RAYS

FULL SHADE

SHADOW

SHADOW

PLAN

EL.

PLAN SHADOWS

PLAN SHADOWS (PREFERRED)

45°

45°

EL. SHADOWS - TRADITIONAL (PREFERRED)

EL. SHADOWS

45°

45°

FIG. 6.3

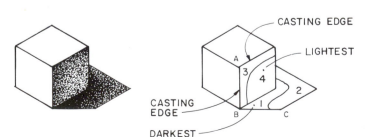

CASTING EDGE

LIGHTEST

CASTING EDGE

DARKEST

FIG. 6.4

The sun emits an infinite number of rays that create sunlit areas, shades, and shadows on objects they strike. Shade occurs on a surface turned away from the direct rays of the sun, and shadows are dark areas caused by the shaded portion of an object blocking the sun's rays. Shadows are geometrically related to areas in full shade that cast them. (People commonly use the words "shade" and "shadow" interchangeably. In architectural drawing terms, they are often used incorrectly. For example: "In the shade of the old apple tree" is incorrect. "In the shadow of the old apple tree" is correct.) In addition, the defining edges of shadows converge to vanishing points. This perspective nature of shadow edges can readily be observed on the ground when the altitude angle is low—in early morning and late afternoon.

Rays of the sun are assumed to be parallel when drawing multiviews and paralines. For perspectives, the rays are usually drawn parallel, but there is a method that mimics reality, thereby interpreting rays as not parallel. In this chapter, all rays are parallel and are indicated by short, dashed lines. The traditional and preferred sun angle for casting shadows in elevation is 45° with the sun originating over the viewer's left shoulder. This angle further assumes the direction of sun is along the diagonal of a cube (the consequent altitude angle is 35°16'). If 45° is used for casting plan shadows, the effective length of shadows is too long when an accompanying 45° is used in elevation. Shorter shadows in plan are preferred. (Only the cube portion of the illustration in Fig. 6.3 is toned in plan shadows.)

VALUES IN SHADE AND SHADOW

In drawing, the word "value" expresses the degree of lightness or darkness. Given an object and background of approximately the same value, shadows are darker than shade. However, the shaded side of a near black object will be darker than its shadow on a white background.

Light is reflected from the atmosphere and nearby surfaces back into both shades and shadows. This causes the values of shades and shadows to be lighter the further they are from casting edges, and darker when closer. Fig. 6.4 shows relative values of shades and shadows. The darkest value within these areas is at the intersection between casting edge AB and shadow line BC.

Although it is common practice for the edges of shadows to be drawn with the lightest of lines, distant shadow edges are really less distinct. Atmospheric conditions, such as overcast skies, haze, and fog lessen the difference in values of an object and background, diffuse edges, and generate mood.

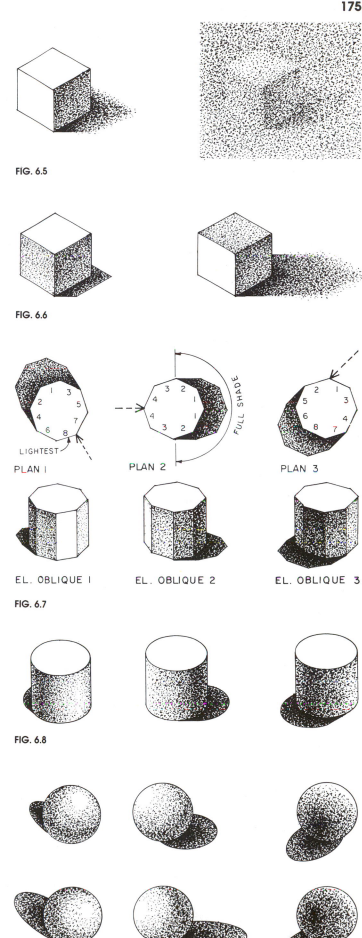

FIG. 6.5

When the altitude angle is 45° both horizontal and vertical surfaces in sunlight are equally light (Fig 6.5). If the altitude angle is much greater, vertical surfaces are in partial or full shade, and shadows are shorter and more defined. Conversely, if the angle is significantly less than 45°, horizontal sunlight surfaces become partially shaded, and shadows are longer and less defined at a distance from casting edges.

The value of shade darkens as light strikes vertical surfaces at less than right angles. The surfaces most perpendicular to the rays of the sun are the lightest in value, and sides directly opposite are the darkest. Only in Plan 2 of the three octagonal prisms in Fig. 6.7 does the sun light two surfaces equally (surfaces 4/4 are the lightest and 1/1 the darkest).

FIG. 6.6

PLAN 1   PLAN 2   PLAN 3

EL. OBLIQUE 1   EL. OBLIQUE 2   EL. OBLIQUE 3

FIG. 6.7

Light areas, shades, and shadows for the three cylinders respond to the same solar angles as the prisms above, but the shaded tones are continuous and vary from sunlight to partial shade to full shade.

FIG. 6.8

The top three spheres in Fig. 6.8 are also rendered for the same solar angles as the prisms and cylinders above. The lower set of spheres responds to a greater solar angle.

Shade patterns for the spheres vary in roughly elliptical areas from pure white (perpendicular to the direction of the sun) to the darkest area of shade (opposite the pure white). The shadow pattern from a sphere is also elliptical and the casting edge is the point of intersection between the bottom of the sphere and the horizontal surface. Shadows for the six spheres are the darkest at this intersection and cause the darker area in the shadow to also be roughly elliptical.

FIG. 6.9

CONSTRUCTING PLAN SHADOWS

The simplest to most complicated shadows in plan are drawn using descriptive geometry techniques. Solving plan shadows, like descriptive geometry problems, requires two views (the plan and one elevation) and the angle of the sun. Another similarity is that when enough examples have been seen and problems solved, plan shadows can be pre-visualized and practical shortcuts applied.

Casting both plan shadows and elevation shadows employs the same descriptive geometry method: The horizontal component of the shadow is found in plan and the vertical in elevation. Figs. 6.10 through 6.16 demonstrate the vast majority of techniques for the construction of both. In these illustrations, Plan and Elevation are givens, as is the direction of the sun's rays in both views (angle A and C, as shown on page 173).

Note that the illustrations in Fig. 6.10 are organized in the same order as in Chapter Two. You may find it helpful to go back and review particular techniques.

1. A horizontal line casts a parallel and equal-length shadow on a horizontal casting plane.
2. The distance from a horizontal line to its shadow is proportional to the height of the line above the casting surface.
3. and 4. Sloping and oblique lines will cast non-parallel shadows.
5. The length of shadow for a vertical line is in the direction of the sun's ray in plan and dependent on the elevation angle of the sun's ray.
6. The shadow from a vertical line not touching a horizontal surface will not touch the line in plan.
7. Regardless of whether a casting surface is horizontal, sloping, or oblique, the plan shadow will be in the same direction as the horizontal angle of the sun's rays.
8. In this illustration, the horizontal direction of the sun's ray makes sloping cutting plane 1,2 in Plan. This plane and the consequent horizontal direction are transferred into Elevation, point A_1 is found there, and then projected back to Plan.

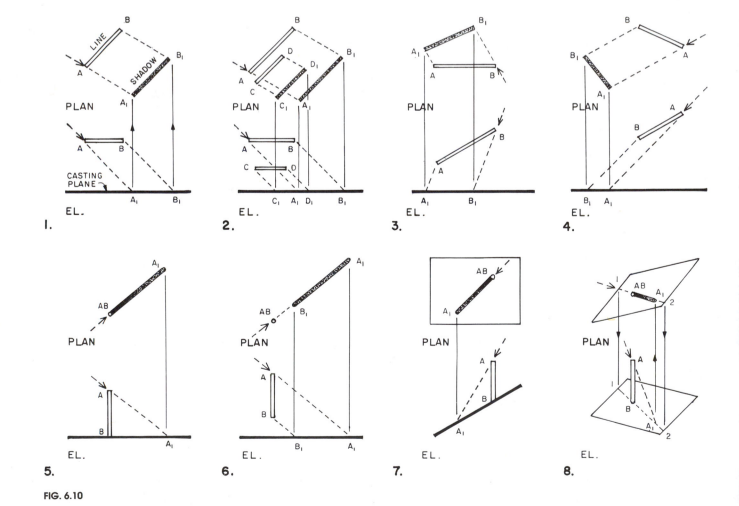

FIG. 6.10

9. A horizontal line casting a shadow on an oblique plane. Same type of solution as #8.

10. Intersecting lines casting shadows on a sloping plane.

11a. and 11b. Given a horizontal (bearing) and altitude angle, finding the elevation angle and casting a shadow on an oblique plane (shadow not shown in Elevation).

12. and 13. Any shape horizontal plane will cast a same-size and same-shape shadow on a horizontal surface.

14. and 15. The size of a plane, or planes, and the distance above the casting plane can cause part of the shadow to be covered up or fall on another plane.

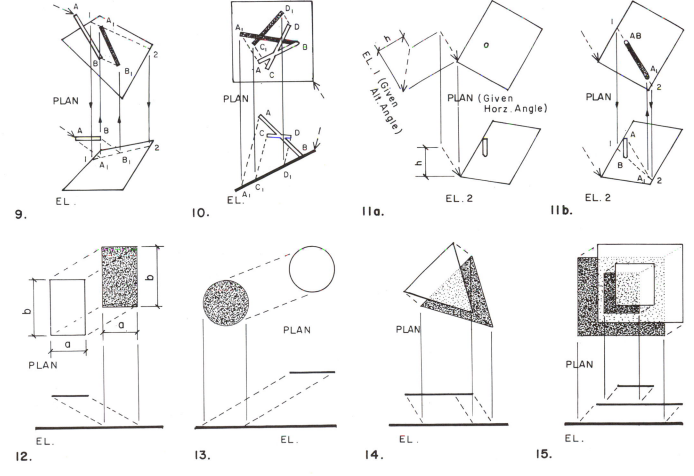

FIG. 6.11

16. A vertical plane casting a shadow. Horizontal lines of this plane cast equal parallel shadows, and vertical lines cast shadows in the direction of the sun's rays.
17. This vertical plane is a circle (h dimension is the diameter) casting an elliptical shadow (see pages 155 and 156).
18. Vertical plane ABCD casting a shadow on an oblique plane using cutting planes (shadow not shown in Elevation).
19. A solid floating above a horizontal casting surface. Part of the shadow is under the solid. The top and bottom planes of the solid generate duplicates connected by shadows from the vertical lines. The shadow lines do not connect with the bottom corners of the object (B does not connect with B1), proving the object does not sit on the casting plane.
20. Only the centers of the circles need be projected into Plan. The shadow is constructed by using the circles and parallel lines.
21. If all imaginary lines within shadows in this illustration are drawn, the shadow on a parallel plane will be in the form of a plan oblique.
22. In this illustration, only plane AEC casts its own parallel shadow.

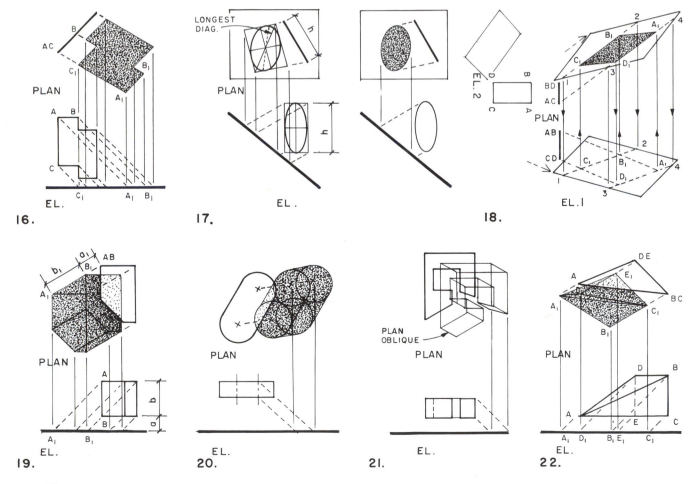

FIG. 6.12

23. and 24. Solids supported by vertical solids. Note a_1 and b_1 are proportionate to a and b.

25. Dimension a_1 is determined by dimension a and the elevation angle. If the Plan and Elevation angles had been 45°, a would equal a_1 and a_2.

26. Lines and planes not parallel to the casting surface will not cast equal-length, parallel, or equal-sized shadows.

27. Gable roof in which the outer limit of the shadow is defined by eave line AD.

28. Same gable roof with ridge line BE as the controlling outer limit of shadow. One side of the roof is in shade.

29. Shadow of a hipped roof.

30. Shadow from L-shaped roof, which has both a gable and hipped roof. The convenient starting shadow line for this example is the ridge line.

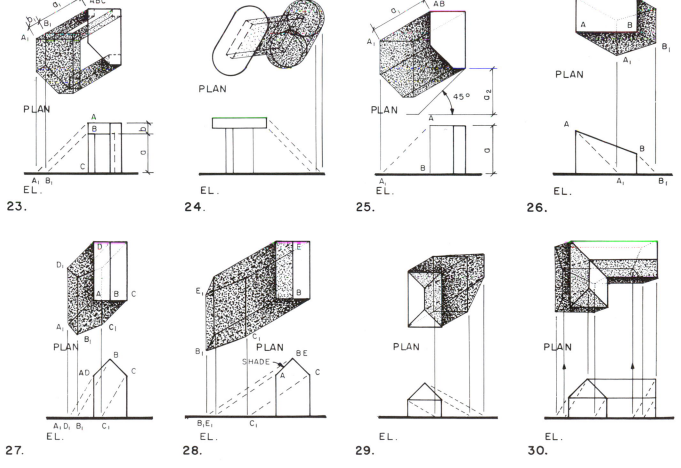

FIG. 6.13

31. Compositions with more than one element often cast composite shadows overlapping one another. The shadow from the lowest element is darker than the shadow from the taller element. This generates a shadow within a shadow.

32. Same objects as illustration 31 but vertical angle changed; shadows from three elements are now separate.

33. Shadow from higher element is darker on the ground than on the lower-level object. This graphic treatment modifies actual light conditions but effectively separates the intermediate-level object from the ground.

34. To find point x in Plan, x was first projected backward in Elevation, originating point y in Elevation. Point y was then projected into Plan to find point x.

35. If a shadow line in plan cannot be directly found by direct projection from an elevation, imaginary points can be used in a similar manner to illustration 34. In example 35, point y was arbitrarily located along AB in Elevation. Point x was found in the same view, then both x and y were taken into Plan to find line ab (ab must be parallel to AB).

36. Same object and sun angles as 35 but object has an oblique top. Points w and x were used in the same way as 35 to establish the direction of ab (ab must be parallel to $A_1 B_1$).

37. It is often easier in complex problems to use two elevations for shadow casting in plan. The vertical sun angle in Elevation 2 was found by direct projection of AA_1 from Plan. Note that shadows within shadows and differential values within shadows give this illusion a clear three-dimensional representation.

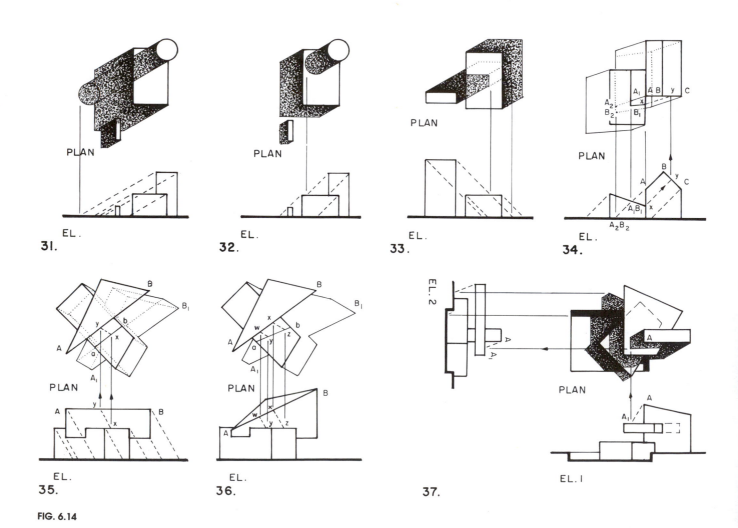

FIG. 6.14

38. An arbitrary selection of points on the object were used to find the shadow line on the curved ground surface.

39. Gable roof casting a shadow on a sloping plane.

40. This casting surface is a bent plane and horizontal line AB casts bent shadow line $A_1 B_1$.

41. Shadows on a bent plane. (This is similar to illustration 34 in which point y is found by back projection from Elevation.)

42. Same forms as illustration 41, but casting surface has been folded downward along line PR.

43. The casting surface has been folded a second time.

44. Truncated triangular prism on an oblique plane. On any flat casting surface, the rays for plan shadows will be parallel, and any cutting planes established in plan will originate parallel cutting planes in elevation.

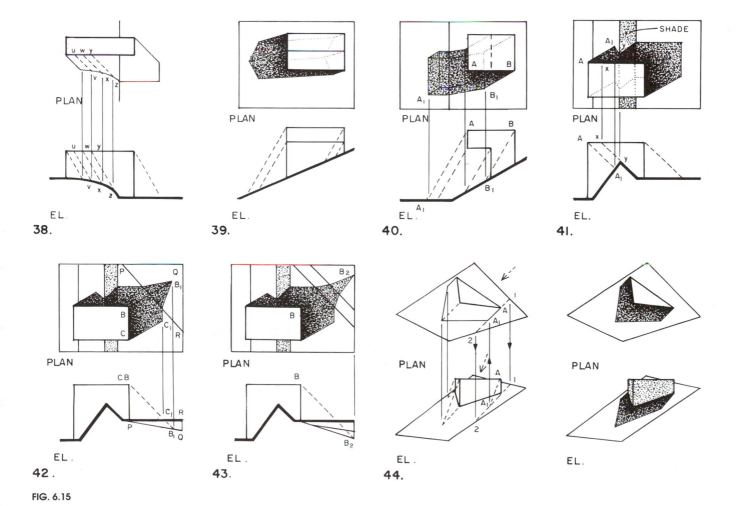

38.   39.   40.   41.

42.   43.   44.

FIG. 6.15

45. Vertical cutting planes employed to find plan shadows on contours. Each plane is in the direction of the sun's ray in plan. The more planes selected, the more accurate the shadow lines. Nine planes—A through I—were uniformly located along the top edge of the solid in Plan. Every cutting plane can be thought of as a section slicing, on the bottom edge, through the ground. Where the sun's rays hit the ground in section locates points in Elevation 1 and 2 (A_1, B_1, C_1, etc.), which are then projected back into Plan. (This shadow pattern is much the same as the one on page 127. If the cubic form had not had a corner chopped off, the shadow would have extended to point x.)

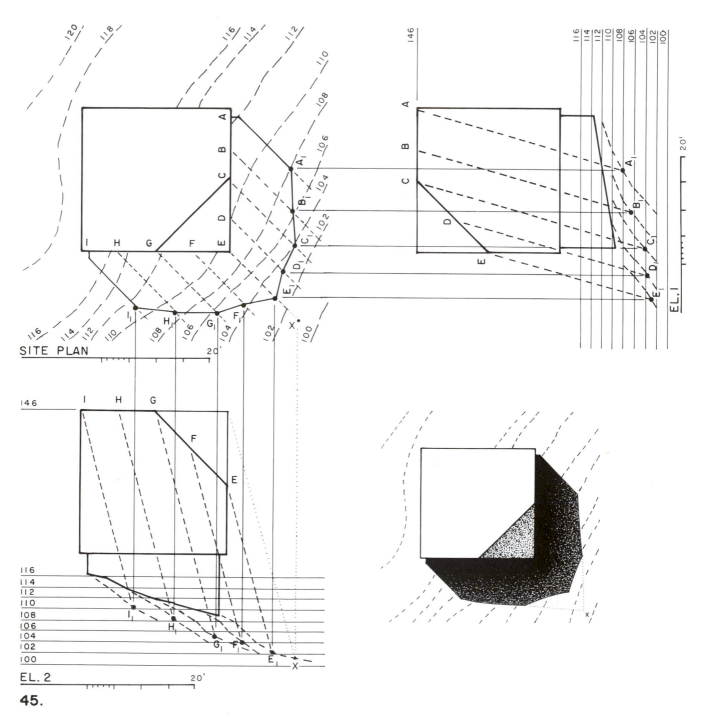

SITE PLAN

EL. I

EL. 2

45.

FIG. 6.16

A SHORTCUT TO CONSTRUCTING PLAN SHADOWS

Rather than projecting back and forth from elevation to plan, shortcuts can be used to construct plan shadows—as long as you know the general principles of shadow casting. The major shortcut depends on realizing that shadow line lengths in plan are proportional to their heights in elevation.

First, scale vertical measurements in elevation and use the same scale, or any other convenient scale, to draw individual shadow lines. Then connect the ends of lines to complete the shadow pattern in plan. Many buildings have flat roofs and are on flat ground. In these cases, only a few pertinent lines need be scaled and no projects have to be made.

Unlike some shadows for the abstract illustrations 1 through 45, shadows for architectural plans are always cast downward. There are two reasons for this convention: First, we see shadows downward in real life, and second, if shadows were cast upward, the building would tend to be pushed off the page. The shadow, then, psychologically supports the plan.

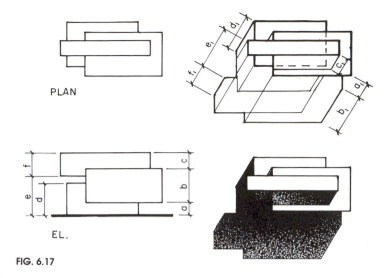

FIG. 6.17

PLAN SHADOWS: SOME EXAMPLES TO NOTE

The values in the shadow from Fig. 6.17 are diagrammed by numbers (the lightest value has the highest number). When rendering shadows, different tones should be continuous and not specifically identifiable.

Fig. 6.19 shows shadows made by stippling, a very time-consuming process. Nevertheless, great subtlety can be achieved and, since drawings are pure black and white, high-quality reproductions (including enlargements for presentations) are guaranteed. (All of the stippled drawings in this chapter have been done with a #3x0 (.25 mm.) pen. Fig. 6.19 has dots made with a #2 (.70 mm.) and #00 (.30 mm.) pen for a coarser texture.)

The example in Fig. 6.20 has uses sticky-backed transfer patterns for shadows, with stippling over the plastic.

A shadow on a light material is lighter than the same shadow on a darker material (Fig. 6.21). This enlivens shadows and gives them a believable transparency. Values for materials can be arbitrarily selected; transparency alone is what makes this an interesting drawing. (The site plan on page 170 uses this principle. The street at the top of the drawing is asphalt—the darkest material in the drawing—and the gridded concrete pavement the lightest. The tree was assigned a medium gray and casts a shadow on both the asphalt and concrete.)

In Fig. 6.22, the percentages of gray used in the drawing in Fig. 6.21 are diagrammed.

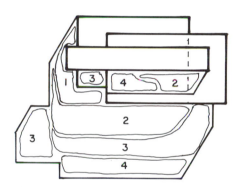

FIG. 6.18

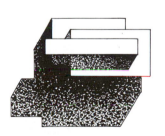

FIG. 6.19

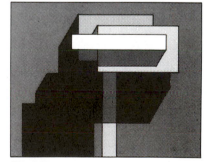

FIG. 6.21

FIG. 6.20

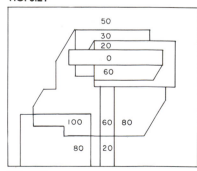

FIG. 6.22

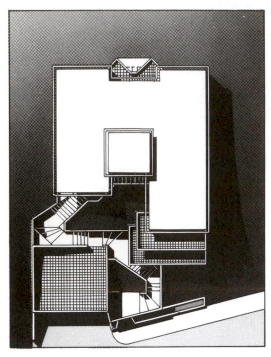

FIG. 6.23

The ground in Fig. 6.23 slopes from the upper right corner of the drawing down to the lower left (note the shadow lines from the flat roof are consequently curved in two directions). If the ground had been a uniform slope from right to left, these shadow lines would have been straight lines. A graded, sticky-backed tone was used to indicate the increasing shade on the ground. The tread edges and walls in shadow were left white to enliven shadows.

The same site plan is repeated in Fig. 6.24, with trees and shadows from trees overlapping built features. The trees were treated as semi-transparent planes with the use of a set of nine gray markers with both chisel and fine points on marker paper, along with a drafting pen and tempera paint in a ruling pen. The muddiness of different-toned areas was reduced by drawing lines across these areas.

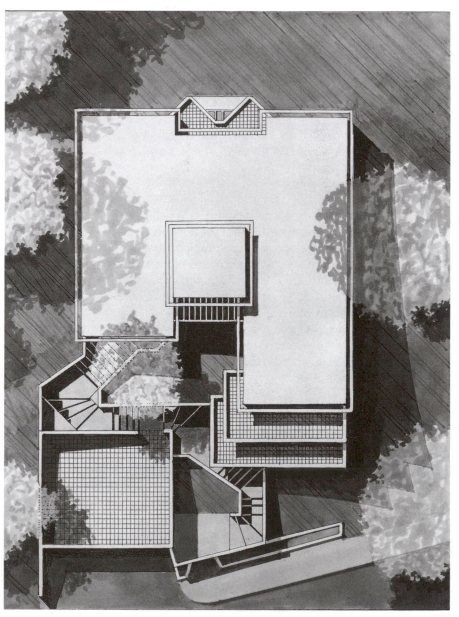

FIG. 6.24

Fig. 6.25 was created with mixed media: sticky-backed transfer tones for the roads, stippling for the ground, and linework/crosshatching for the roofs. The shaded sides of the roofs have two values to articulate different planes. The sunny side of the roofs are the only whites in the drawing and therefore come toward the viewer.

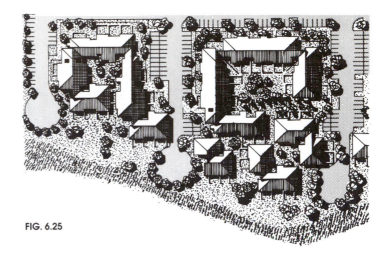

FIG. 6.25

Shadows can be built up using various hand methods to give a drawing a less mechanical appearance. In Fig. 6.26, small circular patterns were made with a pen.

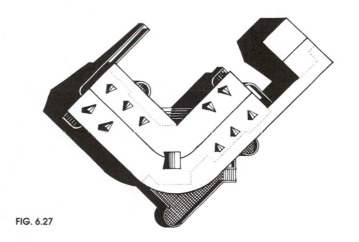

FIG. 6.26

On the other hand, black-and-white drawings without any shades or ground detail (Fig. 6.27) make a strong visual impact and reproduce well, regardless of the reduction for portfolios or publication. Exterior walls are left white within shadows to define forms that would not have been seen otherwise. The dotted lines indicate the building line and porches under the roof. These lines add secondary, subordinate information to the drawing.

Drawing only the shadows and leaving other defining lines out of Fig. 6.28 generates the same high graphic impact as in Fig. 6.27. Because the eye tends to fill in the form, the suggestion of shade and shadow is as effective as a more complete rendering. The same result is obtained from the use of high-contrast film in photography.

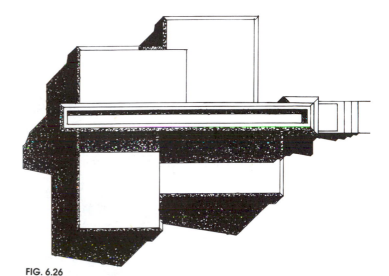

FIG. 6.27

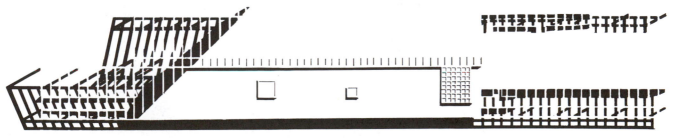

FIG. 6.28

The roofs in Fig. 6.29 have been removed in order to cast both interior and exterior shadows. Casting shadows in complicated problems with multiple geometries relies on all methods, but the shortcut of direct measurement should be the primary technique used (direct projection from elevations would require many drawings).

Fig. 6.29 was inked on vellum and pencil, shadows were added, and tone was applied to all floors. This makes the white walls pop out and, more important, allows material indications to appear in both light areas and shadows. On a design level, the graphic treatment is sympathetic to the architecture because it incorporates old and new elements. (Other drawings of this house can be seen on pages 98, 124, 167, 197, and 214.)

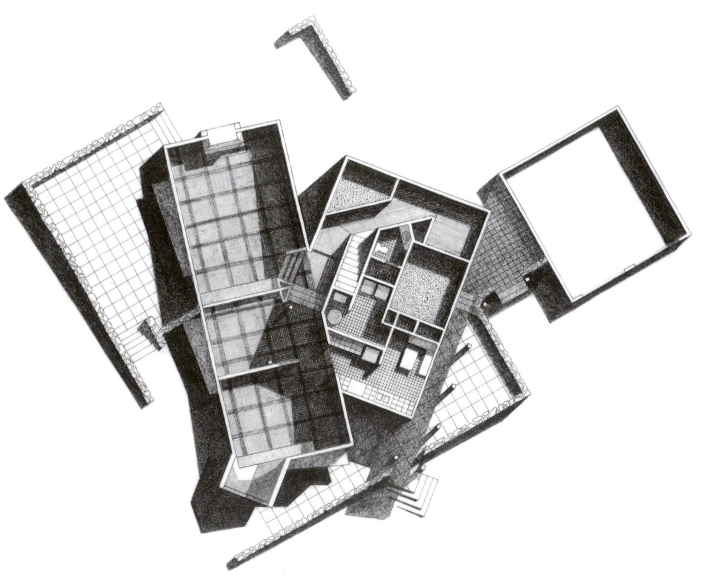

FIG. 6.29

CONSTRUCTING ELEVATION SHADOWS

The same methods used to cast shadows in plan are used to cast shadows in elevation: direct projection from one view to another; selection of imaginary points along a line not associated with the ends of a line; using them for direct projection; and cutting planes on sloping or oblique planes. Most plan shadows are generated from elevations and projected into plan. Elevation shadows reverse this procedure: The shadow points are first found in plan and projected into elevation. In addition, elevation shadows can sometimes be drawn by using two elevations, with or without a plan.

Many shadow patterns can be obtained by more than one method or, for a particular problem, by a mixture of methods. It is even advisable to use more than one method to check the solution found by another method.

The following illustrations frequently show more than one method. Illustrations are cross-referenced in parentheses to other similar problems.

46. This illustration is exactly the same as #1, only the plan and elevation have been reversed. The light source is now upward lighting, occasionally used in movies for a goulish effect.
47. The same configuration as #46 with traditional downward lighting.
48. Line does not touch surface and shadow in elevation does not touch the line.
49. Intersecting lines casting shadows on a folded plane.
50. Direction of sun's rays in Plan transferred into Elevation by cutting plane 1,2. Problem also can be resolved by establishing vertical angle in Elevation (cutting plane 3,4), projecting it into Plan, finding the length of shadow, and then projecting back into Elevation.
51. Two parallel planes casting shadows in Elevation. Note the front plane casts a shadow on the other plane as well as the casting plane.
52. A circle casting an elliptical shadow on a nonparallel casting surface (see page 155). Drawing an ellipse within a rhomboid: Besides the major axis of the ellipse being in the general direction as the longest diagonal of the rhomboid, a circumscribed square can be drawn in Plan, tangents to the circle (ab shown) made and transferred to the rhomboid. The ellipse must touch these tangents as well as the conjugate axes.
53. Sloping triangle casting a shadow on a vertical plane.

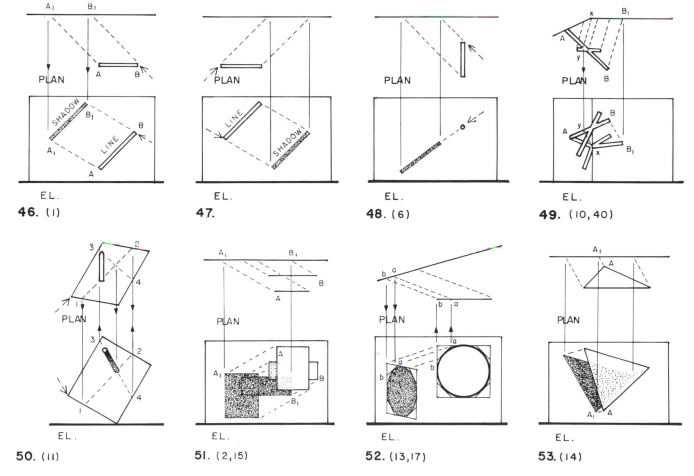

46. (1)   47.   48. (6)   49. (10, 40)

50. (11)   51. (2, 15)   52. (13, 17)   53. (14)

FIG. 6.30

54. Vertical lines, or vertical lines of an object, always cast parallel, equal-length shadows on vertical planes.

55a. Use of a second elevation (Elevation 2) to find shadows in another elevation (Elevation 1).

55b. Same plane casting same shadow by transferring direction of sun in Elevation 1 to Plan, finding points, and projecting back into Elevation 1. Only a few projections are shown.

56. Two pillars casting shadows. Rectilinear pillars, posts and columns always cast shadows wider than the forms in elevation. Part of shadow will be on the ground. Round objects cast shadows of the same width.

57. Same pillars and sun angles with shadows on a sloping casting surface.

58. Shadows from columns and beam. Elevation 2 used as a check.

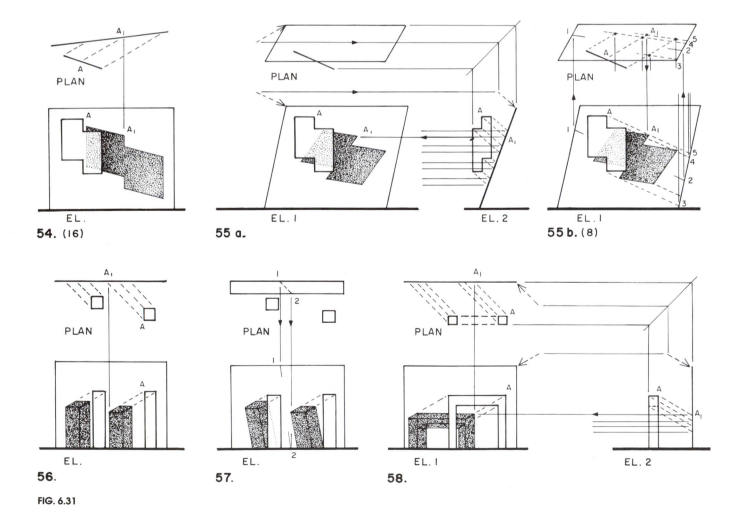

54. (16) **55 a.** **55 b.** (8)

56. **57.** **58.**

FIG. 6.31

59. Shortcut with traditional 45° light source from over viewer's left shoulder. Distance a in Plan is proportional to a_1, and a_1 equals a if both angles are 45°.

60. Columns supporting slab from Illustration 59. Composite shadow on a parallel casting surface.

61. Columns not at edge of slab. Shadows on sloping casting surface. Imaginary points x and z determine shadow line on left-hand column.

62. If a solid does not touch a surface, shadow will not touch solid.

63. Rectangular hole in slab lets light through in elevation shadow. Imaginary extension of vertical casting surface allows point A_1 to be found. This part of shadow falls on ground (not shown).

64. Change of vertical angle eliminates sun coming through hole. Slope of shadow line A_1, x same as z B_1.

65. Shadow from square prism on gable roof building. Imaginary points xy used to find shadow under eave.

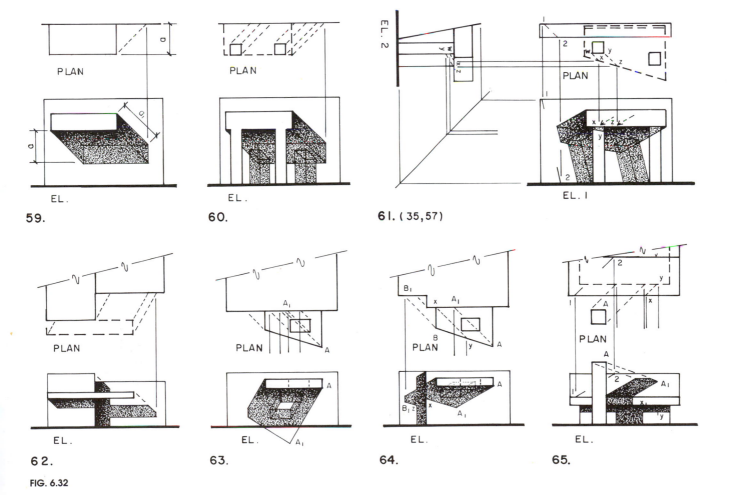

59. 60. 61. (35, 57)

62. 63. 64. 65.

FIG. 6.32

66. Shadow from horizontal slab falling on different in and out surfaces of a solid.

67. Shadows on parallel surfaces will have parallel shadows. Part of solid in partial shade.

68. Shadow on tilted ground plane in front of object as well as shadow on object. Illustration has all techniques used, including two elevations.

69. Dormer casting shadow on gable roof. Shadow line BA₁ found by projecting from Elevation 2 to both Plan and Elevation 1 rather than using cutting planes. This verifies shadow line BA₁ in Elevation 1 is in the direction of sun's rays.

70. Dormer cantilevered out from face of building.

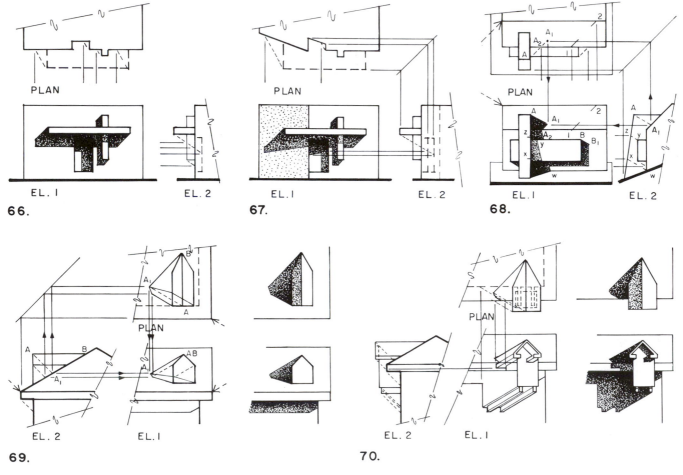

FIG. 6.33

71. Stairs with horizontal side wall. Points of intersection between treads and risers (zxv) were back projected to locate where the shadows came from (point y casts point z, etc.) in Elevation 2. All points in Elevation 2, including A_1, were then taken into Plan and finally into Elevation 1. Shadow lines on top two risers in direction of sun's rays. Top two treads have shadow lines parallel to side wall in Plan shadow.

72. Stairs with sloping side wall. Slope of shadow lines in Plan (xz, tv, etc.) are parallel to one another. Direction of these lines found by an imaginary extension of top tread's plane in Elevation 2, which gives a more accurate B_1 to x line than the shorter xz line. Elevation B shows shadows caused by steeper vertical angle for the sun's rays and point A_1, falling on a riser rather than a tread.

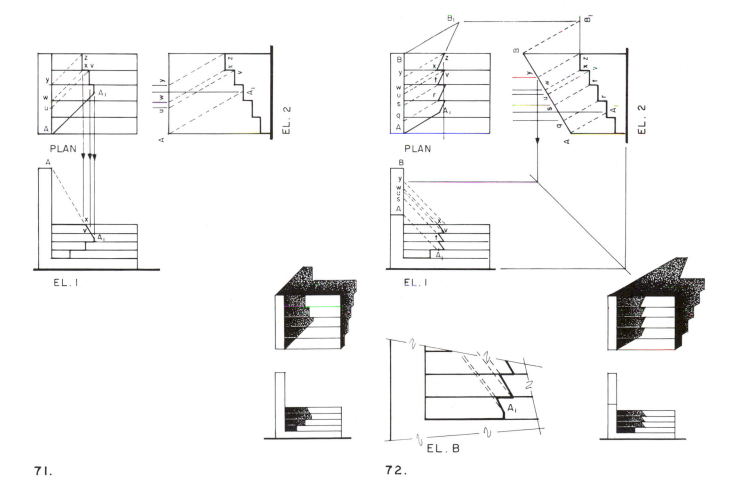

71.

72.

FIG. 6.34

73. Similar to Fig. 6.16 In #73, series of horizontal planes (1, 2, 3, 4 and 5) is drawn in Elevation 1 and projected to Plan, where they become plans at various levels. Then a set of diagonal cutting planes (A, B, C, etc.) concurrent with the sun's rays is taken through the object in Plan. At the points where these cutting planes intersect the plans at various levels, projections are made back into Elevation. This generates profiles of the object in Elevation that correspond to each cutting plane. Finally, points d, e, f, etc. along the casting edge (bottom of the square overhead slab) are projected from Plan to Elevation, and the sun's rays are taken through points e, f, g, h, etc. to find points along the shadow line in Elevation. The three small rendered elevations demonstrate how the shadow changes as the vertical angle of the sun's rays changes. Small Elevation 1 has rendered shade caused by line ST on the concave surface. Elevation 1a also has shade below ST and Elevation 1b has shadow from ST fading into shade.

74. Same procedure as #73 but additional horizontal planes and plans needed for right side of object (shadow is the same up to profile H).

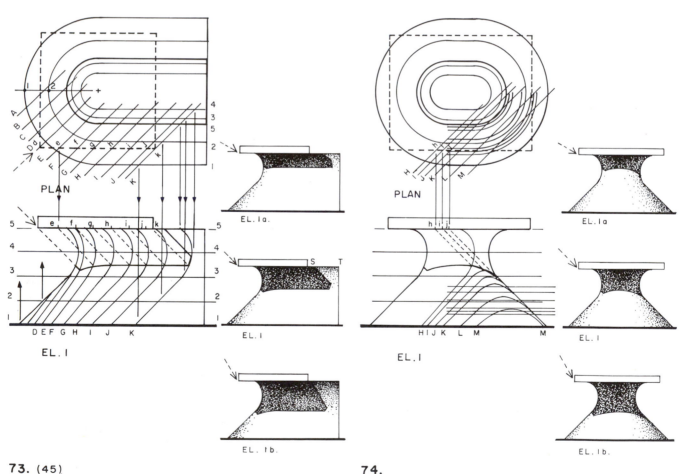

73. (45)

74.

FIG. 6.35

ELEVATION SHADOWS: SOME EXAMPLES TO NOTE

Window glass is transparent, reflective, or both depending on the viewer's angle relative to the glass and the type of glass (mirror glass is only reflective). For the professional and nonprofessional renderer, this presents special problems. First, elevations are flat, orthographic multiviews and cannot show actual reflections; There is no perspective convergence in a multiview. Second, no shadows occur on glass. What looks like shadows are, in reality, reflections of glass framing members. For these reasons, abstraction is necessary when drawing glass in elevations. Various abstractions—including faking it—are shown in the examples that follow.

When glass is rendered with a varying tone (shown in Fig. 6.36), the tone is first applied to the glass. Then, framing members are drawn over the tone. In the perspective, reflections were applied over the tone and the sunlight portions of the framing members applied with white tempera paint in a ruling pen. This technique also works over plastic, sticky-backed transfer tone.

In Fig. 6.37, the tonal range has been compressed—all blacks and grays with no whites. This gives the drawing a moody, brooding quality. The drawing was first executed in ink on vellum, an overall light gray tone was applied with the Cotton Ball technique, and pencil shading then added. The shading was rubbed over with a stump to obtain a smooth tone.

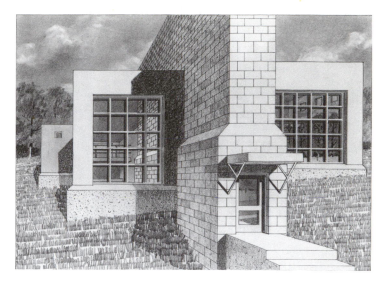

FIG. 6.36

FIG. 6.37

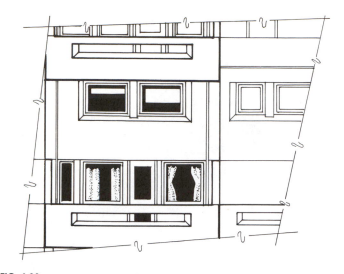

FIG. 6.38

Drawing shadows in elevation more often than not requires the simplification of architectural detail as well as abstraction of shadow patterns.

The large-scale elevation in Fig. 6.38 shows fixed/operable frames and joints between precast concrete panels. The shadows—cast only on curtains and shades—are rendered in a realistic manner without reflections.

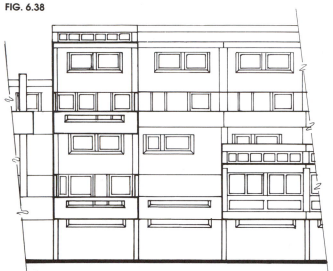

FIG. 6.39

The smaller-scale elevation in Fig. 6.39 abstracts window frames by reducing the number of framing members shown and panel joints abstracted to a single line.

The elevations in Fig. 6.40 show even less detail and reduced lineweight contrast. In order to establish the different planes in space, shadows were drawn black on the nearest planes and changed to primarily 80% for distant planes. Twenty-percent gray was also added to distant planes in sunlight.

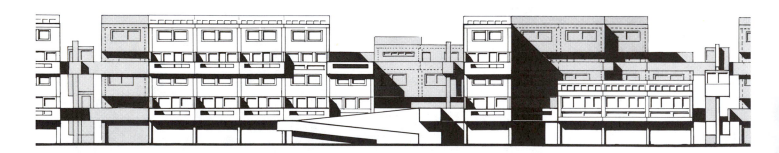

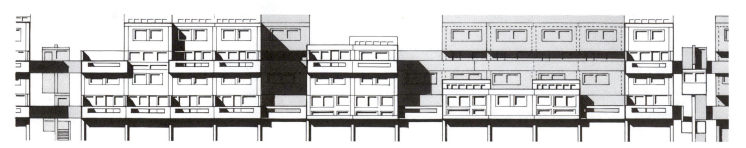

FIG. 6.40

On overcast days (Fig. 6.41), light, besides being more diffuse and casting less distinct shadows, comes from multiple directions because of atmospheric refraction. Nevertheless, diffuse light and shadows can be an effective manner for rendering presentations. In this interior elevation, light enters from the large triangular skylight. Light also comes into the house from the opposite side of the building, casting light shadows on the stair.

Although Fig. 6.41 depicts a selected combination of section and elevation beyond, it is not a true section because, among other things, the second floor is not shown. This technique comes from Beaux-Arts drawings, where important spaces were rendered in full shade and shadow with the building profile ghosted in light tone.

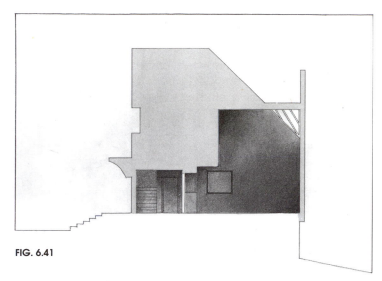

FIG. 6.41

These interior shades and shadows were drawn with a range of B pencils and, for reproduction purposes, the profile accomplished with 30% solid (not screened) transfer tone. A gray pencil tone was applied to the square window in the center of the drawing. If it had been left white it would have attracted the viewer's eye too much.

The background trees in Fig. 6.42 are dark, thereby pushing the lighter-toned building forward in abstract space. Glass indicates reflections from the sky and, as a general rule, glass should be rendered darker on sunlit surfaces and lighter on shaded surfaces.

The window tones were made using the Cotton Ball technique; a streak was made with a kneaded eraser; the reflections of frames drawn with pencil; and window frames in sunlight erased with an erasing shield (the members were large enough to erase rather than ruling over the tone with tempera paint). The background trees were done with a coarse kitchen sponge and ink dabbed against a sheet of plastic drafting film held against the edges of the elevation. Corrections to the small amount of ink bleeding under the plastic were made with "white-out" for ink. A few trunks and branches were then drawn with a pen and ink, and a few others with a brush and white tempera paint.

FIG. 6.42

The size of any drawing in relation to the page is of critical importance. Fig. 6.43 can be interpreted as a lonely house in the landscape or as an isolated object juxtaposed with the earth. This elevation has a different image than Fig. 6.42, even though the elevation types are different.

The elevation was given a heavier outline (#0, .35 mm.) than Fig. 6.42 in order to push it forward from the white sky. Windows are abstracted with even tone and shadows.

FIG. 6.43

CONSTRUCTING ISOMETRIC SHADOWS

When casting plan and elevation shadows, the true horizontal angle of the sun's ray (azimuth or bearing) is used in plan, and the vertical angle (usually not the altitude angle) is used in elevation. Isometrics are three-dimensional drawings, which means that both of these angles must be applied in a single drawing.

Although any altitude angle can be employed, each will generate changes to its components. The easiest method for constructing isometric shadows is to assume a 45° altitude angle. This causes the horizontal component to be horizontal on the drawing page. Additionally, a 45° triangle can be used (the shadow line direction of a horizontal line will consequently be approximately 21°.)

75. In this illustration, the horizontal direction of the sun's ray is drawn first (line Ax). As a principle, any vertical line casts a parallel vertical shadow line on a parallel plane. Point A_1 is found by using a 45° triangle (the altitude angle). A_1 is then connected to B (line will be the consequent 21° angle).
76. A shadow from line AE will either fall entirely on the ground or partly on the ground and partly on the vertical plane. Shadow line Ee is drawn first. A_1 must be on line eX. A 45° projection from A locates A_1.
77. Similar to both #75 and #76.
78. Shadows on sloping plane. Line $A_1 C_1$ establishes direction of all shadows from vertical lines on a sloping plane. If direction of shadow had been at right angles to plane, shadows from vertical lines would have been parallel to sides of sloping plane.
79. Shadow from gable roof.
80. Imaginary points x and y locate shadow line from broken ground plane. A_1, B_1, and C_1 found two ways: by imagining forms extend to lower level of ground (A_3) or assuming shadow line from AA_2 goes horizontal down to b and continues horizontally to A_1.
81. Lines not parallel to casting surface will not cast a parallel shadow.
82. Shadow point E located by drawing imaginary casting surface wxyz at the level of E and casting an imaginary shadow on this plane (A_2B_2 must be parallel to A_1B_1.)

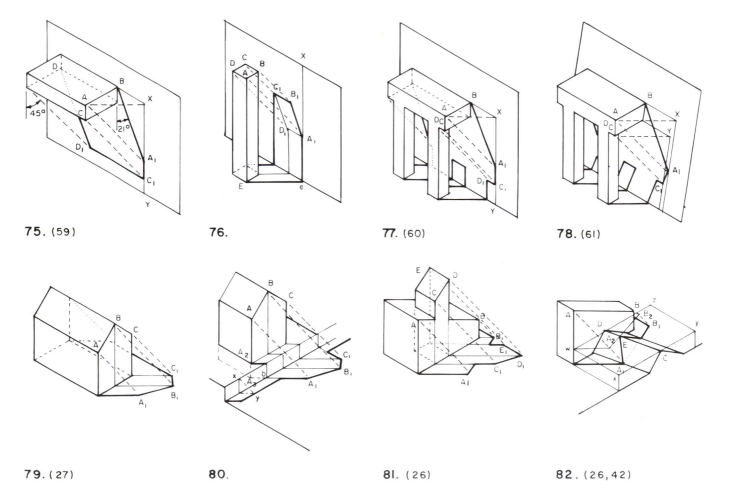

75. (59)   **76.**   **77.** (60)   **78.** (61)

79. (27)   **80.**   **81.** (26)   **82.** (26,42)

FIG. 6.44

The paraline in Fig. 6.45 is drawn with a diffuse light source. Individual planes are treated as transparent.

This drawing was executed on Strathmore drawing paper with a full range of B pencils.

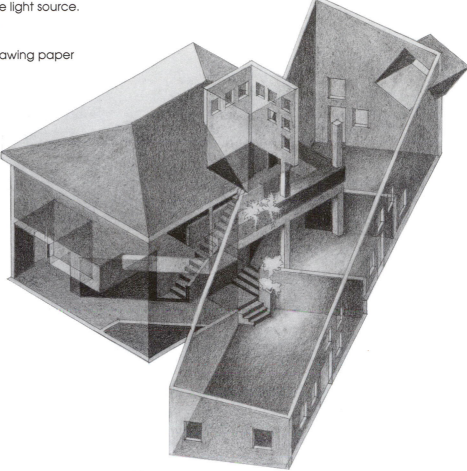

FIG. 6.45

SUN CONTROL

During summer, hot sun is unwelcome inside or outside of buildings in almost any geographic location. Roof overhangs, or any projecting horizontal plane, protect a building from the south sun and, if the overhang dimension is calculated correctly, can also allow the welcome warmth of the winter sun to enter. Deciduous trees on the south side of a building function as even better sun-control devices by blocking the summer sun and, when leaves fall, allowing sun to enter in cold months. Yet what happens when there are no existing trees on a site, or if they're planted in the wrong place? For trees to be a viable solution, they must be mature in size, which takes years of growth.

The heat from the sun is the greatest from midday to sunset. During this time of day, the rays get lower in the sky and come more from the west. Roof overhangs alone will not stop this sunlight from entering the building. Only the arrangement of large areas of glass in a way that won't receive the west sun, the construction of vertical elements to block the west sun, or the presence of trees will provide adequate sun control. A combination of one of these methods coupled with roof overhangs can be effective.

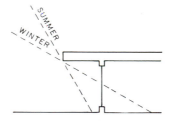

CONTROL OF SOUTHERN SUN

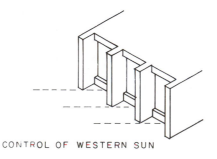

CONTROL OF WESTERN SUN

FIG. 6.46

CHAPTER 7

PRESENTATION GRAPHICS AND REPRODUCTION

Graphic design is a broad, general term applied to architectural graphics, advertising, packaging, page layouts, posters, video, and a wide variety of other two-dimensional applications. Many individual designers and groups have originated visual ideas in the past, and their contributions flow in and out of current graphic design.

At the turn of the twentieth century, one major group, the Analytical Cubists, led by Picasso and Braque, abandoned perspective and realism to explore the abstract two-dimensional surface of fragmented forms, simultaneous views of objects, overlapping images, transparencies, and sharp angles. One small but significant feature appeared in some paintings: stenciled letters. This suggested the visual importance of typography in the emerging sensibilities of modern art. It is not possible to overstate the Cubists' contribution to design then or now.

The maverick American architect Frank Lloyd Wright had a marked influence on European architecture and design when his work was published in the 1910-1911 Wasmuth Volumes. Many of his drawings for these books were rendered in pure black and white without grays. European designers, particularly the Dutch De Stijl group, were impressed by Wright's hovering planes and asymmetrical compositions, accentuated by the stark drawings. Wright's architectural ideas were transformed by the Dutch, while his presentation graphics were largely ignored. The De Stijl architects preferred more intellectual paraline drawings and drew few perspectives, as opposed to write Wright, who drew mostly perspectives and almost no paralines.

Revolutionary Russia was another fertile ground for visual ideas. Even before the Communist Revolution, painters were exploring twentieth century art. After the revolution, the Constructivists and other groups looked upon art as an instrument of radical, often political, change. The visual impact of printed words mixed with drawings and photographs was paramount for their graphic designs. Elemental shapes—squares, rectangles, triangles, and circles—floated in many of their compositions with a leaning toward the use of diagonals. Throughout the fine and applied arts of revolutionary Russia was the unstable effect of restless dynamism.

The Bauhaus was a German design school started by Walter Gropius shortly after World War I. The influence of the Bauhaus on the twentieth-century design matched the Beaux-Arts' influence on nineteenth-century architectural design. Under Gropius' guidance, a brilliant faculty (mostly painters) was assembled to teach design applicable to all of the practical arts: architecture, industrial design, graphic communications, textiles, furniture, etc. With an integrated technological outlook, this universal design approach was first taught in a foundation program that included an abstract two-dimensional design course (perhaps the first of its kind). The importance of the Bauhaus was in the application of a universal design attitude to all visual artifacts, including many not normally thought of as modern design subjects: furniture, industrial products, graphics, and film.

Other movements, such as Surrealism, Futurism, Dada, Italian Neorationalism, Art Deco, and the Finnish designer Alvar Aalto were also influential in early twentieth-century design. Each group's ideas filtered into design in general and graphic design in particular. Lurking in the background and always provoking thought was Japanese design. Throughout history and still today, Japan has produced some of the greatest decorative art ever known.

All of these design groups abhorred the nineteenth-century École des Beaux-Arts. This school, its graduates, and buildings represented backward design attitudes inappropriate for new generations who felt that architecture and design could radically change the world for the better. Karl Marx once made a political/historical statement that, if transposed to design, would express the Modernists' feelings about the École: "The past hangs like a nightmare on the minds of the living." Not until "The Architecture of the École des Beaux-Arts" show held at the Museum of Modern Art in 1975-1976 did this attitude change. The show occurred during the bloom of the sentimentally overindulgent Post-Modern Movement.

Beaux-Arts presentation graphics were limited to traditional plans, sections, elevations, and auxiliary elevations, with no paralines and very few perspectives. The plans were always fiercely symmetrical and drawn in a variety of media, often with cast shadows. All lettering on them (of which there was little with student work) was visually subordinate to the drawings; main titles were in print and any text cursive (script). Beaux Arts sections were never sections in a technical sense, but were interior elevations rendered in shade and shadow with a ghosted profile of the building (see page 195). Elevations were likewise rendered with shades and shadows (usually in black and white wash or watercolor). Buildings were set in nature, never in a contextual relation with other buildings. Like Bauhaus, Beaux-Arts students and architects considered buildings international, suitable for any geographic location regardless of local building customs or climate. (See page 133 and top example on page 195 for Beaux-Arts-influenced examples.)

The importance of any historical or graphic design overview is based on the feeling that most ideas are recycled, with or without radical transformation, for current usage. Every designer has been influenced by the work of others, and the best apply their own creativity to generate an original mixture. In *Pioneers of Soviet Architecture*, Selim O. Kahn-Magomedov, gave the following definition of Lissitsky's 1920s designs: ". . . the horizontal and vertical displacement of volumes relative to each other; overhangs of one volume over another; the siting of a large and bulky inchoate shape over smaller scattered ones; the soaring into space of a large volume supported only on a small area of its lower surface." This could well be the description of a Frank Gehry building from the early 1990s.

Chapter 7 explains abstract design ideas and some associative meanings taken from the fine and applied arts. Freehand tracings from various sources are related to presentation drawings and graphic design in general. Many references are made to Frank Lloyd Wright's drawings simply because he practiced for over sixty years, designed more than 500 buildings and, consequently, made many presentation drawings. The last part of this chapter covers conventional reproduction techniques.

COMMUNICATING WHAT TO WHOM AND WHY

Design presentations to other architects, instructors, clients, or lay committees differ from one another and so require a variety of approaches. In any project, an architect may be faced with separate sets of problems. For example, while a color rendering done in extreme photorealism—crowds of carefully drawn people and the latest model automobiles—is often shown to laypersons, this type of drawing may be too precious and distracting for a professional audience.

Titles on drawings convey information but are often not included in presentations for two reasons: First, presentations are usually assembled in a hurry, particularly when done in school, and time runs out before titles can be added; Second, many architects feel words distract from design content. The practice of excluding titles is reasonable in a school situation, but inappropriate when communicating with laypeople. A drawing with no titles would be rejected by any building department or contractor.

Numbering spaces on presentation drawings that are cross-referenced to a printed list is a common practice and standard for magazine publication. This method allows clients and readers to access necessary information, without having too much distracting text on the drawing itself.

Making the designer name or logo exceedingly large on drawings is inappropriate. In any presentation, the architectural design or process is of primary importance, followed by the quality of drawings, and then the graphic design. The designer's name is least important.

There are many questions that should be answered before a presentation is done. For instance, what distance will the drawings be seen from? Is the presentation meant to demonstrate architectural process rather than product? Does a project call for something close to sensory bombardment (multimedia) or a graphically understated group of beautiful drawings? Another, often forgotten question, is how will the drawings be reproduced?

Working drawings are the most straightforward, standardized type of graphic communication. Construction information is conveyed to contractors and to building departments for approvals. Unlike other presentation types, titles and sheet numbers should dominate working drawings. Cross-reference symbols are next in the visual hierarchy. The reason for this order is simple: Working drawings contain many sheets and each sheet has many drawings. A contractor has to turn pages often to follow cross references, so the graphics must be designed for quick recognition.

BORDERS, BOUNDARIES, AND EDGES

Working drawings always have borders. Prints from originals are used at a construction site, and these prints are made by hand-placing the original against photosensitive paper (the eventual print). If there were no borders and the drawings went to the edges, any misalignment in the contact printing process would risk eliminating part of the drawing. The border on the left hand binding edge is roughly twice the dimension of the other borders.

Whether presentation drawings have borders or not is optional, but do give it careful thought.

All architectural drawing represents in two dimensions what we think about objects and spaces in three dimensions. This differs from many other kinds of graphics that are often two-dimensional representations of two-dimensional subjects. This is why there is a fundamental spatial relationship in architectural work between the page and drawing. A small drawing on a page can imply one idea while a large drawing on a small page implies something else. For example, psychologist Erik Erikson asked Native American children to draw themselves. On a large piece of paper, one child drew a very small tree, the horizon, and an extremely small vertical line—which represented the child's self—under the tree. The implications are clear.

A small drawing on a large page makes a dramatic statement. Borders on such a drawing would be questionable. As a drawing gets larger, relative to the page size, the drawing starts to have a relationship to the edge and other ideas or questions come forward. Is the drawing a snapshot of an infinite scene or a defined play within a proscenium opening? The lack of borders on a page implies limitlessness, while light borders merely define the picture and heavy borders act as a proscenium opening.

In the author's sketch in Fig. 7.1, the drawing comes forward from the border (in front of the proscenium) while in Fig. 7.2 it recedes from the heavier border. The photograph on page 8 is another example of objects ahead of a proscenium and the drawing on page 80 indicates an infinite screen receding from the picture plane.

AUTHOR

FIG. 7.1

AUTHOR

FIG. 7.2

Another way to think about a border is whether the two-dimensionality of the page is trying to get into the three-dimensional representation—or is the drawing attempting to escape from the two-dimensional confines? In many of Frank Lloyd Wright's drawings, the sky and the sides of the drawings only are defined by lines. The open bottom of the drawings allows the earth to be basic, unlimited, supportive, and organic. Effectively, Wright was allowing two-dimensionality to flow into the drawing.

WRIGHT – YOUNG

FIG. 7.3

In some other of Wright's drawings, such as the perspective for the 1947 Ayn Rand House, the sky is typically defined and the building shoots out past the partial side border. In a few renderings, trees protrude above the top border. Wright's picture framing is worth a special study. (For Wright-influenced broken borders, see pages 132, middle example; page 146; page 158, top example; and page 195, top example.)

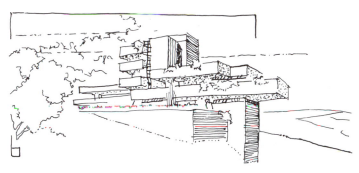

WRIGHT – AYN RAND

FIG. 7.4

Giovanni Piranesi was a great draftsman and etcher in the eighteenth century. His fantasies of Roman ruins and prisons comprise some of the most magnificent and powerful drawings ever made. In many respects Piranesi was an iconoclast, and a few of his drawings questioned the very nature of an image plane. In one rendering, he went so far as to cantilever an object out from the picture plane and cast a shadow on the title block. Piranesi effectively broke the three-dimensional illusion with another three-dimensional illusion of his own.

PIRANESI

FIG. 7.5

Fig. 7.6 demonstrates and expands on Piranese's idea. The rendering of this illustration was done on a matte photograph of Fig. 6.36.

FIG. 7.6

GREEK VASE

FIG. 7.7

MICHELANGELO

FIG. 7.8

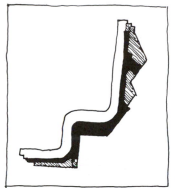

E. M. ESCHER

FIG. 7.9

HENRY MOORE

FIG. 7.10

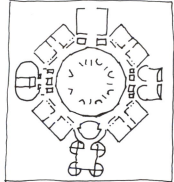

AALTO – BAKER

FIG. 7.11

KAHN – BANGLADESH

FIG. 7.12

WRIGHT (MAHONEY) – RHODES

FIG. 7.13

POSITIVE/NEGATIVE

Positive/negative relationships have always been paramount to all of the arts. Figure/ground is the term applied in two-dimensional work, and positive/negative is used for both two-dimensional and three-dimensional compositions. Figure is the positive element, such as a block of printed material or a drawing, while the ground is the area between these positive elements. Figure and ground visually react with each other and the edges of a drawing. Both should be thought of as equally important design elements.

Greek vases from the fifth century B.C. were one of the most finely considered examples of figure/ground. (The figures were often painted in orange and the ground in black.) Many centuries later, Michelangelo's ceiling paintings for the Sistine Chapel showed abundant uses of this design consideration. M.C. Escher played with figure/ground in many of his provocative visual explorations. In Fig. 7.9, the figures and ground are both flying geese. The sculptures of Henry Moore have a fluid relationship between positive form and the negative space around and through his pieces.

On its most fundamental level, architecture can be abstracted to positive/negative—walls and roofs enclosing volumes.

Residual space, or figure/ground, occurs often in architectural plans. Alvar Aalto's 1947 plan for Baker House (a dormitory at M.I.T.) has two geometries, and the circulation is the residual product between the two. The National Assembly Hall in Dacca, Bangladesh, by Louis Kahn, is another example of circulation as residual space.

Marion Mahoney, who worked for Wright in his most creative years, made the most beautiful drawings to ever come out of Wright's office. Her perspective of Wright's 1906 Rhodes House is a delicate example of figure/ground. The outline of the roofs combines with the branches of the trees and foliage to form designed negative shapes. At a smaller scale, the trees' lineweight emphasizes the space between trunks and branches rather than the continuation of trunks and branches. (The lineweight in the tracing is representative of the original, but some subtle textures were excluded.)

The foiling or overlapping of trees with the foliage of other trees and the foreground brushes against the building also generate three-dimensionality in Mahoney's drawing. Note that the edges of pavement are rendered with dots rather than straight lines. This softening of lines was also used for the junction of building and ground because the technique was sympathetic to his "organic" philosophy.

Designing is the act of arranging or establishing order, of which there are two types: finite, which is limited to one situation; and infinite, which is open-ended and continuous. Either can be rhythmic or fractured, even random.

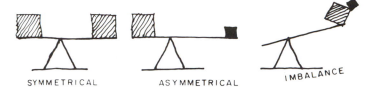

FIG. 7.14

Design ideas are conceived in the human mind, not originated in a hermetically sealed, purely mathematical or intellectual vacuum. When one thinks of order, symmetry and balance easily come to mind. Both words have meaningful connotations. A few cultures in history have approached design with perfection in mind, but those days are only a part of distant history. Until the twentieth century, symmetry was the norm for important buildings and graphic design (painting and sculpture were usually not saddled with symmetry—neither nature nor the human figure is perfectly symmetrical). Major buildings were bilaterally symmetrical and representative of powerful persons, religions, or governments.

Historically, asymmetry was relegated to less important buildings and usually not considered worthy of serious design. With the advent of Modern Art, these attitudes changed and asymmetry became the banner of design.

Personal attitudes are another catalyst for changes in design directions. Do we, like the Classic Greeks, seek a perfect balance in life? Or is it true, as many designers believe, that this is merely nostalgic longing?

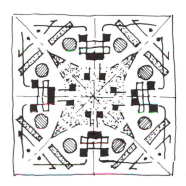

SYMMETRY

FIG. 7.15

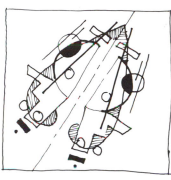

BILATERIAL SYMMETRY

FIG. 7.16

Whatever your opinion, three-dimensional design ideas affect two-dimensional approaches. Alexander Calder's mobiles move in finite space, allowing for the analogy of a person walking through architectural volumes to be made. Art historians write about the dynamic S-curve of the human figure in sculpture. These two examples are fluid, and fluidity offers another order for graphic design.

ALEXANDER CALDER

FIG. 7.17

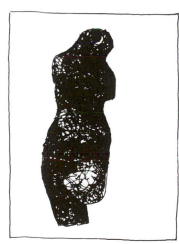

INDIA 2400 - 2000 B.C.

FIG. 7.18

INFINITE ORDER

Patterns and linear development are two kinds of infinite order that can go on forever, or at least as far as the eye can see. Similar to finite order, infinite order can be simple or complex, symmetrical or asymmetrical.

Urban street layouts and construction column grids are two examples of patterns. The centuries-old Japanese house layout uses the tatami mat as a basic model for design. In early twentieth-century art, Piet Mondrian, an artist sometimes allied with the Dutch De Stijl group, explored grids in his search for spirituality in mathematical art. There are countless other examples of patterns in man-made environments, nature, and personal behavior.

TATAMI MAT

FIG. 7.19

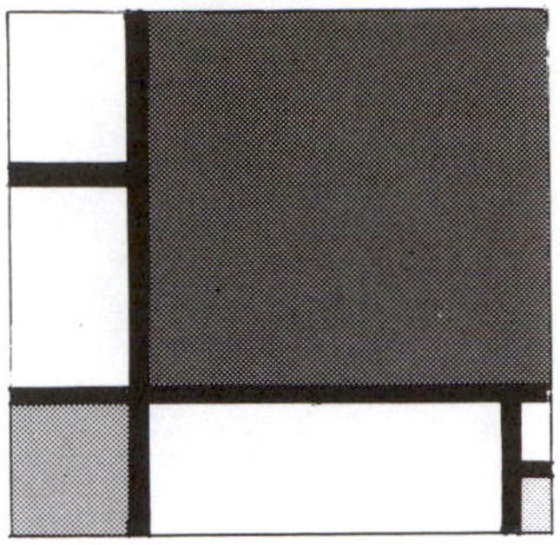

MONDRIAN

FIG. 7.20

Grids and patterns are essential tools for laying out printed pages, as well as a way of organizing a set of presentation drawings. Once grids or patterns have been established, the designer can responsibly play within this form of order. When a book or longer work is laid out, it is possible to have more than one grid rhythmically repeated to meet particular graphic needs.

ONE WAY COLUMN GRID

FIG. 7.21

PLAY

FIG. 7.22

Linear development, as the name implies, is organization around a line. Linear cities, as an architectural example, were proposed by urban planners from the Soviet Union in the 1920s. They imagined linear growth between existing cities along transportation lines. Though the plans for these linear cities were preliminary, Le Corbusier designed a more detailed plan for a twenty-mile development in Algiers. Many such schemes were attempted during the 1960s and became known as megastructures.

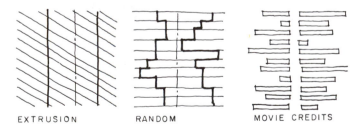

EXTRUSION   RANDOM   MOVIE CREDITS

FIG. 7.23

Linear design can be abstractly seen as an endless extrusion or as patterns around a line, with or without repetition. Often, linear design is practically applied in lists of minor titles and credits for movies.

The space between two lines determines if there is tension between them: If two lines are distant from one another, they are separate; at a closer distance, an attraction between them can be felt; and, when very close together, two lines visually become one, without tension. Michelangelo's painting of Creation on the Sistine Chapel ceiling depicts God giving life to Adam. The two fingers almost touch and the tension can be abstracted as the distance between the ends of the two almost-touching lines.

The amount of tension is what determines whether to poché between lines for cut elements (such as roofs and floors) in multiview drawing. To poché is to darken between lines by stippling, shading, blackening, or coloring). If two such lines are so close together that they visually became one, any darkening creates thin planes that come forward. On a large scale, when two lines have tension between them, they can be left as two lines, with or without light pochéing. This also makes the cut elements come forward. Dark pochéing in such situations makes a receding plane, which, for legibility or reduction purposes, may be desirable.

SEPARATE   TENSION   ONE LINE

FIG. 7.24

MICHELANGELO

FIG. 7.25

Another kind of tension can be seen in the imbalance of Lissitsky's 1920s design for Lenin's Tribune. One expects the structure to be upright. Instead, this design challenges that visual norm and generates tension.

 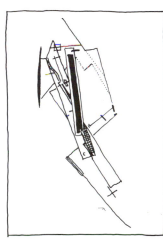

LISSITSKY – LENIN   HADID – PEAK CLUB

FIG. 7.26   **FIG. 7.27**

Beginning in the 1980s, a group of designers strongly influenced by Frank Gehry designed complicated assemblages that, in part, reflect our current state of nervous technology. One common thread between the Russians and Gehry's disciples is the tension in their designs cause by their use of diagonals. Zaha Hadid's 1982 competition entry for the Peak Club outside Hong Kong is a beautiful example of the same sensibility. Within her complex arrangement were three major rectilinear solids set at angles to one another. When these elements were put together with other components, a dynamic tension was achieved.

Opting for a diagonal layout of presentation graphics is yet another method of presenting architectural material. Blocks of type, photographs, and drawings can be arranged on diagonals, if the motivating architectural ideas are in the same vein.

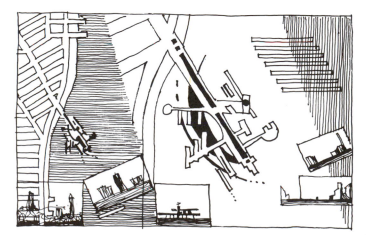

USE OF DIAGONAL LAYOUT

FIG. 7.28

PROPORTIONS AND PLACEMENT

Proportions that relate to mathematics have been around for a long time. The Classical Greeks developed proportions into the "golden section" in the fifth century B.C., Albert Dürer used another system to analyze the alphabet in the fifteenth century, and Le Corbusier invented a system he called "the Modular" for architecture. All systems are based on what individuals or a society find visually appealing at a given time. Proportions for the female figure prove the point: Classical Greek statues look different from Rubens' paintings of women, which differ from contemporary high-fashion models. Le Corbusier spoke the truth when he talked about the Modular: If it doesn't look right, don't use it.

That architects prefer proportions similar to their own bodies is one intriguing, but never-proven theory. H.H. Richardson designed many outstanding heavily proportioned buildings in 19th-century America. He weighed over 300 lbs. Certainly, with Wright this also seems to be true. He was a short man and most of his houses hug the ground. Wright also used low ceilings as a spatial surprise for forthcoming taller spaces. He even changed conventional building details to obtain the proportions he preferred. Exterior soffits are normally attached to ceiling joists that run from the inside out, but Wright broke with tradition and lowered exterior soffits so that his buildings would have a lower proportion of height to length.

The decision of where to place a drawing on the page should involve the elements of figure/ground, tension, balance, and proportion—all of which should be measured with a developed eye rather than formula.

Architectural pages are usually horizontal for two reasons: First, the human field of vision is similar to a horizontal ellipse (more wide than high); and second, the majority of buildings are longer or wider than they are high, with the obvious exception of tall buildings.

A single drawing balanced around the center lines of a page tends to be static and uninteresting, while placing it in a slightly unbalanced location is more dynamic. Moving a single drawing either higher or lower on the page, while keeping it asymmetrically balanced about the center line, is less dynamic yet more comfortable for some viewers.

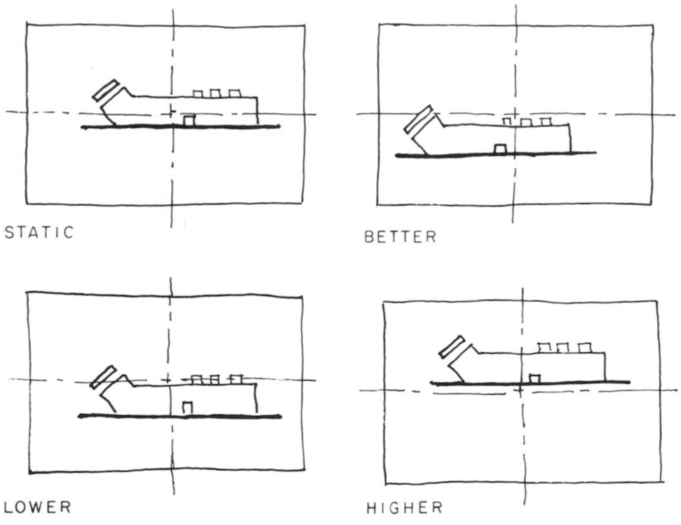

STATIC

BETTER

LOWER

HIGHER

FIG. 7.29

LINEWORK

Differential lineweight was explained and used in earlier chapters 2, 4, and 5 to establish spatial depth. There, the technique was applied to working drawings and presentation illustrations, yet there are still other options for lineweight usages.

The perspectives of Wright's Rhodes House showed profiling to form negative spaces. Heavy outlining of the building's silhouette alone is an old method still used today by a few drafters. This technique was applied in Fig. 7.30 to a tracing of a photograph of Strawberry Hill, a seventeenth-century Gothic Revival castle in England.

It is also possible to devise a method that profiles only certain elements, achieving a two-dimensional pattern unrelated to profiling or spatial indications. In his whimsical drawings of celebrities and entertainers, illustrator Al Hirschfeld has employed many uses of lines, including varying the thickness of a curved line to accentuate the curvature.

In the realm of theory, artist and Bauhaus instructor Paul Klee wrote *Pedagogical Sketchbook* in 1923, after taking charge of the foundation program. In this classic book, Klee postulates that a point moves to become a line, the lines move to form a plane, and a plane moves to generate a mass or volume.

STRAWBERRY HILL

FIG. 7.30

TITLES AND TYPOGRAPHY

Unlike other graphic situations, titles and typography in architectural presentations should be subordinate to drawings when architectural content, rather than process, is the object. This is not to say that titles are not important, because they are. An analogy to a sculptural work is appropriate: If the work has a base, the base should be less notable than the sculpture.

Title blocks are often used in both architectural and engineering practice. Engineers, seldom concerned with graphic design, simply box in the information. Architects, on the other hand, avoid the engineering approach. If title blocks are used to give consistency to architectural presentations, the box can be eliminated in favor of a line above or below the information. When the information is lengthy, the line can be stretched along the page bottom.

Architectural working drawings have boxed-in title blocks organized with a practical graphic design strategy. A set of working drawings is always bound on the left-hand edge with the title of the project and the architect's name parallel to the binding edge. The reason for this is that drawings are rolled for storage, and the main titles must be visible when rolled. Sheet titles and page numbers, like all other information, are done horizontally for normal reading when the set is in use.

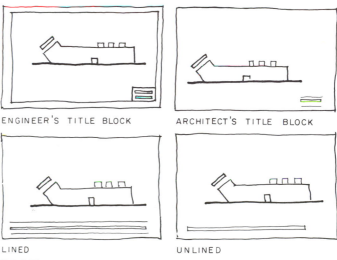

ENGINEER'S TITLE BLOCK   ARCHITECT'S TITLE BLOCK

LINED   UNLINED

FIG. 7.31

ASYLUM FOR THE MENTALLY HEALTHY
MEDEA & VAN GOGH, ARCHITECTS

EXTERIOR DETAILS   23 OF 56

WORKING DRAWINGS

FIG. 7.32

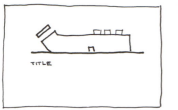 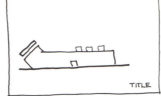

APPROPRIATE WEIGHT   ASYMMETRICAL BALANCED

FIG. 7.33

Visual weight and balance are two key considerations when titles are not used in a block. A title that is too heavy will pull the viewer's eye away from the drawing, the most important element on the page.

Slightly heavier title weight can be used if the title is asymmetrically balanced with the drawing. Visual weight is determined by the size of the font and its lightness or boldness. Lighter fonts can be made larger without becoming visually dominant. A drawing with grays and blacks will support a heavier title, and visual weight for line drawings should be lighter than the drawing itself.

Besides titles, written information, such as explanations of architectural process or design, sometimes accompanies drawings. Unlike text for magazines, advertising, and posters, printed material should be, like borders and titles, in a subordinate key.

Before World War II, architects hand-lettered drawings. Since then, press-on letters, stencils, templates, and lettering machines have become preferred alternatives. Computers have also greatly expanded design options, while saving considerable time.

The spacing between lines (known as leading in printing and computer graphics programs) should be less than the height of letters. This generates tension between lines, which, in turn, ensures both readability and the visual effect of seeing of a body of print. If the spacing is greater, each line reads distinctly separate and the graphic body is lost (poetry is often done this way). Less spacing, similar to two lines close together, emphasizes the graphic body of the text, but makes text less readable.

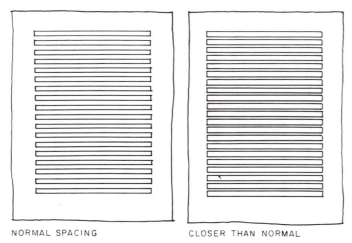

NORMAL SPACING   CLOSER THAN NORMAL

FIG. 7.34

Text can be flush left with a common margin and paragraphs indicated by the space between them. Many consider this style to be modern. Indenting paragraphs is an older, yet widely accepted practice. Whether to justify (align) the right side of copy has both pluses and minuses. If the right is justified, the space between words must be made uneven, thereby affecting readability. If the right is not justified, readability is ensured but the graphic block gets destroyed. Designers seem to prefer the former, providing the column width is not too narrow (the narrower the column, the fewer words per line and the more the space between words must be adjusted).

Typography—the style of printed material—extends beyond considerations of justifying margins and leading. Students, architects, and drafters should be aware of how copy is handled. An advertisement for beer uses printed material differently than one for high-fashion women's clothing, and neither resemble what would be used in a textbook or corporate report. Observing the usage of type in non-architectural sources will help spark ideas for architectural graphics.

Magazines, for instance, sometimes use a large capital letter to begin a paragraph, but this would be too eye-catching for normal architectural presentations. However, the same idea could be employed by using a larger but more subdued beginning letter or "initial cap." Variations can be mixed with margin alignment. In the example on the right above, only the beginning sentences of each major section are indented and start with a larger capital letter. There is no extra space between paragraphs; the distinction is made by not justifying the last sentence on the right.

Typeface, font, and style are terms used to describe particular letter faces. Ever since Western writing was invented in Mesopotamia some four or five thousand years ago, the typography has been a major design concern. Examples of serif letters (letters with curved or straight stroke marks at the beginning and/or end) were used in ancient Rome, and sans serif (without strokes) can be seen on marble inscriptions in Greece made before the birth of Christ.

Serif letters became the dominant typefaces until designers from the De Stijl group, the Russian revolutionaries, and the Bauhaus started designing new sans serif alphabets. These groups from the 1920s preferred the simplicity and purity of sans serif letters. Sans serif became, and still is, considered the modern choice by most architects.

There are literally hundreds of letter faces available for press-on letters, computer programs, and printing. A particular face may have one name from one source, and the same face, or a near-duplicate, will be called something else by another source. All faces are always available in different point sizes and often in bold, light, extended (wider), condensed (narrow), and outline (hollow).

Helvetica, a 1960s Swiss-designed font, was popular among architects for its crispness and neutrality. Because this style of letter is very legible, it is often used for building signage. Helvetica's neutrality prevents it from having a distinctive character.

Helvetica Bold has a heavy appearance and is hardly ever used in architectural graphics. The light version is more visually appealing to architects than either Helvetica or Helvetica Bold.

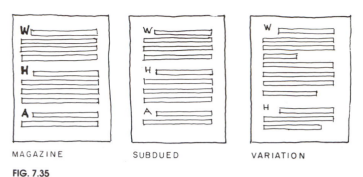

MAGAZINE   SUBDUED   VARIATION

FIG. 7.35

SANS SERIF   SERIF   SERIF

FIG. 7.36

HELVETICA

HELVETICA BOLD

HELVETICA LIGHT

FIG. 7.37

AAABCDEFGHIJKLM
MNOPQRSTUVW
WWWXYZ & abcde
efghijklmnopqrstuvv
wwwxyyz 1234567

AVANT GARDE GOTHIC LIGHT

FIG. 7.38

ABCDEabcde

EUROSTILE EXTENDED

FIG. 7.39

Avant Garde Gothic Light has more style than Helvetica Light, plus the advantage of different shapes for certain letters. Due to its style, Avant Garde Light can be used with lowercase letters only. Microgramma and Eurostile Extended (both similar) have become increasingly popular in graphic design. The font, with its block-like character, is architectural and structural-looking.

ABCDEFGHIJKLM

ELECTRONIC

FIG. 7.40

ABCDEFGHIJ

BROADWAY ENGRAVED

FIG. 7.41

ABCDEFabcdef

PACKING CASE

FIG. 7.42

Medea & Van Gogh - Architects
000 WEIRD WAY   TRANSYLVANIA, ROMANIA

COMBINED

FIG. 7.43

When selecting a letter style for a presentation, it should be compatible with the architectural design, or on rare occasions, contrast it. For instance, when a building has a high-tech thrust, a font similar to Electronic could be used. (NASA, by the way, is an excellent source for high-tech graphics.) Another building might make overt references to American Art Deco, and in this case Broadway Engraved would be appropriate. Should a building design have mixed parentage—exposed steel with wood—either a serif or sans serif font would be equally good.

Architects admire certain other architects and sometimes emulate their graphics. Le Corbusier was a hero to many. "Corb" used packing-case stencils for project titles, and abbreviated the name of the project to three or four letters, accompanied by his own file number.

Fonts do not have to be the same, or even variations within the same family. Mixing lettering styles, as in the imaginary letterhead in Fig. 7.43, can add visual variety. The name of the firm is in American Typewriter Light with capitals and lowercase letters. A much smaller and darker Microgramma face, only in capitals, balances the lighter American Typewriter above. The line separating the two intentionally touches the "g" in the architects' names. The American Typewriter with capitals and lowercase letters is traditional, but the font is lighter than normal, therefore providing a modern touch. This letterhead seems to say that this is a firm with a solid structural base, yet it also has a modern flair.

PERSPECTIVES AND RENDERING

Perspective drawing is neither a natural way of drawing nor an absolute representation of reality. If it were natural, children would begin drawing three-dimensional objects in perspective—but they don't. Their drawings look like paralines. If perspective were an absolute representation, it would not have taken tens of thousands of years for humankind to discover it. Perspective is a common, learned psychological convention.

Perspective as we know it was discovered by the Florentine architect Fillipo Brunelleschi in the early years of the fifteenth century Italian Renaissance. His discovery was rooted in the tradition of Western, rational thought, with the human being as the center of all things. Other cultures, however, have made their own representations of linear three dimensionality. In classical China, for instance, perspective was based on symbolic philosophy rather than Western photographic realism. In Chinese perspective, lines do not converge toward the horizon, but instead vanish to the observer's position, opening up the view to an infinite Cosmos.

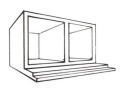

WESTERN PERSPECTIVE

FIG. 7.44

AXONOMETRIC

FIG. 7.45

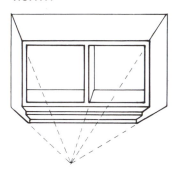

PERSPECTIVE FROM CHINA

FIG. 7.46

Western perspective also assumes that the viewer is in a fixed position, but early "perspectives" from India show multiple vanishing points and sometimes even multiple horizon lines. To the Western eye, these drawings look like failed attempts at perspective. This may be true, as Western influences were present in India at the time. There is also another creditable theory, namely that artists assumed the viewer was moving.

The late-Renaissance invention of anamorphic drawing does not even use straight lines. This type of drawing is intended to be viewed through any one of a number of devices—a half sphere, cylinder, cone, etc.—in order to appear "correct" to "our" way of visualizing.

Anamorphic drawing indirectly creates a paradox: The horizon in Western perspective is assumed to be a straight line, but both the earth (the horizon) and the human eyeball are curved.

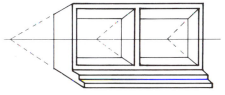

PERSPECTIVE FROM INDIA

FIG. 7.47

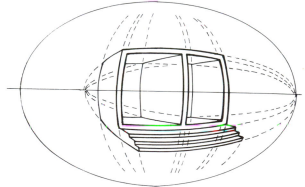

ANAMORPHIC PERSPECTIVE

FIG. 7.48

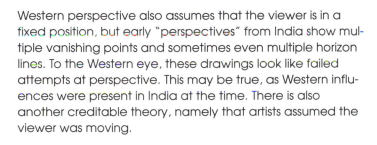

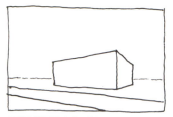

PERSPECTIVE PULL

FIG. 7.49

NEUTRALIZED

FIG. 7.50

When perspective lines converge at a sharp angle, the viewer's eye follows the lines off the page. This can be offset by placing a human figure, tree, or other vertical element across the converging lines. This forces the eye in another direction and lessens the perspective pull.

POOL OF LIGHT

FIG. 7.51

POOL OF LIGHT

FIG. 7.52

Professional renderers depict a building in a pool of light with a dark foreground shadow caused by an imaginary tree or cloud. The background is darker than the pool of light but lighter than the foreground. This technique originated in landscape painting.

FIG. 7.53

The line drawing in Fig. 7.53 does not use a pool of light, nevertheless, the compositional elements and treatments are worth repeating. (Drawings for this house have appeared on numerous pages in other chapters.) First, the perspective is located low on the page. Second, lineweight gets lighter for objects further back in space. Third, the borders are broken to allow the two-dimensional surface of the page to flow into the three-dimensional illusion. Fourth, the trees create a tall rhythmic overlap with other elements. Fifth, the strong perspective pull of the street is lessened by the foreground trees and ferns.

Multiviews, paralines, and perspectives are usually thought of as literal representations of reality, but presentations can vary from photorealism to abstraction. What balance to strike between the two depends on what is being communicated to whom and why.

If drawings are to be used by a shopping center developer to attract investors or shoppers, photorealism is close to mandatory. The "what" for this type of project involves lots of activity and people, convenience, up-to-date kitsch style, and the fun of shopping. An architecture editor of a theoretical publication would hardly be interested in the why or what of the previous project, but would instead focus on the serious architectural content behind the building design. A more abstract presentation would be appropriate in this case.

The majority of projects fall between the extremes, so that the what, whom, and why become inseparable.

Architects put human figures in drawings, if for no other reason than to help the viewer realize scale. The person and tree in Figs. 7.54 and 7.55 are treated differently. On the left is an example of near-photorealism, while the drawing on the right is abstract and sketchy. Either of these imbalanced thumbnails could be the basis for an elevation or perspective, but the one on the right would be sympathetic to a freehand drawing. The sketch on the left would work with either a freehand or hard line drawing. One alternative to this is to abstract the two objects even more and use them as a contrast to a hard line drawing.

LITERIAL

FIG. 7.54

ABSTRACTED

FIG. 7.55

A number of architects use a single figure as a symbol in a drawing. In Peter Eisenman's perspective in Fig. 7.56, the lone realistic figure is used to asymmetrically balance the composition. Drafters sometimes make the single figure in a drawing a famous architect. In Eisenman's drawing, the man is Mies van de Rohe. Mies' later buildings were normally symmetrically balanced with a column grid for infinite order. Many of Eisenman's buildings have highly intellectual, mathematical grids, so the reference to Mies is understandable.

Actual photographs can be integrated or computer-scanned into a drawing. Mies van de Rohe, for instance, integrated landscape photographs with some of his drawings. The final product had an eye-catching, surreal quality.

EISENMAN

FIG. 7.56

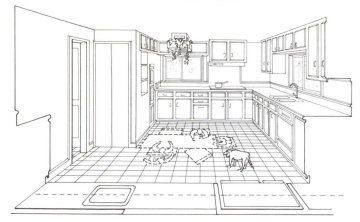

FIG. 7.57

The perspective on page 198, a competition entry from a facility for the mentally handicapped, combines a photograph with a perspective. The photography was done on a client-organized site visit; the two architects are looking at the proposed site. A photographic negative was printed on wash-off plastic drafting film and portions removed for the perspective. Fig. 7.57 shows a client's dog watching people and furniture. This abstraction is a humorous comment on the two-dimensional illusion of perspective. Note the foreground play between plan, section and perspective.

MOOD, TECHNIQUE, AND THEATRE

Line drawings have an abstract, neutral character suitable for most projects. However, there are occasions when this neutrality negates the essence of an architectural design.

The elevation pictured in Fig. 7.58 is for a World War II memorial dedicated to the Japanese-Americans who served in that war. (The site plan is on page 170 and other elevations are on page 36). The line elevations belie the design and the elevation shown here fortifies the architectural content. Mood and technique are the essential difference between the two.

Understanding the content of this memorial is essential to its appreciation. A dead tree is the major vertical element and this ancient, mythological Japanese symbol talks with a large existing rubber tree. Beneath the dead tree are its "fallen leaves"—metal plates inscribed with the names of soldiers who died. At the base of the dead tree is a metal sculpture made from weathering structural steel shapes. This type of steel rusts and stains surfaces. This sculpture is a near-literal translation of the flag raising at Iwo Jima. The line elevations capture the Iwo Jima image but lose the all-important staining effect, evocative of tears. (One could even find these drawings insulting because of this "omission.") The elevation in Fig. 7.58, on the other hand, is solemn in disposition, even though it lacks the power to stain. Mood and technique have been unified, and, perhaps, the drawings generate their own truth.

This elevation was pencil-rendered on an instant copy (Xerox) reduction from the line elevation. Note how the patchwork-quilt-like pencil strokes for the leaves are not literal representations of leaves, but their overall texture is. The ground cut in section also has a texture—circular strokes—and this technique has a compositional relationship with the tree texture. Although the metal sculpture is dark, a full range of values was used for the overall illustration. Consequently the drawing does not have a brooding mood.

FIG. 7.58

Presentations for school and professional projects include drawings, verbal, and, at times, written information; slide shows and videos are often included. Although not theatrical, one way to heighten slide shows is to use a 2 1/4" x 2 1/4" format. The quality of 2 1/4" is significantly better than 35 mm; negatives, slides and prints from the intermediate format are sharper and have richer, deeper tones. The cost, however, of cameras and projectors is many times the cost of 35 mm.

Another non-theatrical way to enhance presentation drawings is to appropriate someone else's drawing approach. "Developing your own style over time" is a misleading cliche, unintentionally made and sold to those who think design/drawing is only ego expression. In fact, no one "originates" style.

Students frequently adopt the drawing methods of architects they admire. Professionals do the same, but the best go deeper, often borrowing from non-architectural sources. In the 1960s, Kallman, Mc Kinnell, and Knowles appropriated Henry Moore's World War II subway sketches of people for their Boston City Hall competition drawings. Moore's sketches were compatible with both the heroic building design and drawings. From the same time period, an English group, Archigram, published comic books to promote their disposable, tongue-in-cheek, high-tech architectural fantasies. In other graphic pieces, they borrowed heavily from commercial advertising. Morphosis, an architectural firm from the 1980s and 1990s, used many sources and techniques for their provocative graphics. They practically originated (with help from the Cubists) composite drawings (see page 126 for similar drawings). Morphosis also directly borrowed from Escher, and their beautiful, post-design silkscreens influenced by the Russian Constructivists, explored old and new design directions.

From enhancement to theater is frequently a small step but one filled with problems: Theater can be both good and bad. Overdramatization can be unappealing if the design content does not warrant the spectacle.

The size of a drawing can be imposing. Beaux Arts drawings were as large as 20' x 26'. For a multi-level school project, the author drew the plans on a continuous 12" roll of paper that stretched over 15'. One student, when assigned a wall section for his three-story building, made the drawing full-sized and hung it out of a window for the reviewers.

Professional presentations are usually not so dramatic but can be even more powerful. Arata Isozaki, for example, designed a house of nine squares for a travelling exhibit. The drawings were engraved and embossed on 24"-square, 2"-thick steel plates.

ROUGHS AND DUPLICATES

All too often, architects, students, and drafters start drawing without any thought given to graphics; drawings more or less just land haphazardly on the page. It is far better to preplan than accept accident. A series of small thumbnail sketches, as small as 2" x 3", done freehand can be good preplanning. In these roughs, borders, balance, tension, positive/negative relationships, and values can be effectively studied. Presentation drawings are worth the time and effort.

Larger roughs are used for working drawings to plan which drawings will be where and on what page. Regardless of whether the drawings are done by hand or are computer-generated, the roughs serve as a necessary guide.

Presentations are usually done on "charrette." (The word is French and roughly means "hurry." The word "charrette" was stenciled on carts taking Beaux-Arts student drawings from their studios to school). One sound practice is to obtain drawing duplicates while on charrette in case of calamitous events (spilled ink or coffee, rain, cats, and dogs are notorious villains). Without a duplicate, drawings must be started all over again; important and valuable time is lost.

Whenever possible, rendering should be done on duplicates. This practice offers two advantages in addition to lessening the effects of total catastrophe: First, duplicates allow for experimentation with different methods; and second, spare copies can be used to make tests on an identical surface as the final drawing.

REPRODUCTION AND ORIGINALS

Reproduction methods are always changing, particularly as new software, digital methods, and interfaces become available. These and other technological advances sometimes make older processes obsolete and it is impossible to outguess future trends. By the time a person reads a paragraph in this section, the method described may be outmoded and replaced by something better. Nevertheless, graphics, drawing execution, and reproduction are intertwined. Not being aware of available processes severely limits graphic possibilities. With the above risks in mind, an understanding of current and traditional methods (excluding computer generations) is a good starting point.

Novices think of originals as drawings done on a piece of paper or plastic drafting film and reproduction as the process which produces copies. This is limited thinking based on a lack of knowledge. To offer a simple, dramatic example of another option, a drawing can be partially inked on plastic drafting film, photographically reversed onto another sheet of plastic drafting film, and drawing continued (the second sheet of film is known as a second-generation original). What were black-lines, areas of black, printing, and sticky-backed transfer tones, become white on black. In this example, which is the original?

Each successive generation loses some quality; the amount lost depends on how the first generation was done, what drawing surface was used, and the particular reproduction process employed. There would be very little loss in the example described above (ink on plastic drafting film photographically reversed). This second-generation original could be used for publication. Third-generation originals, regardless of process, have limited application.

There are two basic types of reproduction that affect how originals are made: opaque reproduction and transparent reproduction. When a drawing is executed with opaque reproduction in mind, white-out and white paint in ruling pens can be used for corrections. Correction fluids in a transparent process will end up as black areas. Additionally, any pencil smudges on the front or picked up on the back from the drafting board surface will print as gray on a duplicate. Regardless of these small drawbacks, there are some graphic benefits with transparent reproduction. Linework, such as column grids, can be put on the back of a sheet; you can then draw on the front side and erase without disturbing the grid. Reverse duplicates (printing the front on the back) provide similar opportunities: furniture, mechanical ductwork, etc. may be added and erased on the front while keeping the drawing on the back undisturbed.

Contact printing and enlargement/reduction are two other reproduction basics. Contact printing is, as the name implies, when the original is printed in direct contact with the eventual duplicate. Contact is made by simply placing the original over a light-sensitive material (the eventual duplicate) and adding a piece of glass over both, or by using a vacuum frame to ensure maximum contact.

Enlargement and reduction require optics; the better the optics, the better the reproduction. When drawings are reduced for portfolios and the like, the drafter must account for problems inherent in the process. Closely spaced lines, when reduced, tend to be visually darker (more tension between them) or to become one when the image is greatly reduced. The drafter should compensate by not drawing lines that might close in with other lines.

The more a drawing is enlarged, the more quality will suffer. The opposite is also true: the closer in size to the original, the closer the quality. Reduction noticeably lessens drafting errors, while enlargement magnifies. (Magnification is not necessarily a bad thing. Pencil illustrations drawn on rough drawing surfaces and then enlarged will have a nice grainy quality). Enlargements by the instant-copy process are inexpensive, the quality is often good, and large reproductions can be presented. (Originals are made smaller, which takes less time.) One practical strategy for high-quality presentations and reductions is to make the drawings at an intermediate size, enlarge them, add detail for presentation, and reduce the originals for portfolio.

Line and continuous-tone have fundamental differences that interface with reproduction methods.

Line, as a reproduction word, means any pure black and white illustration—in other words, no grays. Plastic-backed transfer tones, despite having tone, are considered line originals. Large areas of black are also line for reproduction purposes. Continuous-tone originals employ a range of grays. Paintings and pencil-shaded drawing are continuous-tone. Different reproduction techniques are used for line and continuous-tone work.

THE DIAZO PROCESS

By far the most used and least expensive line duplicates are made with the diazo process. Only contact printing is used and the quality of the print is determined by the degree of transparency (vellum is only 85-90% transparent and plastic drafting film is close to 100%) and the density of the original linework (ink is close to 100% opaque, and the density of pencil depends on the grade of lead used and the pressure applied when drawing). Continuous tones reproduce poorly.

Final prints made with the diazo process are positive reproductions (black on the original appears black on the print). When printing, the original is placed on top of an emulsion-coated paper and the two are then run through a large machine. The combination is first exposed to light, then to ammonia fumes which develop the print. Originals with faint linework have to be run through the machine at a slower speed (more exposure) in order to capture the image. An overall, unwanted gray background comes with this increased exposure.

Various kinds of emulsion-coated paper or film can be run through the machine, but 20# blue is commonly used. Two or three other colors are standard and 32# brown or black-line presentation prints, suitable for pencil shading or markers, can be had at slightly greater expense. Diazo sepias are second-generation, same-sized transparencies that can be corrected with a special fluid or eraser (a sepia is less transparent than vellum).

Taping a piece of vellum or other material over an original will decrease transparency and can be used to generate intentional gray areas—backgrounds for plans, elevations, paralines, etc. (It is difficult to obtain exact alignment.) Tape should be applied to only one edge, parallel to the longest dimension of the page. The reason for this is that the original and emulsion-coated paper must go over a roller in the machine, and the difference in diameter between the two is enough to rip them apart if taped on two edges. Machine operators always feed originals into the machine with the longest dimension as the leading edge.

Following are other characteristics of diazo printing:

1. Neither opaque nor rigid originals can be reproduced.
2. Some people mistakenly refer to diazo prints as blueprints. They're not. A blueprint has white lines on a dark blue background. Blueprinting is nearly obsolete.
3. Since prints are paper, shrinkage of up to 1/16" in 30" may occur. This may or may not be critical.
4. Prints fade over time. The more exposure to direct sunlight, the quicker the prints will fade.
5. Maximum input: 48" by any length (from rolls).
6. Print paper comes in standard sizes. The size of originals should match one of these standards if a large quantity of printing is expected. (For short printing runs, diazo prints can be trimmed.)
7. For maximum accuracy, diazo printing can be done in a vacuum frame.

PHOTOGRAPHY

Still photography is the oldest modern reproduction method. Etching and engraving are, of course, older, but with the exception of printing money and a few other applications, these two reproduction methods are little used. Traditional photography is based on reflected light from an object passing through a lens to expose grains of silver on a negative. The negative is then developed and contact-printed or enlarged onto photographic paper. Digital photography, commercially available since the late 1980s or early 1990s, uses an entirely different process and will probably replace traditional silver-based photography.

Because of its long history, still photography, of all the reproduction methods, has the richest library of techniques available for both artistic and commercial applications. Like any process, a little knowledge about it allows a lot of freedom. For example, the first-generation original for the site plan on page 170 was drawn with ink on plastic drafting film and the second-generation original was a matte- (versus glossy-) finished photographic contact print. The pencil work was done on this second generation original. (Matte print surfaces have varying degrees of "tooth," or texture, according to what manufacturer makes the product. Tooth is necessary for pencil shading and, conversely, a smooth surface will not take pencil shading.)

Photographing onto photosensitive plastic film is another method for producing a second-generation original (the uncoated version of this film is the same as plastic drafting film and commonly known by the trade name Mylar™). The photosensitive Mylar™, when exposed and developed, is a transparency, either positive or negative, and available as either fixed or wash-off. Photosensitive Mylar™ is primarily responsive to black; exposure to continuous tones will drop out light grays and medium grays darken. Close approximations of continuous tones are made by placing a halftone screen (usually black lines on plastic) over the film in a vacuum frame before exposure. Tones are consequently broken up into a pattern of smaller or larger positive, roughly square, dots.

The perspective on page 198 uses the above process. First, a medium format, 2 1/4 x 2 1/4" negative of the site was enlarged onto a 10"-square positive wash-off Mylar™ using a coarse 65-line halftone screen. Second, a line perspective was drawn on a vellum overlay. Third, the wash-off was then put over the perspective and pertinent areas removed with a wet electric eraser. Fourth, the perspective was traced with a 4 x 0 (.18 mm.) pen. Fifth, 65-line screened sticky-backed transfer tones, varying from 20% to 70%, were applied to create the second-generation original.

Fig. 7.59 shows a true-sized photographic print from a portion of the 10" square original showing the coarser screen. This print was reduced for this book and enlarged 100% for presentation (equivalent to 20" square with a 33-line screen).

A segment of the 20" square photograph is shown in Fig. 7.60. At the normal reading distance of 10" to 16", the close-up appears too grainy, but at 8' to 15' the grain and drafting errors are not noticeable. Always consult with someone at a high-quality reprographics house before attempting the technique described above. Computer scanning accomplishes the same results as above with much less effort.

Halftone screens are used in all black-and-white offset printing. The lines per inch vary from 55 lines to 300. As the screen gets finer, detail becomes sharper and blacks blacker. A 65-line screen is standard for newspapers (the paper is cheap and coarse), whereas a 133-line is used in book publication, and 300-line, used in some fine-arts books, requires special inks and papers. Eighty-five to 100 lines per inch is the finest that will be reproduced by the instant copy process (commonly known by the trade name Xerox). Special-effect screens are available for conversion of continuous-tone originals to halftones and, if judiciously used, can have creative applications for architectural graphics. Color printing also uses screens. Originals are shot with four negatives—three for the primary printing colors and another for black. In the final product, each color is printed separately, generating a fine matrix of closely spaced dots.

There are two types of negatives, one sensitive to only line (black) and the other sensitive to continuous-tone. When continuous-tone originals are photographed, the white of the paper or board will reproduce as an unrepresentative light gray, which reduces graphic punch. This gray can be removed in the photographic process and the final halftone is known as a halftone dropout. (All reproductions of pencil drawings in this book are dropout halftones.)

FIG. 7.59

FIG. 7.60

DO-IT-YOURSELF PHOTOGRAPHY

Every architect and student must, at times, take photographs of buildings, models, or drawings. There are few problems with slide developing but prints (unless you are short on time or money) should be made by photographic or reprographic houses. While snapshots of Aunt Martha at her birthday party, developed at the local one-hour service, may look fine, chemicals are often not fresh (color tones will be out of balance: the white of a drawing will be slightly yellow or blue). There is a dramatic difference between prints made by a do-it-yourself photographer and those done by a house. Amateurs take a negative and then to obtain a print, the negative must be enlarged. Photographic houses shoot the negative at final print size and contact print, thereby eliminating quality loss caused by passing the image through an enlarging lens. Even more important, the amateur has limited abilities, equipment, and materials.

Here are some important things to know when taking photographs in 35-mm:

1. Alignment of the film plane and the original is critical. If the two are not perfectly aligned, parallel lines in the drawing will converge on the print and right angles will not end up as right angles. (Professional houses use a vacuum frame and camera on a track; both are perfectly parallel to one another). A 35-mm camera with a removable viewfinder allows for the use of a gridded screen. Right angles in the drawing can be aligned with the film.
2. Macro lenses are designed for maximum sharpness at close focusing distances and are corrected the most for flatness. If possible, borrow or rent a macro.
3. Always use a tripod to avoid camera shake.
4. Always use a cable release or camera timer to avoid camera shake.
5. Color and black-and-white film are both rated by an ISO speed (printed on the box and cartridge). The lower the speed, the sharper the picture. Kodachrome slide film, rated at either ISO 25 or 64, still produces the truest colors and sharpest results (Japanese color films tend to be brighter).
6. Color films are also rated in degrees Kelvin for the response to different light sources. Daylight is 5,600° K, a perfect incandescent lightbulb is 3,200° K, and a photoflood, 3,400° K. The light source and film must be matched. (Conversion filters that screw over the lens are available to change one light source to another temperature or light source.)
7. When artificial light is used for copying drawings, at least two cheap photographic clamp lamps should be set at 45° to the original, exactly equal distances from each other and the center of what is being photographed.
8. A large piece of white material should be used when photographing a model. This bounces light back into the shade side of the object.
9. Concerning exposure, all camera and hand-held meters are standardized for 18% gray. If you shoot a white

object and take a meter reading off of it, the photograph will show the white as 18% gray. Likewise, a black object will turn out as 18% gray if metered the same way. The palm of a human hand is close to 18%, regardless of a person's color. An 18% gray card, available at all decent camera stores, is an absolute source for taking meter readings. Always measure from the card and take one exposure at that reading, one with a half-stop more exposure and one with one half-stop less. This practice is known as bracketing and ensures a perfect exposure.

10. It is advisable to have film developed shortly after exposure because the color balances shift with time.

PHOTOGRAPHY WITHOUT NEGATIVES

Photostats are black-and-white photographic prints made without negatives. They cost roughly one-half to one-third the cost of a negative/print and, under most circumstances, produce equal results. For architects and students, photostats are an inexpensive alternative for portfolios and submissions for publication.

In this process, originals are enlarged or reduced onto line-sensitive paper in a vacuum frame. Halftone screens are sandwiched between the glass and print paper when reproducing continuous-tone originals. Dropout prints can also be made and the quality is better than an unscreened continuous-tone print made from a negative; the whites are not light gray.

The following are important things to know about photostats:

1. Photostatic services are usually not included in reprographic or photographic houses.
2. Firms that provide quality photostats are difficult to find and often not listed in the Yellow Pages. Consult with a reprographics company to find locations.
3. Only one print is available per shot, therefore, if many prints are needed, the cost of negative/prints is less.
4. Line photostats are acceptable for publication, including this book, but screened "stats" are not.

PHOTOGRAPHIC VERSUS REPROGRAPHIC COMPANIES

Professional photographic houses normally do commercial work for advertising, and reprographic firms are generally geared for architectural and engineering reproductions. The latter provide, at least, the following services: Diazo printing, photographics, xerography, color-laser copying, megachromes (full digital printing, including computer-disk readouts), and CAD support. Photographic houses usually do not provide as full a range of services as reprographic firms do, and probably neither has photostatic services.

Both can provide valuable advice before you create presentations, as well as suggestions on how best to reproduce work after completion. This cannot be overemphasized: Answers to questions expand knowledge and knowledge expands opportunities.

ORGINAL

FIG. 7.61

INSTANT COPY

FIG. 7.62

LASER COPY

FIG. 7.63

THE INSTANT-COPY PROCESS

"Instant copy" has been used in previous chapters to avoid the common proprietary name Xerox. Other manufacturers such as IBM, Canon, and Kodak also make instant-copy machines. An older model from one manufacturer sometimes produces better-quality copies than a newer machine from the same company. No single manufacturer produces the best-performing machine over time.

The best performance and quality should not be confused with convenience features like sorting and stapling. Standard machines deposit toner onto 8 1/2" x 11", 8 1/2" x 14" (legal), and 11" x 17" paper. Paper weights vary from typical 20# bond to 110# card stock in white plus color. Any customer-provided paper within these weight limitations—including brown wrapping, special drawing, watercolor, or gridded paper—can be printed on, if the shop or operator will do it. The majority of machines will enlarge to 200% and reduce by 50%.

In the opaque process of instant copying, the machine reads the original and deposits toner in a number of different ways. Standard machines do not reproduce continuous tones well. An original and instant copy from a standard machine are shown in Figs. 7.61 and 7.62.

Laser copies from machines that make digital readouts produce good-quality reproductions (Fig. 7.63), but the cost is significantly higher. Normal copies cost pennies, while laser copies cost dollars.

For presentations, brochures and portfolios, a screen dropout photostat produces even better and less expensive instant copies on a standard machine than from a laser machine.

The author has used a flexible brochure system based on instant copies of dropout, screened photostats for years. All projects show one page with an illustration and text plus additional pages oriented to what aspects a potential client might be interested in. The brochures are individually made up and spiral-bound, including or excluding projects with contracted or expanded presentations. The quality is excellent, flexibility is unlimited, and cost is low.

Fig. 7.64 shows an instant copy from a standard instant-copy machine of the perspective on page 198, same size as the original. Fig. 7.65 is the 200% version (100% enlargement). These examples can be compared with the photographs on page 221. There is very little quality difference but the instant copy is far cheaper.

INSTANT COPY FROM 10" ORGINAL

FIG. 7.64

Instant-copy machines are available that reduce or enlarge onto 36"-wide by any- length bond or erasable vellum paper. Architects often use these machines to reduce working drawing for reproducible "record" sets.

INSTANT COPY ENLARGEMENT TO 200%

FIG. 7.65

APPENDIX

The following descriptive problems are ordered by type in the same sequence as Chapter Two. In a few instances, principles that preceed the sequence must be applied and, consequently, are referenced to the applicable page number. Although accuracy is important, comprehension is even more important.

All solutions can be drawn within the space provided if carefully located. Four-inch triangles are convenient for drawing and an adjustable triangle is highly recommended. Where orientation may be difficult, titles have been underlined. Many problems can be solved by measuring and remeasuring or by using dimension transfer lines. If not indicated otherwise, select one method and show the process of construction. Show all projection lines in light lineweight, label all points in drawings according to the description given on pg. 44, and title all new views. Also, letter all true-length lines in both given and new views.

ABBREVIATIONS USED:

Bot	bottom
C.P.	crossing point
dimen.	dimension or dimensions
dimen trans line	dimension transfer line
EL.	elevation
ht.	height
INCL. V.	inclined view
L.I.	line of intersection
meas.	measure
pg.	page
P.I.	point of intersection
pt.	point
ref.	reference
remeas.	remeasure
rt.	right
T.L.	true length
T.S.	true size

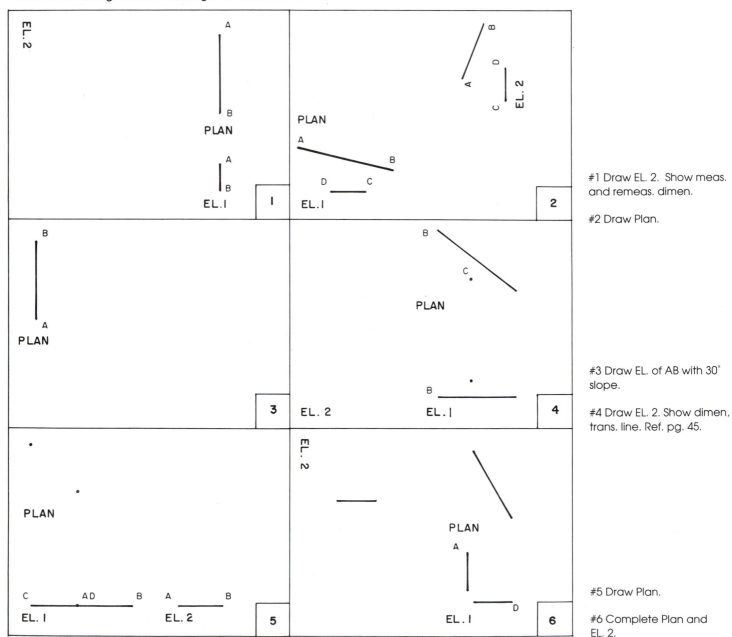

#1 Draw EL. 2. Show meas. and remeas. dimen.

#2 Draw Plan.

#3 Draw EL. of AB with 30° slope.

#4 Draw EL. 2. Show dimen. trans. line. Ref. pg. 45.

#5 Draw Plan.

#6 Complete Plan and EL. 2.

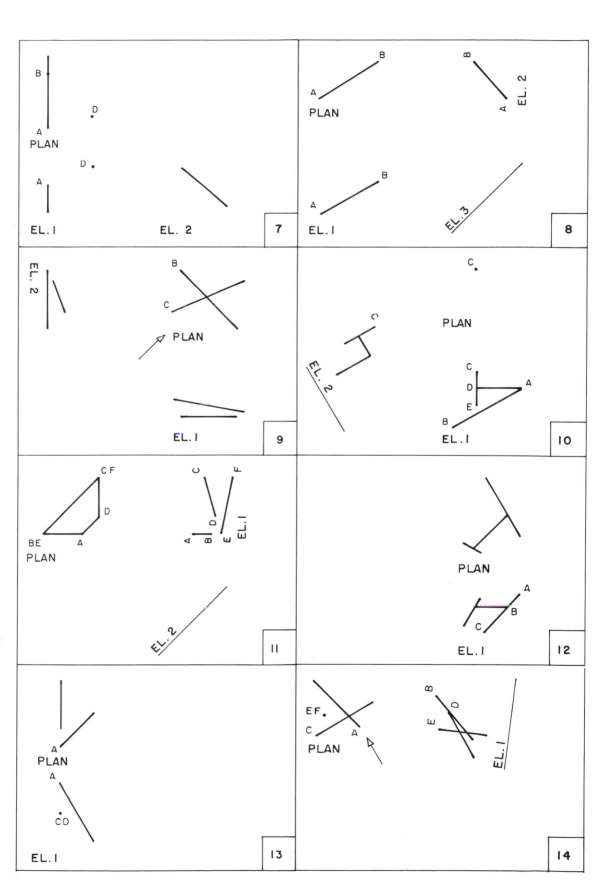

#7 Complete Plan, EL. 1, and EL. 2. Show dimen. trans. line.

#8 Draw EL. 3. Show ht. dimens.

#9 Draw EL. 3 in direction shown. Show ht. dimens.

#10 Draw Plan.

#11 Draw EL. 2. Show dimen. trans. line.

#12 Draw an EL. in which line ABC is T.L. Project from Plan.

#13 Draw an EL. in which line AB is T.L.

#14 Draw an EL. in direction shown. Show dimen. trans. line.

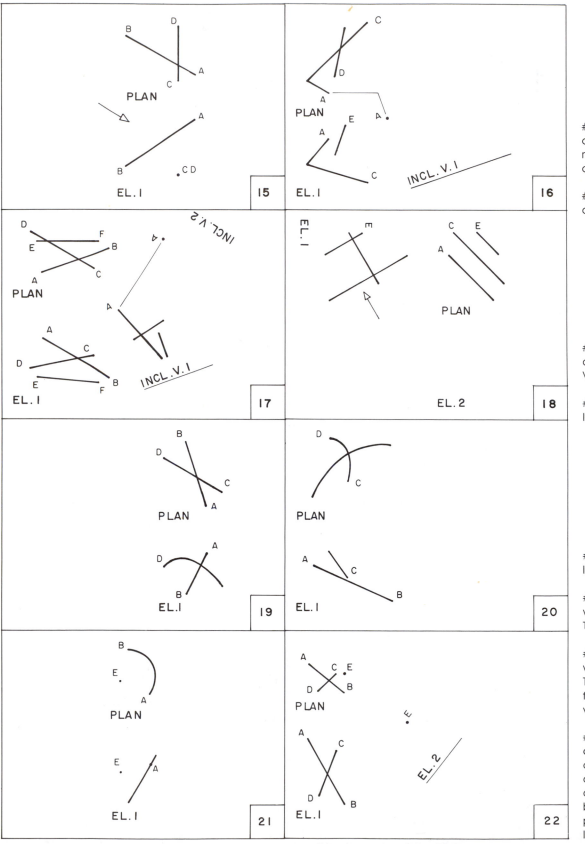

#15 Draw an INCL. V. in direction shown. Show meas. and remeas. dimens.

#16 Draw INCL. V. 1. Show dimens. trans. line.

#17 Draw INCL. V. 2. Show dimens. in EL.1 and INCL. V. 2.

#18 Draw EL. 2 and an INCL. V. in direction shown.

#19 Draw an EL. in which line AB has a 30˚ slope.

#20 Draw an INCL. V. in which curve CD is T.L. and T.S.

#21 Draw an INCL. V. In which curve AB is T>L. and T.S. Draw a rt. angle line from curve to point E in all views. Ref. pg. 57.

#22 Draw EL. 2. Show dimen. trans. line. Then draw an INCL. V. in which a line starting at point E is at rt. angles to CD. Show back projection to complete all views with dashed line. Ref pg. 49.

In the problems on this page, graphically show your test for flatness of all planes. If there is no test, letter reason for flatness or non-flatness. In parentheses following Elevation title, letter whether the view looks at the bottom or top of the plane.

#23 Draw any flat plane in EL.

#24 Show test for flatness.

#25 Draw any flat trapezoid in EL. 1. Ref pg. 87.

#26 Draw any flat plane in Plan.

#27 Draw any flat plane in EL. Show ht. dimens.

#28 Draw any flat plane in Plan. Show dimens. in plane at rt. angles to EL. image plane.

#29 If plane is flat, draw EL. 2. Show meas. and remeas. dimens.

#30 If plane is flat, draw EL. 2. Show dimen. trans. line.

#31 Draw EL. 2, if plane is flat.

#32 If plane is flat, draw INCL. V.1.

#33 If plane is flat, draw EL. 1 and an INC V. in direction shown.

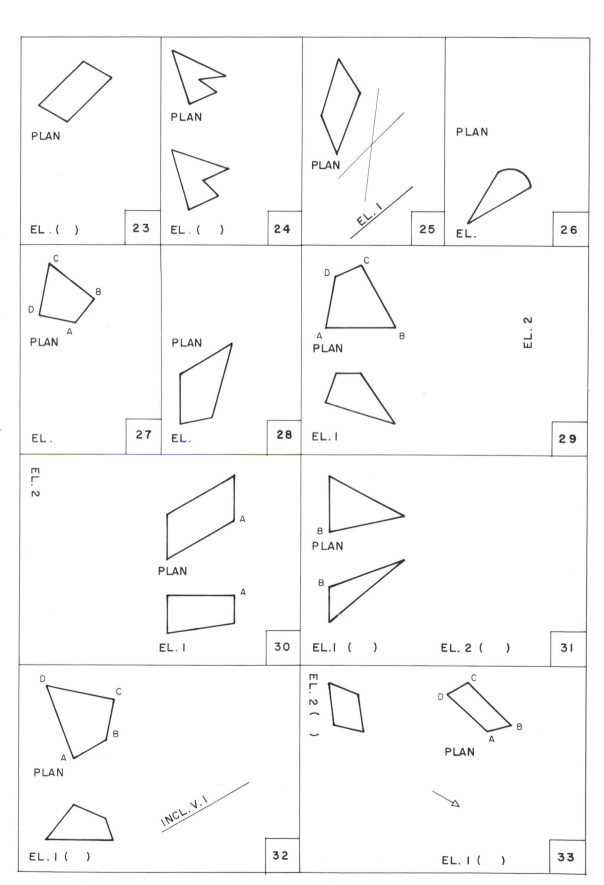

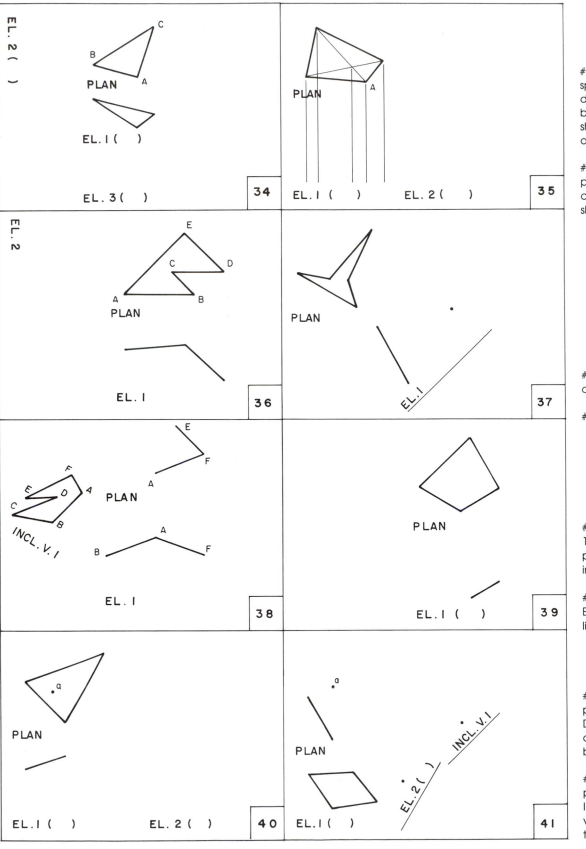

#34 Draw EL. 2 that corresponds to EL. 1. If EL. 1 depicts either the top or bot. of plane, draw EL. 3 showing opposite surface of plane.

#35 In EL. 1 draw any flat plane. Show ht. dimen. chosen. Draw EL. 2 and show consequent dimen.

#36 Using imaginary lines, complete EL. 1.

#37 Complete EL. 1.

#38 Complete Plan and EL. 1. Solve points B and C by projection before employing imaginary lines.

#39 Draw any flat plane in EL. 1 and construct a T.L. line in Plan.

#40 Complete any flat plane in EL. 1 and EL. 2. Draw a T.L. line in all views and transfer point a to both EL.

#41 Complete any flat plane in Plan, EL. 2 and INCL. V.1. Draw a T.L. in all views and transfer point a to all views.

#42 Draw T.S. view of plane.

#43 Draw T.S. view of plane.

#44 Draw T.S. view of plane and label all new pts. EL. 1.

#45 Draw a T.S. trapezoid and Plan to match. Ref.pg. 87.

#46 Draw T.S. view of plane. Show dimens.

#47 Draw T.S. view of plane. Show dimens.

#48 Draw T.S. bot. view of rt. triangle ABC. Ref. pg. 86. Then draw Plan and EL. 2 to match. Show dimens.

#49 Draw T.S. view of plane. Show dimens.

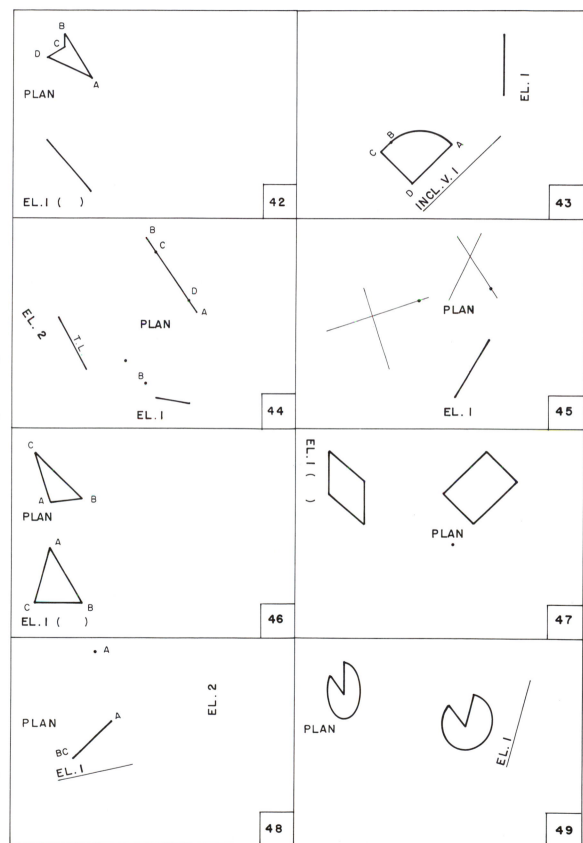

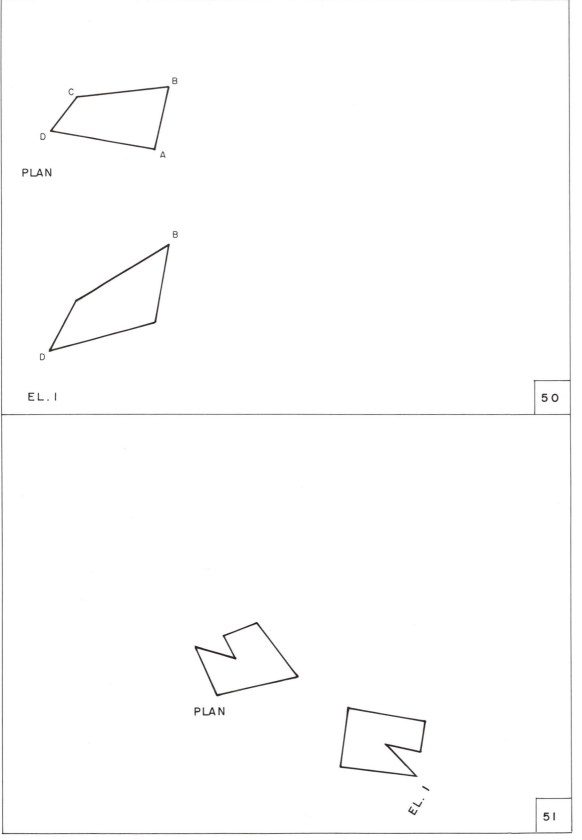

PLAN

B

C

D

A

B

D

EL. 1

50

#50 Establish a T.L. line in EL. 1 and then draw a T.S. view of plane. Show both dimens. and dimen. trans. lines.

PLAN

EL. 1

51

#51 Establish a T.L. line in Plan and draw T.S. view of plane. Show both dimens and dimen. trans. lines.

In the problems that follow, correct the given drawings to correspond with solutions. Indicate back projections with long dashed lines. Ref. pg. 57.

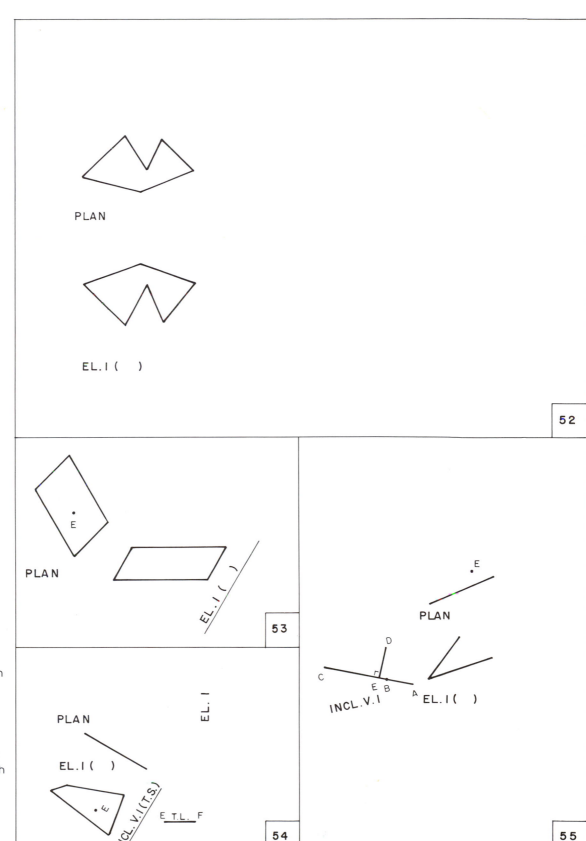

PLAN

EL. I (   )

52

#52 Draw T.S. view of plane. Show both dimens. and dimen. trans. lines.

PLAN

EL. I (   )

53

PLAN

EL. I (   )

53 Construct the direction of a line perpendicular to plane at pt. E.

#54 Draw T.L. line EF at rt. angles to plane in Plan and EL. 1. Then draw EL. 2. Pt. E is on plane. Show both dimens. and dimen. trans line.

#55 Draw line ED in both Plan and EL. 1 of triangle ABC.

PLAN

EL. I

INCL. V. I (T.S.)

E T.L. F

54

E

PLAN

D

C   E   B   A   EL. I (   )

INCL. V. I

55

Reminder: Lines or planes hidden by a closer plane are indicated by short dashed lines. Ref. pg. 58. When given drawings are corrected to show the solution, use this indication as well as back projections.

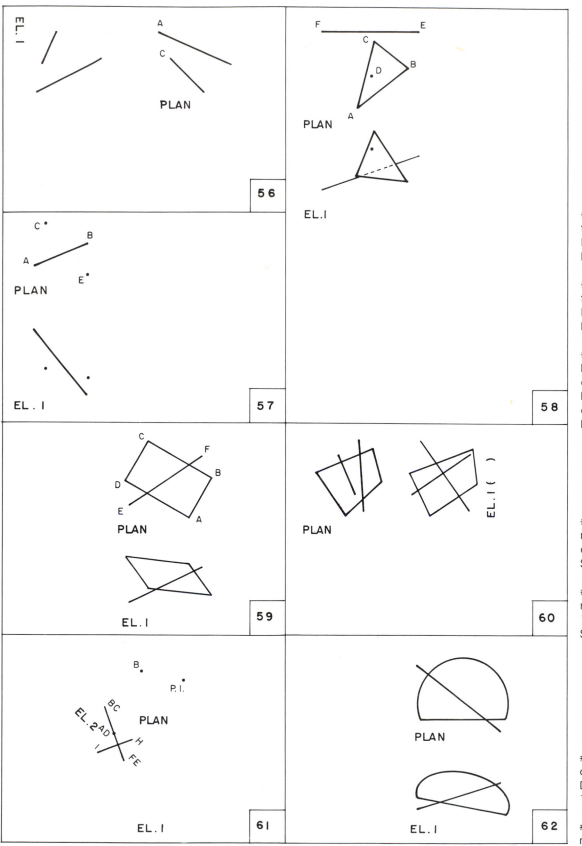

#56 Draw shortest distance from pt. A to line CD. Distance does not have to be T. L.

#57 Draw rt-angled lines from pt. C and E to line AB. Distance does not have to be T. L.

#58 By establishing a T.L. line in El. 1, draw a rt.-angled line from pt. D to line EF in all dwgs. Show all dimens. and dimen. trans. lines plus visibility test.

#59 Using the edge view method, find P.I. of line EF and parallelogram ABCD. Show visibility test.

#60 Using edge view method from T.L. line in EL. 1, find P.I. for both lines. Show visibility.

#61 EL. 2 is an edge view of a hexagon. Ref. pg. 87. Draw Inc. V., Plan, and EL. 1 showing line HI and its P.I.

#62 Using the edge view method, find F.I.

Problems #66, #67, and #68 involve finding the L.I. between planes by the edge view method. Use differential lineweight in final drawings to indicate spacial relationships.

#63 Using cutting plane method, draw P.I.

#64 Using cutting plane method, draw P.I.

#65 Using cutting plane method, draw P.I.

#66 Label points and T.L. lines. Identify top or bot. of EL. 1 and EL. 2. Then using edge view method, draw L.I.

#67 Label points and T.L. line. Identify top or bot. of EL. 1. Then using the edge view method, find L.I. and complete views.

#68 Label points. Identify top or bot. of EL. 1. Then using the edge view method, draw L.I. Finally, construct T.S. of plane DEF.

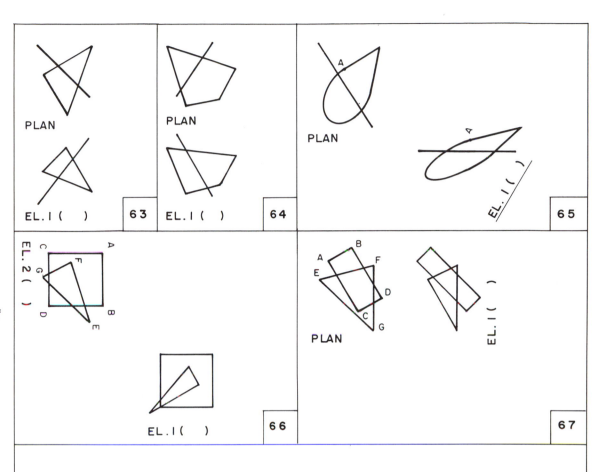

PLAN

PLAN

PLAN

A

EL.I ( )

EL.I ( )   63

EL.I ( )   64

EL.I ( )   65

EL.2 ( )   C   F   A
G
D   B
E

EL.I ( )   66

A   B   F
E   D
C   G

PLAN

EL.I ( )   67

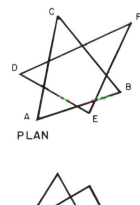

C   F
D   B
A   E

PLAN

EL.I (ABC-),(DEF-)   68

In problems #69, #70, #71, and #72, find the intersection or non-intersection of planes using cutting planes. Employ trial and error. Each line should be resolved one at a time, tested for visibility, and indicated by differential lineweight for spacial position before going on to the next line. This process will help avoid confusion and reveal relationship before the next line is tested.

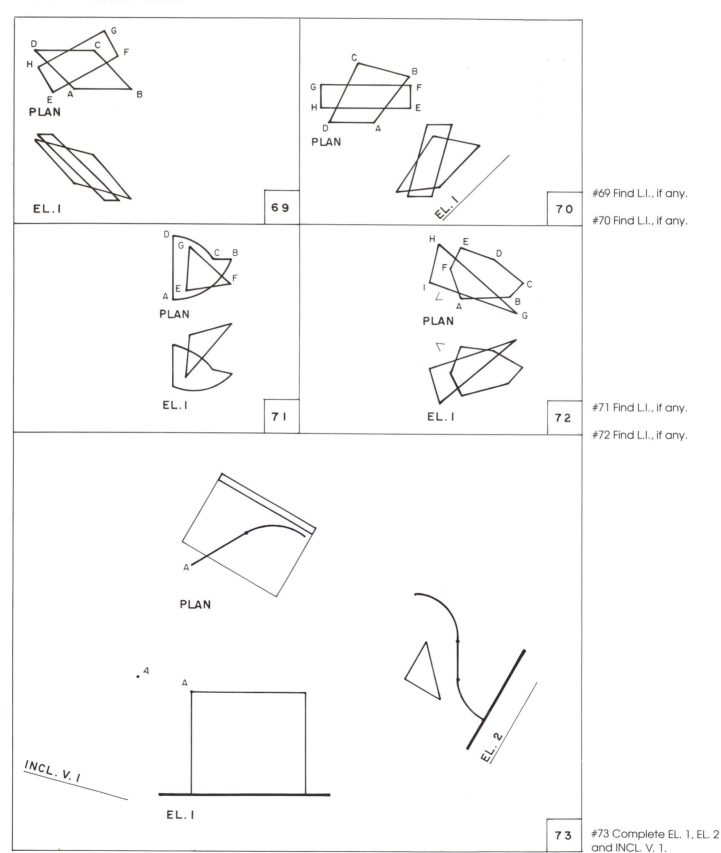

#69 Find L.I., if any.

#70 Find L.I., if any.

#71 Find L.I., if any.

#72 Find L.I., if any.

#73 Complete EL. 1, EL. 2 and INCL. V. 1.

Beginning with #78 are problems involving solids. Points need not be labelled but when drawing becomes difficult, points should be immediately identified. Use differential lineweight to indicate spacial depth.

#74 Draw Plan.

#75 Draw EL. 1.

#76 Draw any flat plane with curves in EL. 1 and INCL. V. I. to match.

#77 Draw flat plane EFGH in all views. Draw L.I. in Plan and EL. 1. Then complete all three views.

#78 Draw EL. 2.

#79 Draw EL. 2.

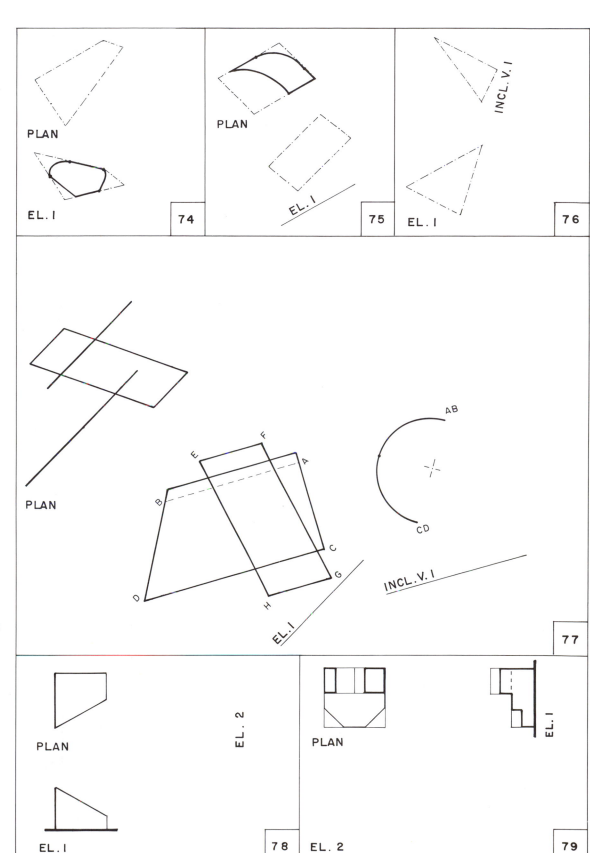

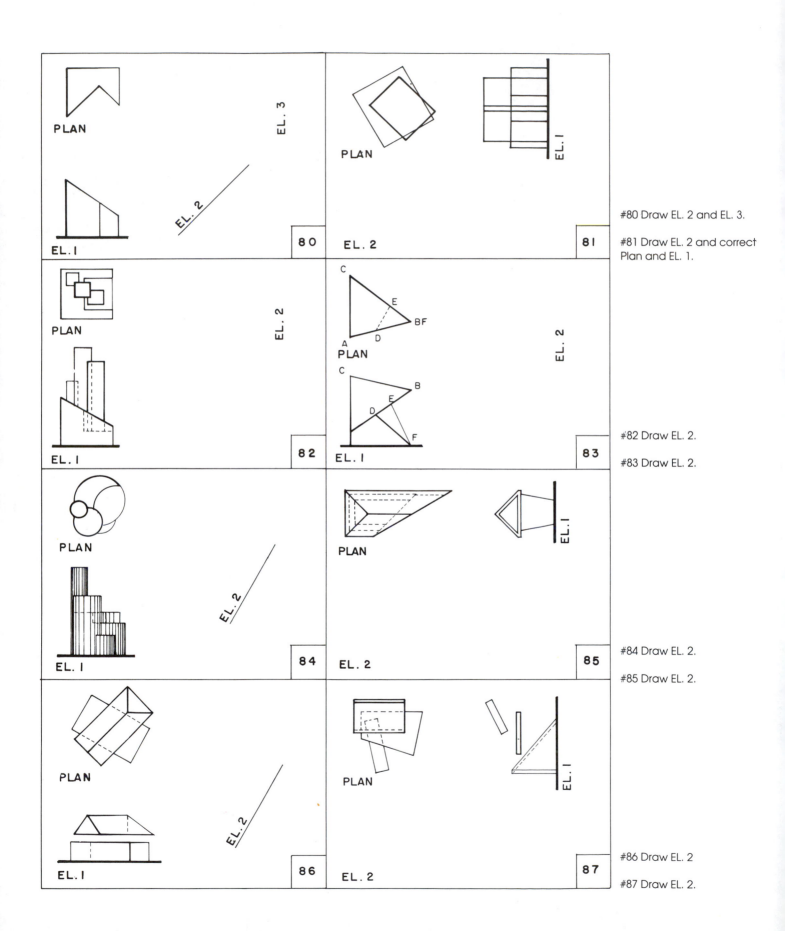

PLAN

EL. 3

EL. 2

EL. 1

80

PLAN

EL. 2

EL. 1

81

PLAN

EL. 2

EL. 1

82

C
E
BF
A D
PLAN

C
B
E
D
F
EL. 1

EL. 2

83

PLAN

EL. 2

EL. 1

84

PLAN

EL. 1

EL. 2

85

PLAN

EL. 1

EL. 2

86

PLAN

EL. 2

EL. 1

87

#80 Draw EL. 2 and EL. 3.

#81 Draw EL. 2 and correct Plan and EL. 1.

#82 Draw EL. 2.

#83 Draw EL. 2.

#84 Draw EL. 2.

#85 Draw EL. 2.

#86 Draw EL. 2

#87 Draw EL. 2.

Problems #92 through #99 have lines missing from some or all given views. Given lines are correct but may indicate hidden lines solid. Complete all drawings; show hidden lines with dashes, and use differential lineweight.

#88 Draw a view of this solid which shows plane ABCD in T.S.

#89 Draw INCL. V.I in direction shown.

#90 Draw INCL. V.I.

#91 Draw INCL. V.I.

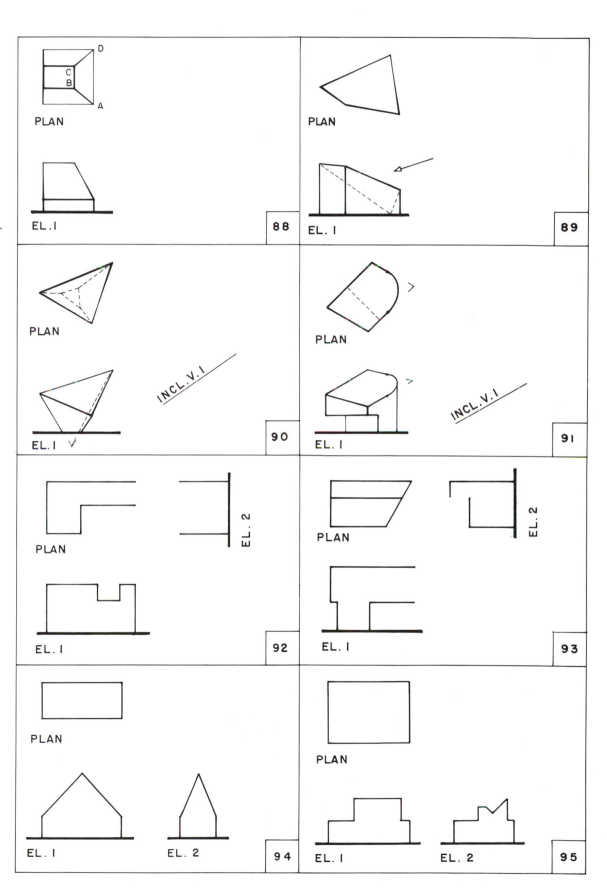

In problems #100, #101, #102, and #103, solids are on flat sloping planes. Draw EL. 2 for each problem using the edge view method.

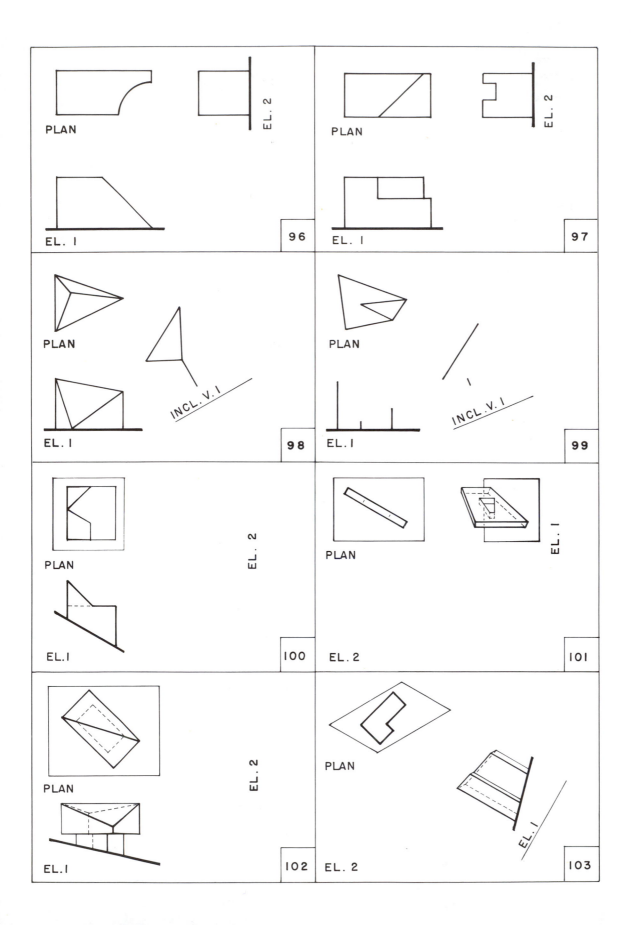

PLAN

EL. 2

EL. I

96

PLAN

EL. 2

EL. I

97

PLAN

INCL. V. I

EL. I

98

PLAN

INCL. V. I

EL. I

99

PLAN

EL. 2

EL. I

100

PLAN

EL. I

EL. 2

101

PLAN

EL. 2

EL. I

102

PLAN

EL. I

EL. 2

103

Problems #104, #105, #106, and #107 are solids on oblique planes and the methods for finding intersections are identical to planes intersecting solids. Using the cutting plane method, find intersections, correct drawings, and use differential lineweight.

Problems #108 through #115 show lines which may or may not penetrate solids. Use either projection or cutting plane methods, with or without new drawings. Show solutions on all drawings but do not indicate lines within solids.

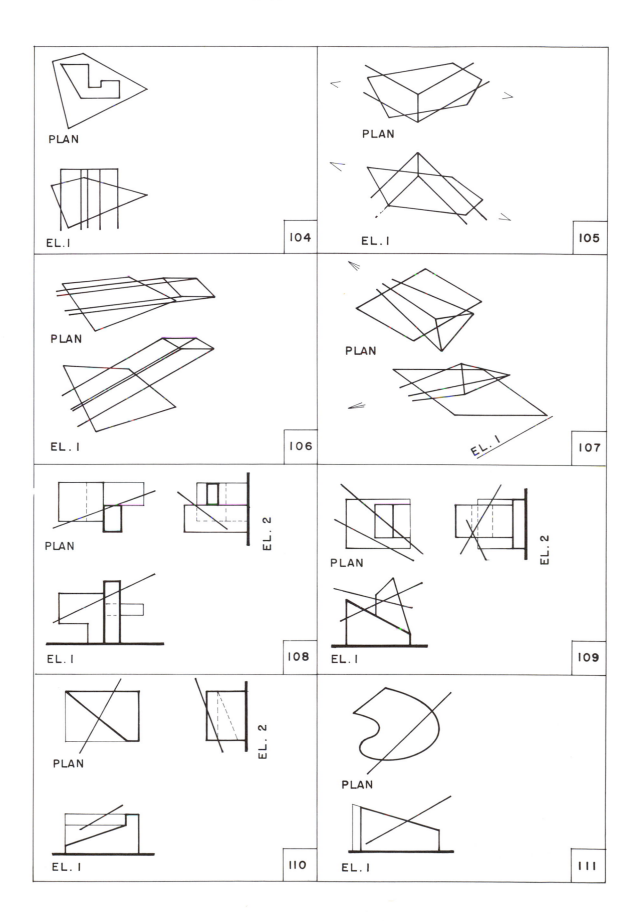

In problems #116 through #121, correct Plan to correspond to the level indicated. Show new plan by crosshatching or differential lineweight.

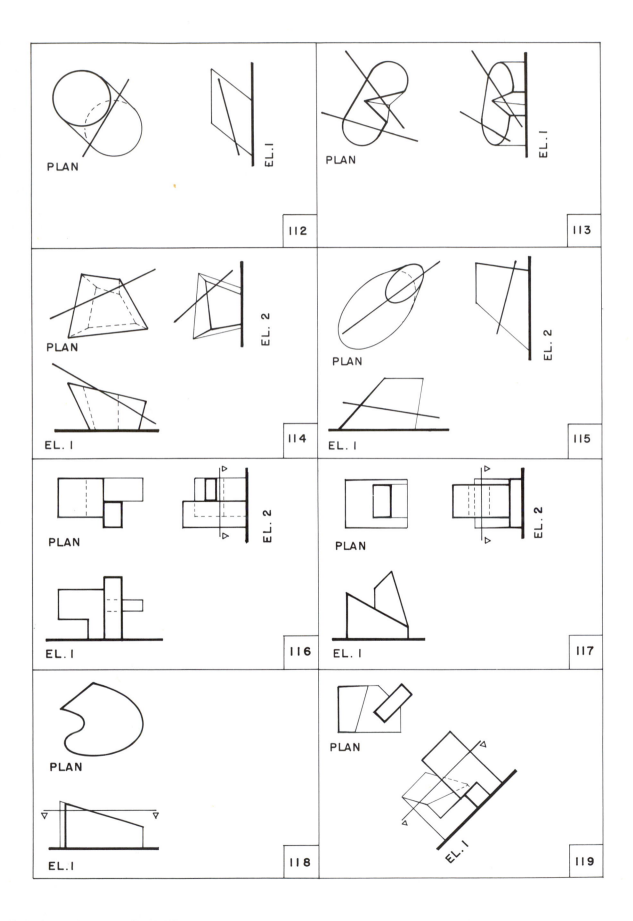

PLAN

EL. I

112

PLAN

EL. I

113

PLAN

EL. 2

EL. I

114

PLAN

EL. 2

EL. I

115

PLAN

EL. 2

EL. I

116

PLAN

EL. 2

EL. I

117

PLAN

EL. I

118

PLAN

EL. I

119

#122 Convert EL. 2 to a section.

#123 Convert EL. 1 to a section.

#124 Convert EL. 1 to a section.

#125 Draw Section 1.

#126 Draw broken Section 1.

#127 Draw broken Section 1. Not all of Section 1 is accomplished by projection. Ref. pg. 124.

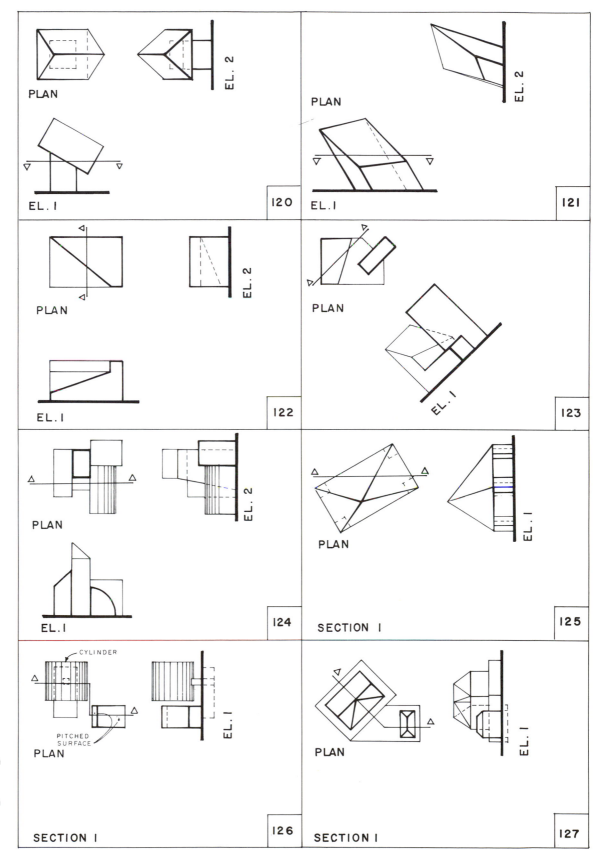

PLAN · EL. 2 · EL. 1 · 120

PLAN · EL. 2 · EL. 1 · 121

PLAN · EL. 2 · EL. 1 · 122

PLAN · EL. 1 · 123

PLAN · EL. 2 · EL. 1 · 124

PLAN · EL. 1 · SECTION 1 · 125

CYLINDER · PITCHED SURFACE · PLAN · EL. 1 · SECTION 1 · 126

PLAN · EL. 1 · SECTION 1 · 127

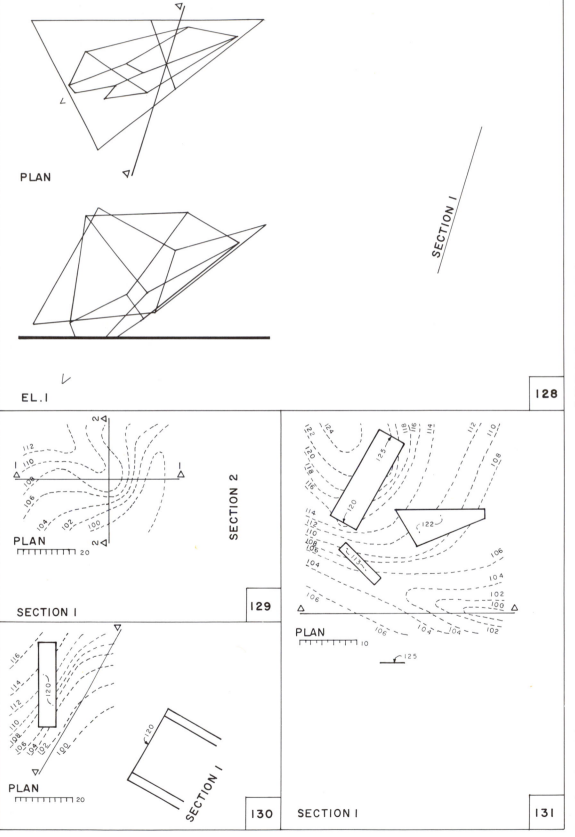

PLAN

SECTION 1

EL. 1

128

#128 A folded triangular plane intersects an oblique, truncated pyramid (ref. pg. 95) with an irregular quadrilateral base (ref. pg. 87) in this problem. Correct Plan and EL. 1 for intersections and hidden lines. Draw Section 1. An incl. v. may be necessary to solve all intersections.

SECTION 2

PLAN

SECTION 1

129

PLAN

125

PLAN

SECTION 1

130

SECTION 1

131

#129 Draw sections 1 and 2. Ref pp. 110 and 111.

#130 Draw Section 1.

#131 Draw Section 1 and object beyond image plane.

245

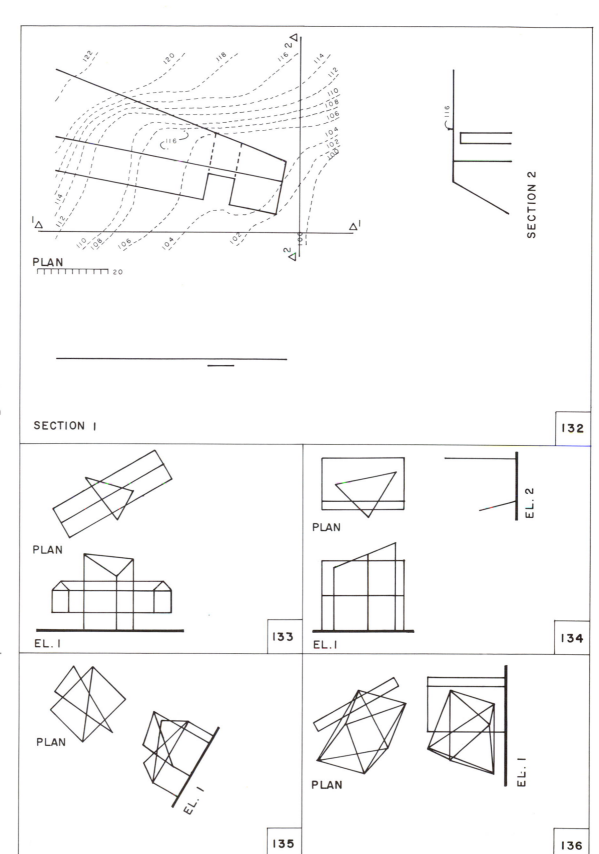

#132 Draw Section 1 and 2. A series of horizontal cutting planes must be used in Plan to find one line of intersection.

#133 Correct Plan and EL. 1.

#134 Correct Plan and EL. 1.

#135 Correct Plan and EL. 1.

#136. In this problem, an irregular octahedron (ref. pg. 95) is intersected by a vertical slab. Correct Plan and EL. 1.

PLAN

SECTION 1

SECTION 2

132

PLAN

EL. 1

133

PLAN

EL. 2

PLAN

EL. 1

134

PLAN

EL. 1

135

PLAN

EL. 1

136

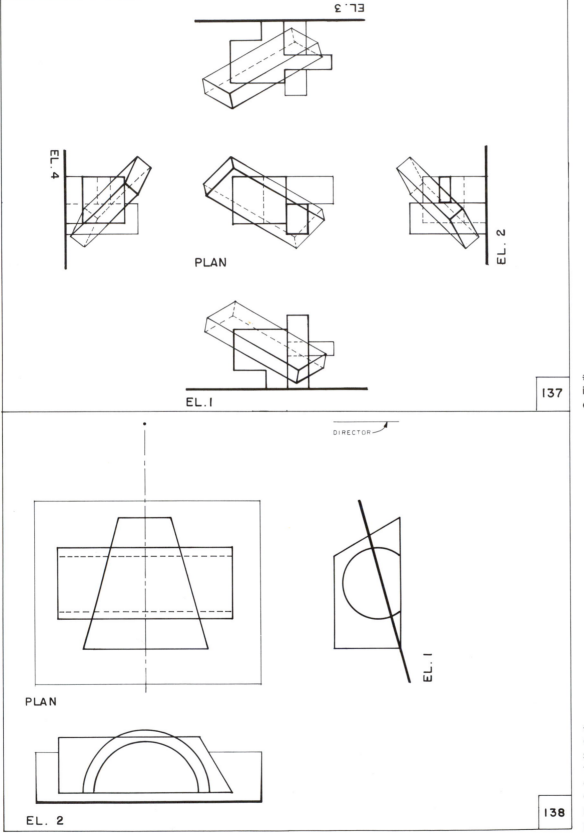

EL.3

EL.4

EL. 2

PLAN

EL.1

#137 Correct all views for intersections and use differential lineweight.

137

DIRECTOR

PLAN

EL.1

EL. 2

#138 A truncated conoid (ref. pg. 95) tunnel intersects a partial cylinder in this problem. Both forms sit on a sloping plane. Correct all drawings but do not show forms below the plane in Plan and EL. 2.

138

The remaining problems in this appendix involve shades and shadows. Although the sequence of problem types follows Chapter Six, the methods for solutions—projection from given or newly constructed views and imaginary points and extension of planes—(ref. illustration on pg. 191) do not follow any sequence.

In problems involving only lines, lines are depicted as thin planes in order to indicate visibility. For accuracy, the center line of each plane should be thought of as the line itself.

The dashed lines with arrows indicate the direction of the sun's rays and are not necessarily projections from view to view. Show shades in all problems where applicable.

#139 Draw Plan shadow.

#140 Draw Plan shadow.

#141 Draw shadows in Plan and EL.

#142 Draw shadows in Plan.

#143 Draw shadows in Plan, INCL. V. 1, and V. 2.

#144 Draw shadows in Plan.

#145 Draw shadow in Plan.

#146 Draw shadows in Plan and EL. 1.

#147 Draw Plan shadows.

#148 Draw Plan shadows.

#149 Draw shadows in Plan and EL. 1.

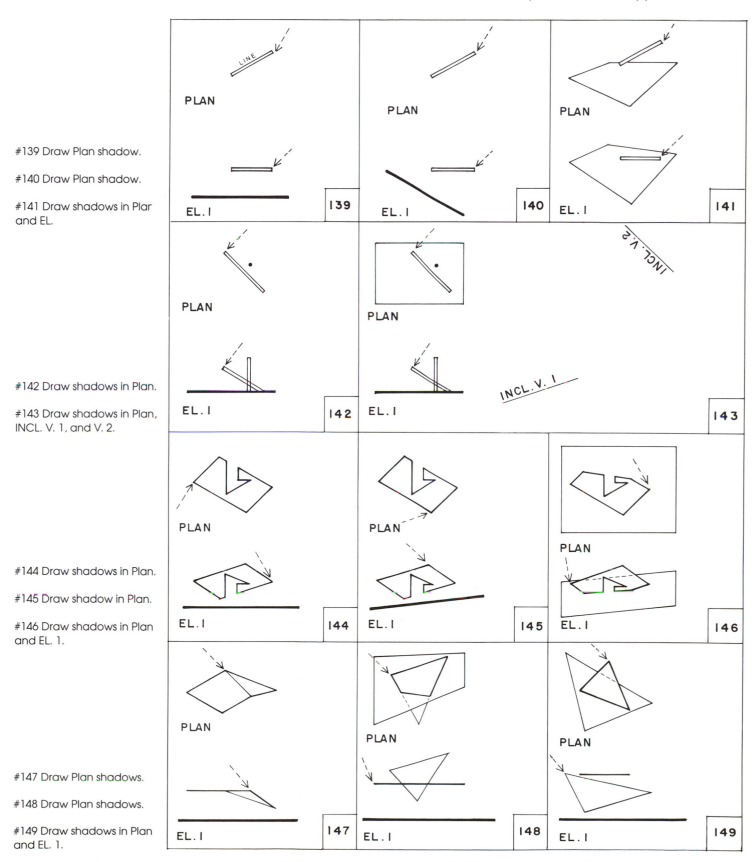

Draw plan shadows in problems #150 through #157.

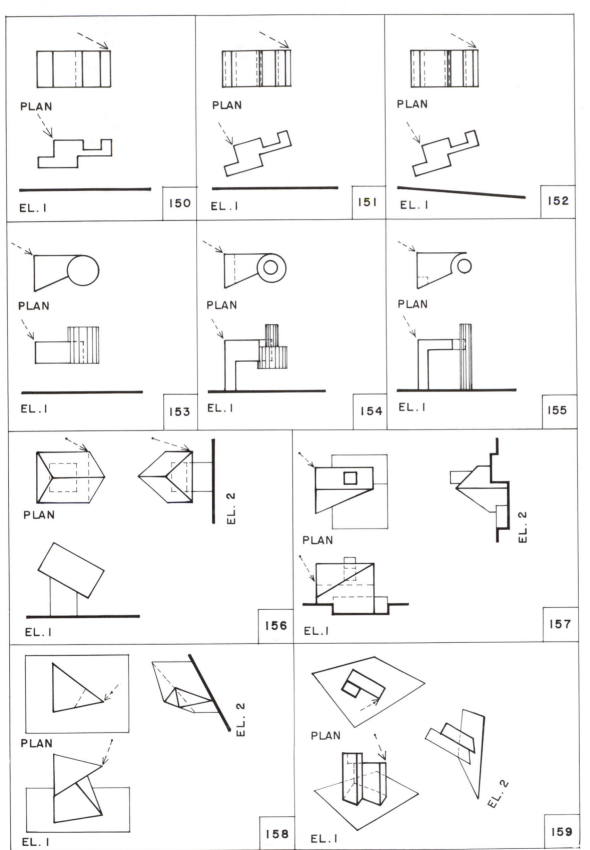

PLAN

EL.1

150

PLAN

EL.1

151

PLAN

EL.1

152

PLAN

EL.1

153

PLAN

EL.1

154

PLAN

EL.1

155

PLAN

EL. 2

EL.1

156

PLAN

EL. 2

EL.1

157

PLAN

EL. 2

EL.1

158

PLAN

EL. 2

EL.1

159

#158 Draw shadows in Plan and EL. 1.

#159 Draw shadows in Plan, EL. 1, and EL. 2.

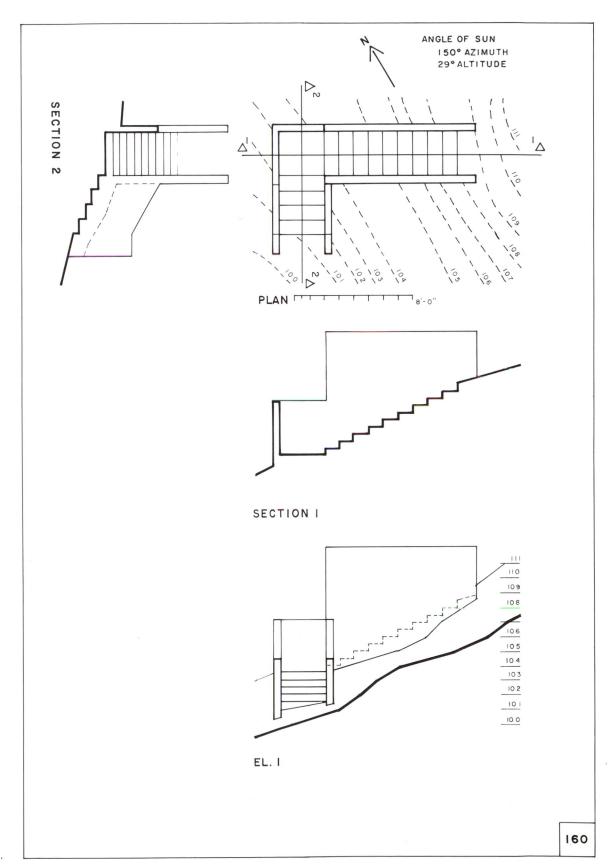

ANGLE OF SUN
150° AZIMUTH
29° ALTITUDE

SECTION 2

N

PLAN ⌐‾‾‾‾‾¬ 8'-0"

SECTION I

EL. I

111
110
109
108
106
105
104
103
102
101
100

#160 Draw plan shadows
on stair and ground. Ref.
illustration 45 on pg. 182
and 71 and 72 on pg. 191.

In problems #165 through #170, draw shadow in EL. 1.

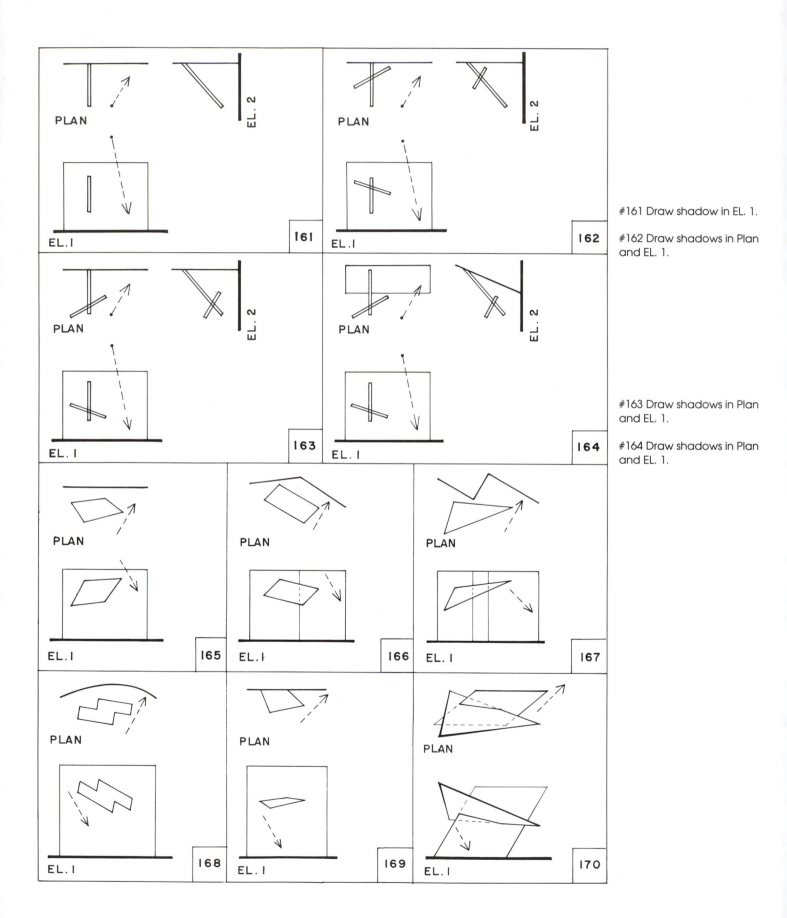

#161 Draw shadow in EL. 1.

#162 Draw shadows in Plan and EL. 1.

#163 Draw shadows in Plan and EL. 1.

#164 Draw shadows in Plan and EL. 1.

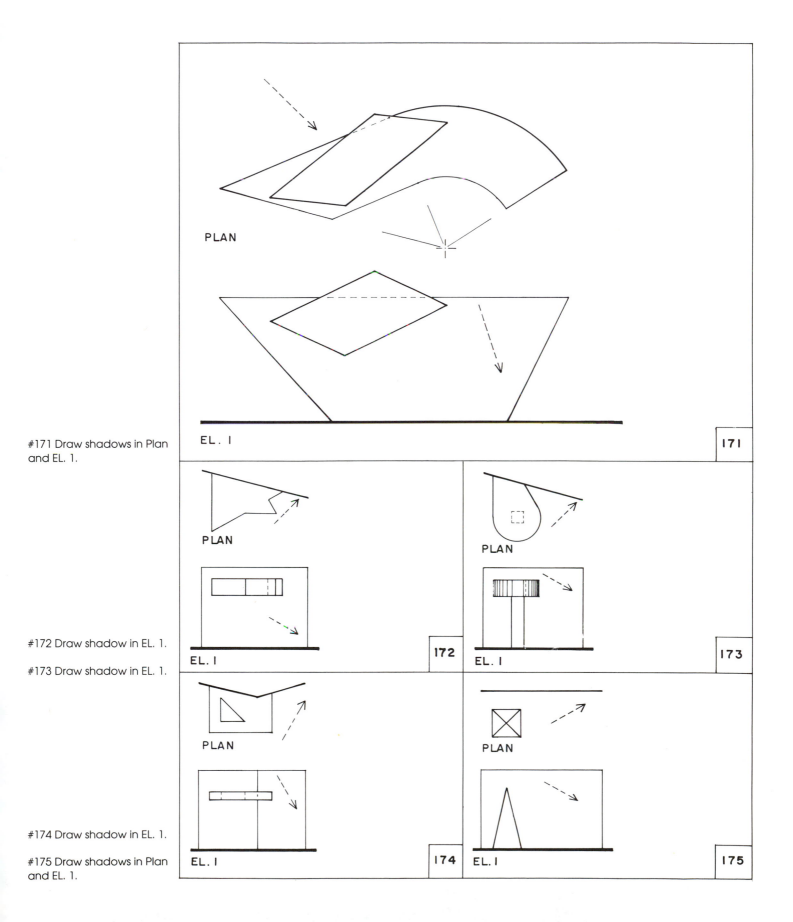

PLAN

EL. 1

171

#171 Draw shadows in Plan and EL. 1.

PLAN

EL. 1

172

PLAN

EL. 1

173

#172 Draw shadow in EL. 1.

#173 Draw shadow in EL. 1.

PLAN

EL. 1

174

PLAN

EL. 1

175

#174 Draw shadow in EL. 1.

#175 Draw shadows in Plan and EL. 1.

In problems #176 through #181, draw shadows in Plan and
EL. 1.

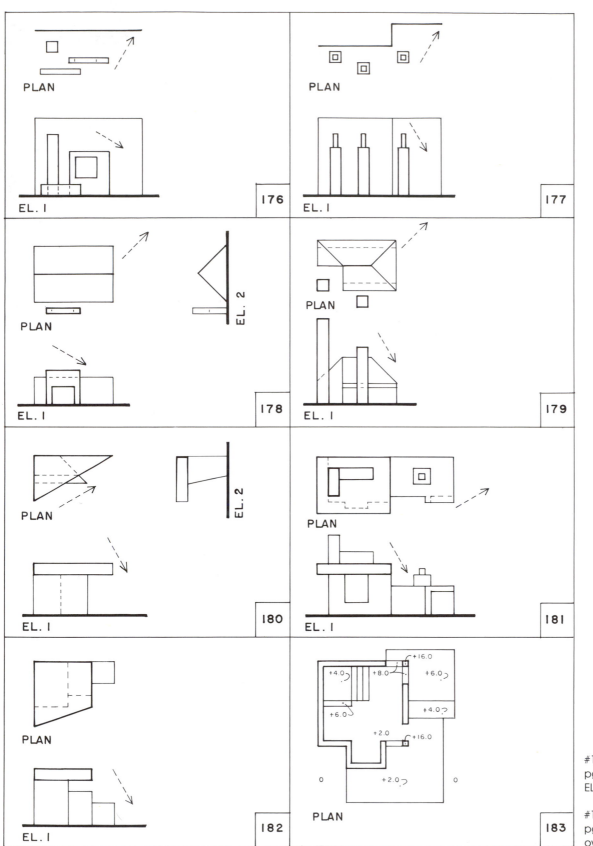

PLAN

EL. 1   176

PLAN

EL. 1   177

PLAN

EL. 2

EL. 1   178

PLAN

EL. 1   179

PLAN

EL. 2

EL. 1   180

PLAN

EL. 1   181

PLAN

EL. 1   182

+16.0
+4.0   +8.0   +6.0
+6.0   +4.0
+2.0   +16.0
0   +2.0   0

PLAN   183

#182 Adapt the shortcut on
pg. 183 to draw shadows in
EL. 1.

#183 Using the shortcut on
pg. 183, draw Plan shad-
ows.

INDEX